OVER 1000 FANTASTIC ANIMAL FACTS

OVER 1000 FANTASTIC ANIMAL FACTS

Miles
Kelly

First published in 2011 by Miles Kelly Publishing Ltd
Harding's Barn, Bardfield End Green, Thaxted, Essex, CM6 3PX, UK

Copyright © Miles Kelly Publishing Ltd 2011

This edition printed 2014

6 8 10 9 7 5

Publishing Director Belinda Gallagher
Creative Director Jo Cowan
Editors Carly Blake, Rosie Neave, Sarah Parkin, Claire Philip
Editorial Assistant Lauren White
Cover Designer Kayleigh Allen
Designers Kayleigh Allen, Candice Bekir, Sally Boothroyd, Jo Cowan, Joe Jones,
Sally Lace, Sophie Pelham, Andrea Slane, Tom Slemmings, Elaine Wilkinson
Production Manager Elizabeth Collins
Reprographics Stephan Davis, Jennifer Hunt, Lorraine King
Assets Lorraine King

ISBN 978-1-84810-543-0

Printed in China

British Library Cataloguing-in-Publication Data
A catalogue record for this book is available from the British Library

Made with paper from a sustainable forest

www.mileskelly.net
info@mileskelly.net

Contents

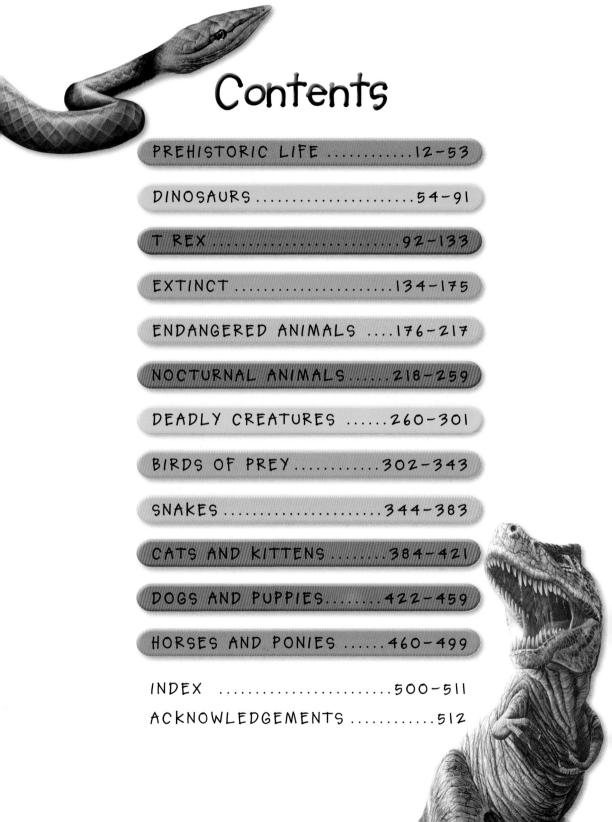

PREHISTORIC LIFE

DINOSAURS

T REX

EXTINCT

ENDANGERED ANIMALS

NOCTURNAL ANIMALS

DEADLY CREATURES

BIRDS OF PREY

SNAKES

CATS AND KITTENS

DOGS AND PUPPIES

HORSES AND PONIES

PREHISTORIC LIFE

1 **The Earth was once covered by huge sheets of ice.** This happened several times during Earth's history and we call these frozen times ice ages. However, the ice ages are a tiny part of prehistory. Before then, the world was warm and lakes and seas covered the land. Even earlier than this, there was little rain for thousands of years, and the land was covered in deserts. Over millions of years weather and conditions changed. Living things changed too, in order to survive. This change is called 'evolution'.

Woolly rhinoceros

Cave lion

▼ A scene from the last ice age, about 10,000 years ago. Animals grew thick fur coats to protect themselves from the cold. Many animals, such as woolly mammoths, survived on plants such as mosses. Others, such as cave lions, were fierce hunters, needing meat to survive.

Aurochs

Woolly mammoths

Megaloceros

Life begins

2 Life began a very, very long time ago. We know this from the remains of prehistoric life forms that died and were buried. Over millions of years, their remains turned into shapes in rocks, called fossils. The first fossils are over 3000 million years old. They are tiny 'blobs' called bacteria – living things that still survive today.

▼ Fossils of *Anomalocaris* have been found in Canada. It had a circular mouth and finlike body parts. Its body was covered by a shell.

3 The first plants were seaweeds, which appeared about 1000 million years ago. Unlike bacteria and blue-green algae, which each had just one living cell, these plants had thousands of cells. Some seaweeds were many metres long. They were called algae – the same name that scientists use today.

4 By about 800 million years ago, some plants were starting to grow on land. They were mixed with other living things called moulds, or fungi. Together, the algae (plants) and fungi formed flat green-and-yellow crusts that crept over rocks and soaked up rain. They were called lichens. These still grow on rocks and trees today.

Jellyfish

5 The first animals lived in the sea – and they were as soft as jelly! Over 600 million years ago, some of the first animals were jellyfish, floating in the water. On the seabed lived groups of soft, feathery-looking creatures called *Charnia*. This animal was an early type of coral. Animals need to take in food by eating other living things. *Charnia* caught tiny plants in its 'feathers'.

◀ *Charnia* looked like a prehistoric plant, but it was actually an animal!

Charnia

6 One of the first hunting animals was *Anomalocaris*. It lived 520 million years ago, swimming through the sea in search of prey. It caught smaller creatures in its pincers, then pushed them into its mouth. *Anomalocaris* was a cousin of crabs and insects. It was one of the biggest hunting animals of its time, even though it was only 60 centimetres long.

▲ The *Cooksonia* plant had forked stems that carried water. The earliest examples have been found in Ireland.

7 By 400 million years ago, plants on land were growing taller. They had stiff stems that held them upright and carried water to their topmost parts. An early upright plant was *Cooksonia*. It was the tallest living thing on land, yet it was only 5 centimetres high – hardly the size of your thumb!

15

Animals swarm the seas

8 **Some of the first common animals were worms.** However, they were not earthworms in soil. At the time there was no soil and the land was bare. These worms lived in the sea. They burrowed in mud for plants and animals to eat.

▼ Trilobites moved quickly across the seabed. Some could roll up into a ball like woodlice do today. This was a means of protection.

◄ *Ottoia* was a sea worm that fed by filtering tiny food particles from the sea.

9 **The next animals to become common were trilobites.** They first lived about 550 million years ago in the sea. Trilobites crawled along the seabed eating tiny bits of food they found. Their name means 'three lobes' (parts). A trilobite had two grooves along its back, from head to tail, so its body had three main parts – left, middle and centre.

▼ *Pterygotus* was a fierce hunter, with large eyes and long claws.

10 **Trilobites were some of the first animals with legs that bent at the joints.** Animals with jointed legs are called arthropods. They have been the most common creatures for millions of years, including trilobites long ago, and later on, crabs, spiders and insects. Like other arthropods, trilobites had a tough, outer shell for protection.

11 **Some of the first hunters were sea scorpions – some were as big as lions!** *Pterygotus* was 2 metres long. It swished its tail to chase prey through water, which it tore apart with its huge claws. Sea scorpions lived 500 to 250 million years ago. Unlike modern scorpions, they had no sting in their tails.

12 For millions of years the seabed was covered with the curly shells of ammonites. Some of these shells were as small as your fingernail, others were bigger than dinner plates. Ammonites were successful creatures and thousands of kinds survived for millions of years. Each ammonite had big eyes to see prey and long tentacles (arms) to catch it with. Ammonites died out at the same time as the dinosaurs, around 65 million years ago.

▲ This rock contains an ammonite fossil. The shell would have protected the soft-bodied creature inside.

◀ *Pikaia* looked a little bit like an eel with fins.

QUIZ
1. Did sea scorpions have stings in their tails?
2. What does the name 'trilobite' mean?
3. What kind of animal was *Ottoia*?
4. When did ammonites die out?
5. What was special about *Pikaia*?

Answers:
1. No 2. Three lobes, or parts 3. A worm 4. 65 million years ago 5. It had an early type of backbone

13 Among the worms, trilobites and ammonites was a small creature that had a very special body part — the beginnings of a backbone. It was called *Pikaia* and lived about 530 million years ago. Gradually, more animals with backbones, called vertebrates, evolved from it. Today, vertebrates rule much of the world — they are fish, reptiles, birds and mammals.

Very fishy

14 The first fish could not bite – they were suckers! About 500 million years ago, new animals appeared in the sea – the first fish. They had no jaws or teeth and probably sucked in worms and small pieces of food from the mud.

15 Some early fish wore suits of armour! They had hard, curved plates of bone all over their bodies for protection. These fish were called placoderms and most were fierce hunters. Some had huge jaws with sharp sheets of bone for slicing up prey.

▲ *Hemicyclaspis* was an early jawless fish. It had eyes on top of its head and probably lived on the seabed. This way it could keep a look out for predators above.

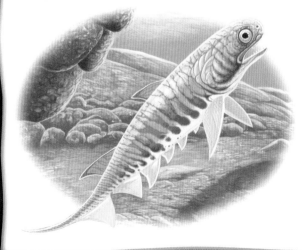

16 Spiny sharks had spines, but they were not really sharks. These fish were similar in shape to today's sharks, but they lived in rivers and lakes, not the sea, about 430 million years ago. *Climatius* was a spiny shark that looked fierce, but it was only as big as your finger!

◄ The fins on the back of *Climatius* were supported by needle-sharp spines. These helped to protect it from attacks by squid or other fish.

17 **The first really big hunting fish was bigger than today's great white shark!** *Dunkleosteus* grew to almost 10 metres long and swam in the oceans 360 million years ago. It sliced up prey, such as other fish, using its massive teeth made of narrow blades of bone, each one as big as this book.

18 **Some early fish started to 'walk' out of water.** Types of fish called lobefins appeared 390 million years ago. Their side fins each had a 'stump' at the base made of muscle. If the water in their pool dried up, lobefins could use their fins like stubby legs to waddle over land to another pool. *Eusthenopteron* was a lobefin fish about one metre long. Over millions of years, some lobefins evolved into four-legged animals called tetrapods.

VERY FISHY!

You will need:
waxed card (like the kind used to make milk cartons) crayons scissors piece of soap

Place the piece of waxed card face down. Fold the card up at the edges. Draw a fish on the card. Cut a small notch in the rear of the card and wedge the piece of soap in it. Put the 'fish' in a bath of cold water and watch it swim away.

▼ *Eusthenopteron* could clamber about on dry land when moving from one stretch of water to another.

Animals invade the land

19 **The first land animals lived about 450 million years ago.** These early creatures, which came from the sea, were arthropods – creatures with hard outer body casings and jointed legs. They included prehistoric insects, spiders and millipedes. *Arthropleura* was a millipede – it was 2 metres in length!

▶ *Arthropleura* was as long as a human and was the largest-ever land arthropod.

20 **Some amphibians were fierce hunters.** *Gerrothorax* was about one metre long and spent most of its time at the bottom of ponds or streams. Its eyes pointed upward, to see fish swimming past, just above. *Gerrothorax* would then jump up to grab the fish in its wide jaws.

21 **The first four-legged animal had eight toes on each front foot!** *Acanthostega* used its toes to grip water plants as it swam. It lived about 380 million years ago and was one metre long. Creatures like it soon began to walk on land, too. They were called tetrapods, which means 'four legs'. They were a big advance in evolution – the first land animals with backbones.

◀ *Acanthostega* probably spent most of its time in water. It had gills for breathing underwater as well as lungs for breathing air.

23 Soon four-legged animals called amphibians were racing across the land. Amphibians were the first backboned animals to move fast out of the water. *Aphaneramma* had long legs and could run quickly. However, prehistoric amphibians, like those of today such as frogs and newts, had to return to the water to lay their eggs.

22 Fins became legs for walking on land, and tails changed, too. As the fins of lobefin fish evolved into legs, their tails became longer and more muscular. *Ichthyostega* had a long tail with a fin along its upper side. This tail design was good for swimming in water, and also helpful when wriggling across a swamp.

24 Some amphibians grew as big as crocodiles! *Eogyrinus* was almost 5 metres long and had strong jaws and teeth, like a crocodile. However, it lived about 300 million years ago, long before any crocodiles appeared. Although *Eogyrinus* could walk on dry land, it spent most of its time in streams and swamps.

◄ *Ichthyostega* had short legs, so it could probably only move slowly on land.

Life after death

25 **There were times in prehistory when almost everything died out.** These times are called mass extinctions. Just a few types of plants and animals survive, which can then change, or evolve, into new kinds. A mass extinction about 290 million years ago allowed a fairly new group of animals to spread fast – the reptiles.

26 **Reptiles' skin and eggs helped them to survive.** Unlike an amphibian's, a reptile's scaly skin was waterproof. Also, the jelly-like eggs of amphibians had to be laid in water, while a reptile's eggs had tough shells for surviving on land. Around 280 million years ago, reptiles such as 1.5-metre-long *Varanosaurus* were spreading to dry areas where amphibians could not survive.

EDIBLE REPTILES

You will need:
100 grams dried milk
100 grams smooth peanut butter   2 tablespoons honey
currants   food colouring

Mix the dried milk, peanut butter and honey in a bowl. Mould this paste into reptile shapes. Decorate with currants for eyes and add food colouring for bright skin patterns. Then cause a mass extinction – eat them!

▲ *Varanosaurus* lived in what is now Texas, USA, and may have hunted fish in swamps.

▶ *Hylonomus* lived in forests in what is now Canada. It hunted insects, spiders and millipedes.

27 The first reptile looked like a lizard. However *Hylonomus* belonged to a different reptile group to lizards. It lived like a lizard, chasing prey on the ground and in trees. It lived 345 million years ago.

28 Some reptiles started to avoid bad weather by sleeping underground. *Diictodon* lived about 260 million years ago and used its large teeth to chop up tough plant food. It may have dug holes to shelter from the heat, cold and rain.

▼ *Diictodon* had strong legs and sharp claws for burrowing.

Wars around the world

29 **Some amphibians fought back against the reptiles.** *Mastodonsaurus* was a big, strong amphibian, 2 metres long, with sharp teeth. It hunted fish, other amphibians, and small reptiles. It lived at a time when reptiles were spreading even faster, about 250 to 203 million years ago. But most other big amphibians did not survive the reptiles.

▼ The nostrils and eyes of *Mastodonsaurus* were on top of its head so that it could breathe and look around whilst hiding underwater.

30 Other amphibians managed to survive the reptile takeover, too. They were mainly small and hid in water or swamps. One was *Branchiosaurus*, which was about 12 centimetres long and hunted small fish in ponds.

▲ *Lystrosaurus* lived in Antarctica when it was a land of lush, tropical plant life. Today it is a frozen continent, covered by thick ice.

▼ As well as sharp teeth, *Moschops* had very strong skull bones, so it may have head-butted rivals in fights.

31 Reptiles showed how the world's lands moved about. *Lystrosaurus* lived about 200 million years ago and its fossils come from Europe, Asia, Africa and Antarctica. This reptile could not swim, so all of these landmasses, or continents, must have been joined together at one time. Over millions of years, they drifted apart to form today's positions.

32 Some plant-eating reptiles had very sharp teeth. *Moschops* was as big as a rhino and lived in southern Africa about 270 million years ago. Its teeth were long and straight, and ended with a sharp edge like a chisel. *Moschops* could easily bite tough leaves and twigs off bushes.

Reptiles take over

33 **Reptiles don't like to be too hot, or too cold.** Otherwise they may overheat, or be too cold to move. Most reptiles bask in sunshine to get warm, then stay in the shade. *Dimetrodon* was a fierce reptile. It had a large 'sail' of skin on its back to soak up heat from the sun.

▲ The name *Dimetrodon* means 'two-types-of-teeth'. It was given this name as it had stabbing teeth and slicing teeth. It measured 3 metres in length.

QUIZ

1. How did *Dimetrodon* get warm?
2. Which types of reptile evolved into mammals?
3. How did some early reptiles swim?
4. Did the first crocodiles like water?

Answers:
1. By basking in the sun
2. Therapsids 3. By swishing their tails from side to side 4. No, they hated it!

34 **The first crocodiles hated water!** An early type of crocodile, *Protosuchus*, stayed on land. It lived in North America about 190 million years ago. It was one metre long and could run across dry land when hunting, using its long legs.

▶ *Protosuchus* had very powerful jaw muscles to snap its teeth shut on prey.

▶ *Chasmatosaurus* had teeth on the roof of its mouth as well as in its jaws.

35 **Some reptiles moved by using their tails.** Many types of early reptiles had long, strong tails. They probably lived in water and swished their tails to push themselves along. *Chasmatosaurus* was 2 metres long and probably hunted for fish. It looked like a crocodile but was more closely related to the dinosaurs.

36 **Some reptiles began to look very much like mammals.** *Cynognathus* was as big as a large dog, and instead of scaly skin it had fur. It belonged to a group of reptiles called therapsids. Around 220 million years ago, some types of small therapsids were evolving into the first mammals.

◀ The jaws of *Cynognathus* were so powerful they could bite through bone. Its name means 'dog jaw'.

Living with the dinosaurs

37 Some reptiles were as big and fierce as dinosaurs – but they lived in the sea. One of these was *Mosasaurus*. It grew up to 10 metres in length and may have weighed 10 tonnes, far bigger than today's great white shark.

I DON'T BELIEVE IT!
Fossils of *Mosasaurus* were found in the same place over 200 years apart! The first was found in a quarry in the Netherlands in 1780. The second was found in the same place in 1998.

38 One sea reptile had teeth the size of saucers! The huge, round, flat teeth of *Placodus* were more than 10 centimetres across. It used them to crush shellfish and sea urchins. *Placodus* was 2 metres long and lived at the same time as the first dinosaurs, about 230 million years ago.

▼ *Mosasaurus* was a huge sea reptile. It had razor-sharp teeth and could swim with speed to catch its prey.

▼ *Archaeopteryx* had a long bony tail, unlike modern birds, which have no bones in their tails.

39 Fossils of the first bird were mistaken for a dinosaur. *Archaeopteryx* lived in Europe about 155 million years ago. Some of its fossils look very similar to the fossils of small dinosaurs. So *Archaeopteryx* was thought to be a dinosaur, until scientists saw the faint shape of its feathers and realized it was a bird.

40 Soon there were many kinds of birds flying above the dinosaurs. *Confuciusornis* was about 60 centimetres long and lived in what is now China, 120 million years ago. It had a backwards-pointing big toe on each foot, which suggests it climbed through the trees. It is also the earliest-known bird to have a true beak.

▲ Fossils of *Confuciusornis* have been found in China. It is named after the famous Chinese wise man, Confucius.

41 Mammals lived at the same time as dinosaurs. These animals have warm blood, and fur or hair, unlike a reptile's scaly skin. *Megazostrodon* was the earliest mammal known to scientists. It lived in southern Africa about 215 million years ago – only 15 million years or so after the dinosaurs began life on Earth. It was just 12 centimetres long, and probably hunted insects.

▼ *Megazostrodon* probably came out at night to hunt for its insect prey. It looked a little like a modern-day shrew.

In and over the sea

42 **One prehistoric reptile had the bendiest neck ever!** The sea reptile *Elasmosaurus* had a neck over 5 metres long – the same as three people lying head-to-toe. Its neck was so bendy that *Elasmosaurus* could twist it around in a circle as it looked for fish and other creatures to eat.

43 **The first big flying animals were not birds, but pterosaurs.** They lived at the same time as the dinosaurs, and died out at the same time too, about 65 million years ago. *Pteranodon* was one of the later pterosaurs and lived about 70 million years ago. It swooped over the sea to scoop up fish.

▼ *Pteranodon* scoops up prey while long-necked *Elasmosaurus* snaps its jaws in search of food.

Pteranodon

44 **The largest flying animal of all time was as big as a plane!** With wings measuring up to 14 metres from tip to tip, the pterosaur *Quetzalcoatlus* was twice as big as any flying bird. It may have lived like a vulture, soaring high in the sky, and then landing to peck at a dead body of a dinosaur.

45 **Some fossils of sea creatures are found thousands of kilometres from the sea.** Around 100 to 70 million years ago, much of what is now North America was flooded. The shallow waters teemed with all kinds of fish, reptiles and other creatures. Today their fossils are found on dry land.

Elasmosaurus

After the dinosaurs

46 A disaster about 65 million years ago killed off the dinosaurs and many other creatures. The main new group of animals was the mammals. Most were small, like rats and mice. *Leptictidium* lived 50 to 40 million years ago. It may be related to moles and shrews.

▲ *Leptictidium* probably hopped like a kangaroo!

48 Often the name of a prehistoric animal can be misleading, like *Palaeotherium*, which simply means 'ancient animal'. However this name was given over 200 years ago, in 1804, because scientists of the time did not know as much as modern scientists. Later studies show that *Palaeotherium* was one of the first animals in the group of hoofed mammals that includes horses.

◀ *Pakicetus* is the earliest-known whale.

47 Whales began life on dry land and gradually returned to the sea. *Pakicetus* lived about 50 million years ago and was nearly 2 metres long. It probably spent alot of time on land as well as in water.

▼ A mother *Uintatherium* and her baby. This strange-looking creature was the largest land animal of its time. Its head was covered in horns and it had small tusks.

49 Around 40 million years ago, the largest animal walking the Earth was *Uintatherium*. This plant eater was over 3 metres long and nearly 2 metres tall at the shoulder – about the same size as a cow. Its fossils were found near the Uinta River in Colorado, USA. *Uintatherium* is thought to be a cousin of horses and elephants.

50 An animal's looks can be misleading. *Patriofelis* means 'father of the cats'. It lived 45 million years ago and was named because scientists thought it looked like an early cat. Later they realized it was really a member of an extinct group of hunting animals called creodonts.

QUIZ
1. What does the name *Patriofelis* mean?
2. How long was *Pakicetus*?
3. In what year were *Palaeotherium* fossils found?
4. How tall was *Uintatherium*?
5. When did dinosaurs die out and mammals start to take over?

Answers:
1. 'Father of the cats'
2. About 2 metres 3. 1804
4. Almost 2 metres tall at the shoulder
5. 65 million years ago

As the world cooled down

51 Before the world started to cool 30 million years ago, palm trees grew almost everywhere – but they became rare. These trees had thrived in warm, wet conditions. But as Earth cooled, other plants took over, such as magnolias, pines, oaks and birch. These changes meant that animals changed too.

▼ *Brontotherium* was somewhere in size between a rhino and an elephant. Males used the Y-shaped horn on their snouts in fighting competitions.

52 *Pyrotherium* means 'fire beast', but not because this plant eater could walk through fire. Its fossils were found in layers of ash from an ancient volcano in Argentina, South America. The volcano probably erupted, and its fumes and ash suffocated and burned all the animals nearby. *Pyrotherium* was about as big as a cow and looked like a combination of a pig and a short-tusked elephant.

53 Many prehistoric animals have exciting names – *Brontotherium* means 'thunder beast'. Where the fossils of *Brontotherium* were found in North America, local people thought they were bones of the gods. They thought that these gods rode chariots across the sky and started thunderstorms, which led to the animal's name.

54 *Andrewsarchus* was a real big-head! At one metre long, it had the biggest head of any hunting mammal on land, and its strong jaws were filled with sharp, pointed teeth. Its whole body was bigger than a tiger of today. *Andrewsarchus* probably lived like a hyena, crunching up bones and gristle from dead animals. Yet it belonged to a mammal group that was mostly plant eaters. It lived 30 million years ago in what is now the deserts of Mongolia, Asia.

▲ *Andrewsarchus* was the biggest meat-eating land animal ever to have lived.

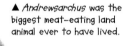

QUIZ
1. What does *Brontotherium* mean?
2. What does *Pyrotherium* mean?
3. How long was the head of *Andrewsarchus*?
4. Where did *Arsinoitherium* live?

Answers:
1. 'Thunder beast' 2. 'Fire beast'
3. One metre 4. Northern Africa

▲ The horns on *Arsinoitherium's* head were hollow and may have been used to make mating calls.

55 Some animals had horns as tall as people! *Arsinoitherium's* two massive horns looked like powerful weapons – but they were light, fragile and made of very thin bone. This plant eater lived in northern Africa about 35 million years ago. It was almost as big as an elephant and may have been an ancient cousin of the elephant group.

What fossils tell us

56 **Fossils are the remains of animals or plants that have been preserved in rock.** Usually only the hard parts of an animal, such as teeth or bones, are preserved in this way. Trilobites had a tough, outer skeleton so usually only this part of their body is found as a fossil. Scientists use the fossil to try to create a picture of how the soft parts, such as muscles and organs, may have looked.

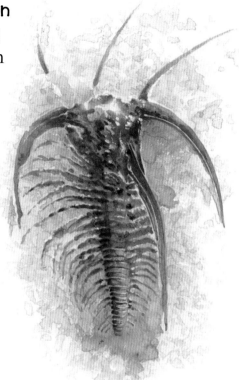

▶ Some early humans are known only from their fossil footprints, not from fossils of their bones. These footprints were discovered in 1978 in Tanzania, Africa.

▲ By examining trilobite fossils, scientists were able to tell that this animal could see in all directions.

57 **Some fossils are known as trace fossils.** These are not fossilized parts of an animal's body, such as bones, but preserved marks left behind by the animal, such as footprints or droppings. By studying the fossilized footprints of an extinct animal, scientists can discover how it walked, how fast it could move and whether it lived alone or in groups.

58 On rare occasions the softer parts of an animal may be preserved as well as the hard parts. Insects may become trapped in sticky sap oozing from pine trees. This sap may then become fossilized as amber, with the insect caught inside. Scientists have found hundreds of insects, spiders and other small creatures perfectly preserved in this way.

▲ Amber spider fossils show that spiders have changed little over the last 30 million years.

QUIZ
1. What is a fossil?
2. What could scientists tell from trilobite fossils?
3. What is amber?
4. What animals did *Archaeopteryx* look like?

Answers:
1. Remains of animals or plants preserved in rock. 2. That they could see in all directions. 3. Fossil tree sap 4. A bird and a dinosaur

◀ Some fossils of *Archaeopteryx* are so well preserved that even the feathers can be seen.

59 One of the most important and valuable fossils ever found was of *Archaeopteryx*, in Germany in 1860. The fossil is about 150 million years old and shows a creature that looked part dinosaur and part bird. It had the feathers and wings of a bird, but the teeth and bony tail of a dinosaur. This shows that birds probably evolved from a type of dinosaur.

60 The importance of some fossils can be misunderstood. *Acanthostega* was one of the very earliest amphibian fossils ever found. However, the man who found the fossil was not an expert on amphibians. When his expedition returned from Greenland, the fossil was put in a drawer at a museum. It was not until over 30 years later that an expert on amphibians happened to see the fossil and realized how important it was.

Prehistoric prowlers

61 Some animals probably ate just about anything. Entelodonts were piglike animals that lived about 25 million years ago. *Dinohyus* was one of the largest entelodonts. Its teeth were sharp and strong, and it had powerful jaw muscles. It ate almost anything from leaves, roots and seeds, to small animals.

62 Some predators (hunting animals) walked on tiptoe but others were flat-footed. Most mammal predators, such as cats and dogs, walk on the ends of their toes. This helps them to run faster. *Daphoenodon* walked on flat feet, like a bear. It is often called a 'bear-dog' as it looked like a dog but walked like a bear.

▼ *Dinohyus* lived in North America and grew to be about 3 metres long. Its powerful neck muscles and large canine teeth suggest it could have broken bones and eaten flesh.

63 Fossils can show if predators hunted by day or at night. *Plesictis* was 75 centimetres long and its fossils show it had large sockets (spaces) for its eyes. This means that it probably hunted at night. It also had sharp claws and a long tail, so it probably scampered through trees hunting birds and insects, gripping with its claws and balancing with its tail.

64 Some predators have changed little over millions of years. *Potamotherium* was an early otter and lived in Europe, 23 million years ago. It looked almost like the otters of today. Its shape was so well-suited to hunting fish in streams that it has hardly changed.

QUIZ
1. Why is *Daphoenodon* sometimes called a 'bear-dog'?
2. Which hunter was active at night?
3. What prey did *Potamotherium* eat?
4. What do scientists think *Entelodon* ate?

Answers:
1. Because it looked like a dog, but walked like a bear 2. *Plesictis* 3. Fish 4. Almost anything

▲ *Potamotherium* had a bendy backbone to allow it to twist about in the water.

Amazing ancient elephants

65 **The first elephant had tiny tusks and almost no trunk.** *Moeritherium* lived in northern Africa about 36 million years ago. It stood just 60 centimetres tall and may have weighed around 20 kilograms – about the size of a large pet dog.

▶ Woolly mammoths had coats of shaggy hair. This hair kept their warm inner fur dry and waterproof in the freezing conditions of the ice age.

66 Some elephants were very hairy. The woolly mammoth was covered in thick, long dense hair to keep out the cold of the ice age. It was larger than a modern elephant and was probably hunted by early people. The last woolly mammoths may have died out less than 10,000 years ago.

67 One elephant had tusks like shovels. *Platybelodon* lived about nine million years ago in Europe, Asia and Africa. Its lower tusks were shaped like broad, flat shovels. Perhaps it used them to scoop up water plants to eat.

69 Some elephants had four tusks. *Tetralophodon* lived about eight million years ago and stood 3 metres tall. Its fossils have been found in Europe, Asia, Africa and America, so it was a very widespread and successful animal.

70 The biggest elephant was the Columbian mammoth. It stood 4 metres tall and may have weighed over 10 tonnes – twice as much as most elephants today. It lived on the grasslands of southern North America.

▼ The Columbian mammoth had tusks that twisted into curved, spiral shapes.

68 Elephants were more varied and common long ago, than they are today. *Anancus* roamed Europe and Asia two million years ago. Like modern elephants, it used its trunk to pull leaves from branches and its tusks to dig up roots. However most kinds of prehistoric elephants died out. Only two kinds survive today, in Africa and Asia.

Animals with hooves

71 **The first horse was hardly larger than a pet cat.** *Hyracotherium* lived in Europe, Asia and North America about 50 million years ago. It was only 20 centimetres tall and lived in woods and forests.

▼ *Hyracotherium* is sometimes called *Eohippus*, which means 'dawn horse'. It had a short neck, slender legs and a long tail.

72 Early horses did not eat grass — because there wasn't any. Grasses and open plains did not appear on Earth until 25 million years ago. Then early horses moved onto them, started to eat grass, and gradually became bigger.

73 Over millions of years, horses gradually lost their toes! The very first horses had five toes per foot, each ending in a small nail-like hoof. *Hyracotherium* had four toes on each front foot and three on each back foot. Later, *Mesohippus*, which was as big as a labrador dog, had three toes on each foot. Today's horses have just one toe on each foot, which ends in a large hoof.

74 Some prehistoric camels had horns.
Synthetoceras had a pair of horns at the top
of its head, and also an extraordinary
Y-shaped horn growing from its
nose. It probably used these
horns to fight enemies
and also to show off to
others of its kind at
breeding time.

▶ The amazing nose horn of
Synthetoceras was present
only on male animals.

HORSE RACE

You will need:
stiff card   crayons
scissors   string about
4 metres long

On the card, draw a picture
of *Hyracotherium*. Colour it in
and cut it out. Make a hole in
the middle, about 2 centimetres
from the top. Thread the string
through the hole and tie one end
to a piece of furniture. Pull the
string tight, then flick it with
a finger to make
Hyracotherium move
along!

◀ *Megaloceros*
may have stored
food for the
winter in the form
of fat in a hump
on its shoulder.

75 Some prehistoric deer had
antlers as big as a person! *Megaloceros*
means 'big deer' and it was as big as
today's biggest deer, the moose. But its
antlers were even bigger, measuring almost
4 metres from tip to tip. *Megaloceros* may
have survived in some parts of Europe
until as little as 3000 years ago.

Cats, dogs and bears

76 **The sabre-tooth 'tiger' *Smilodon* had two huge sharp teeth like sabres (swords) – but it was not really a tiger.** It belonged to a different group of cats to real tigers. *Smilodon*'s teeth were long and sharp but not very strong. It probably used them like knives to stab and slash at its prey, which then bled to death. *Smilodon* then ate it without a struggle.

▶ *Smilodon* had enormously powerful shoulders, so it may have sprung on its prey and held it down.

77 **The earliest cats were similar to those of today.** *Dinictis* lived about 30 million years ago and was strong and stealthy, like the modern-day cougar (mountain lion). It probably hunted like modern cats too, by creeping up close to a victim, then leaping on it to bite its throat or neck.

78 **The first dog, *Hesperocyon*, had a long body and short legs, more like a stoat or mongoose.** It was about 90 centimetres long and lived about 30 million years ago. Only later dogs had long legs and were able to run fast after their prey.

◀ *Hesperocyon* may have hunted in packs. This would have allowed it to hunt animals much larger than itself.

79 The sabre-tooth 'cat' *Thylacosmilus* was not even a real cat! It had a cat-shaped head, body, legs and tail. Yet it was a marsupial – a cousin of kangaroos and koalas. It lived in South America four million years ago.

80 Sea lions did not develop from lions – but from dogs. *Allodesmus* was an early type of sea lion and lived about 13 million years ago. It had strong flippers for fast swimming. Its fossil bones show that it came originally from the dog group.

◄ Early humans had to face many natural dangers, such as cave bears.

81 Early people hunted cave bears, and cave bears hunted early people! The huge cave bear of the Ice Age was as big as today's grizzly bear. Humans called Neanderthals hunted them and used their bones and teeth as ornaments. The bears hunted people too, and left their bones in caves.

Prehistoric giants

82 **The largest flying bird ever was as big as a small plane!** *Argentavis* was twice the size of any flying bird today. Its wings measured 7 metres from tip to tip. It was a huge vulture that fed on the dead bodies of other creatures, tearing off their flesh with its powerful hooked beak.

▼ *Argentavis* lived about seven million years ago in South America.

83 **Some birds were even bigger than *Argentavis*, but they could not fly – and they were deadly hunters.** In South America about one million years ago, *Titanis* grew to 3 metres tall. It raced after its prey, which it tore apart with its huge, hooked beak.

84 **A type of prehistoric kangaroo, *Procoptodon*, was twice as big as those of today.** Yet it could bound along as fast as a racehorse. Like kangaroos of today, it was a marsupial, carrying its baby in a pouch. It lived in Australia.

◀ In South America, *Titanis* was a monstrous hunting bird that chased after mammals such as this early horse.

85 The largest land mammal ever to have lived was a type of rhino – without a nose horn.

Paraceratherium was far bigger than an elephant, at 8 metres long and 6 metres tall at the shoulder. It weighed over 15 tonnes – more than three elephants. This giant creature lived in Asia about 30 million years ago and was a peaceful plant eater.

I DON'T BELIEVE IT!

Giant marsupials may have started stories of the 'Bunyip', a mythical Australian animal.

▲ The huge *Paraceratherium* fed by browsing on trees, stripping off the leaves. Even though it was so big and heavy, *Paraceratherium* had long legs, which means it was probably capable of running.

A giant island

86 For almost 50 million years, South America was like a giant island – with many strange animals that were found nowhere else. Until three million years ago, South America was separated from North America by an ocean. On islands, animals can evolve into unusual kinds found nowhere else in the world.

▶ South America was once separated from North America. This meant that certain animals that survived there, such as *Macrauchenia* and *Glyptodon*, did not live anywhere else in the world.

87 Elephants were not the only animals with trunks! *Macrauchenia* lived in South America about 100,000 years ago. It was about the size of a camel and probably had a trunk to gather leaves to eat. It was not a type of elephant, but a distant cousin of horses and rhinos.

88 Armadillos were once nearly as big as tanks! *Glyptodon* was almost 4 metres long and covered in a thick dome of bony armour. It lived in South America until about 10,000 years ago. Today, armadillos are quite small, but they are still covered in bony plates for protection.

Macrauchenia

Glyptodon

89 One South American creature that has died out was the giant sloth, *Megatherium*. It was a cousin of the smaller sloths that live in trees today – but it was far too big to climb trees. At 6 metres long and 3 tonnes in weight, it was the size of an elephant!

90 When South America joined North America, many kinds of prehistoric animals died out. In particular, animals from North America spread south. They were better at surviving than the South American creatures, and they gradually took over.

▶ *Megatherium* may only have died out in the last few thousand years.

I DON'T BELIEVE IT!
The armadillo is a South American animal that lives in North America, too. Over the past 100 years, it has spread north at a rate of one kilometre every ten years.

49

Our prehistoric relations

91 Monkeys, apes and humans first appeared over 50 million years ago – the first kinds looked like squirrels. This group is called the primates. *Plesiadapis* was one of the first primates. It lived 55 million years ago in Europe and North America.

◀ *Plesiadapis* had claws on its fingers and toes, unlike monkeys and apes, which had nails.

92 Early apes walked on all fours. About 20 million years ago, *Dryopithecus* lived in Europe and Asia. It used its arms and legs to climb trees. When it came down to the ground, it walked on all fours. It was 60 centimetres long and ate fruit and leaves.

I DON'T BELIEVE IT

The first fossils of the giant ape *Gigantopithecus* to be studied by scientists came from a second-hand shop in Hong Kong, over 70 years ago.

▶ The early ape *Dryopithecus* walked flat on its feet, unlike other apes, which walked on their knuckles.

▼ The need to see longer distances on grasslands may have caused the first apes to walk on two legs.

93 **Some kinds of apes may have walked on their two back legs, like us.** About 4.5 million years ago *Ardipithecus* lived in Africa. Only a few of its fossils have been found. However, experts think it may have walked upright on its back legs. It could have made the first steps in the change, or evolution, from apes to humans.

94 **One prehistoric ape was a real giant – over 3 metres tall!** Its name, *Gigantopithecus*, means 'giant ape'. It was much larger than today's biggest ape, the gorilla, which grows to 2 metres tall. *Gigantopithecus* probably ate roots and seeds, and may have hunted small animals such as birds, rats and lizards.

▶ The enormous *Gigantopithecus* could probably stand on its hind legs to reach food.

95 **Scientists work out which animals are our closest cousins partly from fossils – and also from chemicals.** The chemical called DNA contains genes, which are instructions for how living things grow and work. The living animals with DNA most similar to ours are the great apes, chimpanzees and gorillas, both from Africa. So our ancient cousins were probably apes like them. The orang-utan, from Southeast Asia, is less similar.

The first humans

▼ *Australopithecus* walked upright. It spent most of its days searching for food.

96 Our early prehistoric cousins were much smaller than us. One kind was called *Australopithecus afarensis*, meaning 'southern ape from Afar', because its fossils come from the Afar region of East Africa. It was just over one metre tall, lived over three million years ago, and looked part human and part ape.

▶ *Homo erectus* was the first living creature to use fire for cooking and warmth.

97 Very early kinds of humans lived almost two million years ago. They were called *Homo erectus*, which means 'upright human', and they were as tall as us. These first humans spread from Africa, across Asia, and into Europe. However, they all died out about 200,000 years ago.

98 From one million years ago early people made tools out of stone – they had not invented metal. They chipped rocks like flint to form a sharp, cutting edge, and shaped stones into knives, scrapers, or axes. Stone tools have been found with the bones of animals that were cut up for food, along with the ashes of fires used for cooking – and the bones of the people themselves.

▶ The Flores humans probably used stone tools to hunt animals such as the pygmy elephant.

99 Some prehistoric animals were domesticated (tamed) to become the first farm animals. This began around 15,000 years ago. For example, fierce aurochs, a type of wild cow, were gradually bred over time to become quiet, calm animals. They provided people with food and clothing.

100 We are still discovering surprises about prehistoric life. In 2004, scientists found the bones and tools of tiny humans, less than one metre tall, on the island of Flores in Southeast Asia. Their remains are from over 90,000 to less than 15,000 years old. No one knew they existed. In the future we may discover more amazing finds from the past.

QUIZ

1. Were prehistoric humans big or small?
2. What were the first tools made from?
3. When were animals first domesticated?
4. What was discovered on the island of Flores?

Answers:
1. Small 2. Stone 3. 15,000 years ago 4. Flores man

DINOSAURS

101 **Dinosaurs were types of animals with scaly skin, called reptiles.** They lived millions of years ago. There were many different kinds of dinosaurs - huge and tiny, tall and short, fierce hunters and peaceful plant-eaters. But all the dinosaurs died out long, long ago.

Age of the dinosaurs

102 Dinosaurs lived between about 230 million and 65 million years ago. This vast length of time is called the Mesozoic Era. Dinosaurs were around for about 80 times longer than people have been on Earth!

103 Dinosaurs were not the only animals during the Mesozoic Era. There were many other kinds of animals such as insects, fish, lizards, crocodiles, birds and mammals.

104 There were many different shapes and sizes of dinosaurs. Some were smaller than your hand. Others were bigger than a house!

▼ *Jobaria* and *Janenschia*, giant plant eaters.

▼ This timeline begins 286 million years ago at the start of the Permian Period when the ancestors of the dinosaurs appear. It finishes at the end of the Tertiary Period 2 million years ago, when the dinosaurs die out and mammals became dominant.

PALAEOZOIC ERA	MESOZOIC ERA	
PERMIAN PERIOD	TRIASSIC PERIOD	JURASSIC PERIOD
The reptiles, including the ancestors of the dinosaurs, start to become more important than the amphibians.	The first proper dinosaurs appear. These are small two-legged carnivores, meat-eaters, and larger herbivores, or plant eaters.	Many different dinosaurs lived at this time, including the giant plant eaters like Barosaurus.

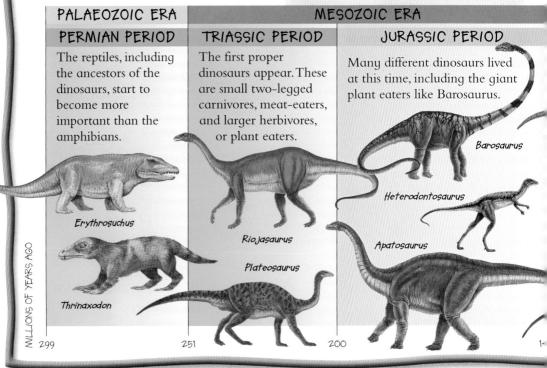

Barosaurus

Heterodontosaurus

Apatosaurus

Erythrosuchus

Riojasaurus

Plateosaurus

Thrinaxodon

MILLIONS OF YEARS AGO

299   251   200   1

105 No single kind of dinosaur survived for all of the Mesozoic Era. Different dinosurs came and went. Some lasted for less than a million years. Other kinds, like *Stegosaurus*, kept going for more than 20 million years.

106 There were no people during the Age of Dinosaurs. There was a gap of more than 60 million years between the last dinosaurs and the first people.

I DON'T BELIEVE IT!

The name 'dinosaur' means 'terrible lizard'. But dinosaurs weren't lizards, and not all dinosaurs were terrible. Small plant–eating dinosaurs were about as 'terrible' as today's sheep!

◄ All the dinosaurs died out at the end of the Cretaceous Period, possibly because of a meteor strike, but no one can be sure.

MESOZOIC ERA	CENOZOIC ERA
CRETACEOUS PERIOD	TERTIARY PERIOD
During the last part of the age of the dinosaurs, both giant carnivores and armoured herbivores were alive.	The dinosaurs have all died out. Mammals, which have been around since the Triassic Period, become the main land animals.

Tyrannosaurus rex

Deinonychus

Brontotherium, herbivorous mammal

Thylacosmilus, carnivorous mammal

Nesodon, herbivorous mammal

Spinosaurus

Tarbosaurus

5

66

2

MILLIONS OF YEARS AGO

57

Before the dinosaurs

107 Dinosaurs were not the first animals on Earth. Many other kinds of creatures lived before them, including several other types of reptiles. Over millions of years one of these groups of reptiles probably changed very slowly, or evolved, into the first dinosaurs.

109 Crocodiles were around even before the first dinosaurs. They still survive today, long after the last dinosaurs. *Erythrosuchus* was 4.5 metres long, lived 240 million years ago, lurked in swamps and ate fish.

Erythrosuchus

108 *Dimetrodon* was a fierce, meat-eating reptile that looked like a dinosaur — but it wasn't. It lived 270 million years ago, long before the dinosaurs. *Dimetrodon* was 3 metres long and had a tall flap of skin like a sail on its back.

110 Therapsids lived before the
dinosaurs and also alongside the
early dinosaurs. They were called
mammal-like reptiles because they didn't
have scaly skin like most reptiles. They
had furry or hairy skin like mammals.

▼ *Ornithosuchus* was one of the early
thecodonts. It was a carnivore that
walked on two legs, a cousin of the first
dinosaurs. The name 'thecodont' means
'socket-toothed reptile'.

QUIZ

1. Did *Dimetrodon* live before
   or after the dinosaurs?
2. Did thecodonts catch small
   animals to eat, or munch on
   leaves and fruits?
3. What are therapsids also
   known as?
4. Did dinosaurs gradually change,
   or evolve into crocodiles?
5. Did all reptiles have
   scaly skin?

Answers:
1. Before 2. Small animals
3. Mammal-like reptiles 4. No, crocodiles
are a separate group. 5. No, some were furry

111 Thecodonts were slim, long-legged
reptiles that lived just before the
dinosaurs. They could rear up and run fast
on their back legs. They could also leap and
jump well. They probably caught small
animals such as bugs and lizards to eat.

112 Of all the creatures shown here,
the thecodonts were most similar
to the first dinosaurs. So perhaps some
thecodonts gradually changed, or evolved, into
early dinosaurs. This may have happened
more than 220 million years ago. But no one
is sure, and there are many other ideas about
where the dinosaurs came from.

The dinosaurs arrive!

113 The earliest dinosaurs stalked the Earth almost 230 million years ago. They lived in what is now Argentina, in South America. They included *Eoraptor* and *Herrerasaurus*. Slim, fast creatures, they could stand almost upright and run on their two rear legs. Few other animals of the time could run upright like this, on legs that were straight below their bodies. Most other animals had legs that stuck out sideways.

Herrerasaurus was about 3 metres long from nose to tail.

The legs were underneath the body, not sticking out to the sides as in other reptiles, such as lizards and crocodiles.

114 These early dinosaurs were probably meat eaters. They hunted small reptiles such as lizards, insects and worms. They had lightweight bodies and long, strong legs to chase after prey. Their claws were long and sharp for grabbing victims. Their large mouths were filled with pointed teeth to tear up their food.

TWO LEGS GOOD!

You will need:

stiff card   sticky tape
safe scissors   split pins

Cut out a model of *Herrerasaurus*; the head, body, arms and tail are one piece of card. Next, cut out each leg from another piece. Fix the legs on either side of the hip area of the body using a split pin. Adjust the angle of the head, body and tail to stand over the legs. This is how many dinosaurs stood and ran, well balanced over their rear legs and using little effort.

Herrerasaurus had a pointed head and a long, bendy neck, which helped it to look around and sniff for prey.

The long tail balanced the head and body over the rear legs.

Herrerasaurus could run rapidly on its two rear legs, or walk slowly on all fours.

Getting bigger

115 As the early dinosaurs spread over the land they began to change. This gradual and natural change in living things has happened since life began on Earth. New kinds of plants and animals appear, do well for a time, and then die out as yet more new kinds appear. The slow and gradual change of living things over time is called evolution.

Plateosaurus

116 Some kinds of dinosaurs became larger and began to eat plants rather than animals. *Plateosaurus* was one of the first big plant-eating dinosaurs. It grew up to 8 metres long and lived 220 million years ago in what is now Europe. It could rear up on its back legs and use its long neck to reach food high off the ground.

117 *Riojasaurus* was an even larger plant eater. It lived 218 million years ago in what is now Argentina. *Riojasaurus* was 10 metres long and weighed about 2 tonnes - more than a large family car of today.

Riojasaurus

118 The early dinosaurs lived during the Triassic Period. This was the first period, or part of, the Age of Dinosaurs (the Mesozoic Era). The Triassic Period lasted from 251 to 200 million years ago.

119 The early plant-eating dinosaurs may have become larger so that they could reach up into trees for food. Their size would also have helped them fight enemies, as many big meat-eating reptiles were ready to make a meal of them. One was the crocodile *Rutiodon,* which was 3 metres long.

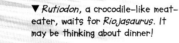
▼ *Rutiodon,* a crocodile-like meat-eater, waits for *Riojasaurus.* It may be thinking about dinner!

I DON'T BELIEVE IT!

Early plant-eating dinosaurs did not eat fruits or grasses — there weren't any! They hadn't appeared yet! Instead they ate plants called horsetails, ferns, cycads, and conifer trees.

What teeth tell us

120 We know about living things from long ago, such as dinosaurs, because of fossils. These were once their hard body parts, such as bones, claws, horns and shells. The hard parts did not rot away after death but got buried and preserved for millions of years. Gradually they turned to stone and became fossils. Today, we dig up the fossils, and their sizes and shapes give us clues to how prehistoric animals lived.

Tyrannosaurus rex

▶ Plant eater *Edmontosaurus* had flat teeth at the back of its jaws for chewing its food.

121 Dinosaur teeth were very hard and formed many fossils. Their shapes help to show what each type of dinosaur ate. *Edmontosaurus* had rows of broad, wide, sharp-ridged teeth in the sides of its mouth. These were ideal for chewing tough plant foods like twigs and old leaves.

▲ *Tyrannosaurus rex* had sharp, knife-like teeth at the front of its jaw for cutting and tearing meat.

122 *Tarbosaurus* had long, sharp teeth like knives or daggers. These were excellent for tearing up prey, and slicing off lumps of flesh for swallowing.

▲ *Tarbosaurus* was 12 metres long and lived 70 million years ago in East Asia.

▼ *Baryonyx was 10 metres long and lived 120 million years ago in Europe.*

123 **Baryonyx had small, narrow, pointed, cone-shaped teeth.** These resemble the teeth of a crocodile or dolphin today. They are ideal for grabbing slippery prey such as fish.

124 **The teeth of the giant, long-necked dinosaur *Apatosaurus* were long, thin and blunt, shaped like pencils.** They worked like a rake to pull leaves off branches into the mouth, for the dinosaur to eat.

▶ *Apatosaurus was 25 metres long and lived 140 million years ago in Western North America.*

FIND DINOSAUR TEETH AT HOME!

With the help of an adult, look in a utensils drawer or tool box for dinosaur teeth! Some tools resemble the teeth of certain dinosaurs, and do similar jobs.
File or rasp – broad surface with hard ridges, like the plant-chewing teeth of *Edmontosaurus*.
Knife – long, pointed and sharp, like the meat-slicing teeth of *Tyrannosaurus rex*.
Pliers – Gripping and squeezing, like the beak-shaped mouth of *Ornithomimus*.

125 **Some dinosaurs, like *Ornithomimus*, had no teeth at all!** The mouth was shaped like a bird's beak and made out of a tough, strong, horny substance like our fingernails. The beak was suited to pecking up all kinds of food such as seeds, worms and bugs.

▲ *Ornithomimus was 3.5 metres long and lived 70 million years ago in western North America.*

Super-size dinosaurs

126 **The true giants of the Age of Dinosaurs were the sauropods.** These vast dinosaurs all had a small head, long neck, barrel-shaped body, long tapering tail and four pillar-like legs. The biggest sauropods included *Brachiosaurus*, *Mamenchisaurus*, *Barosaurus*, *Diplodocus* and *Argentinosaurus*.

▲ *Argentinosaurus* was up to 40 metres long, and weighed up to 100 tonnes.

127 **Sauropod dinosaurs probably lived in groups or herds.** We know this from their footprints, which have been preserved as fossils. Each foot left a print as large as a chair seat. Hundreds of footprints together shows that many sauropods walked along in groups.

128 **Sauropod dinosaurs may have swallowed pebbles – on purpose!** Their peg-like teeth could only rake in plant food, not chew it. Pebbles and stones gulped into the stomach helped to grind and crush the food. These pebbles, smooth and polished by the grinding, have been found with the fossil bones of sauropods.

129 The biggest sauropods, like *Apatosaurus*, were enormous beasts. They weighed up to ten times more than elephants of today. Yet their fossil footprints showed they could run quite fast — nearly as quickly as you!

Mamenchisaurus grew up to 26 metres long and weighed 30 tonnes. It lived in East Asia 160 million years ago.

Barosaurus lived 150 million years ago in North America and Africa. It was 27 metres long and weighed 15 tonnes.

Brachiosaurus grew up to 25 metres long, and weighed up to 50 tonnes. It lived 150 million years ago in North America and Africa.

Diplodocus lived in North America 150 million years ago. It grew to 27 metres long and weighed up to 12 tonnes.

130 Sauropods probably had to eat most of the time, 20 hours out of every 24. They had enormous bodies that needed great amounts of food, but only small mouths to gather the food.

This modern lorry is to the same scale as these huge dinosaurs!

I DON'T BELIEVE IT!

Diplodocus is also known as 'Old Whip-tail'! It could swish its long tail so hard and fast that it made an enormous CRACK like a whip. This living, leathery, scaly whip would scare away enemies or even rip off their skin.

Claws for killing

131 **Nearly all dinosaurs had claws on their fingers and toes.** These claws were shaped for different jobs in different dinosaurs. They were made from a tough substance called keratin – the same as your fingernails and toenails.

Hypsilophodon

132 *Hypsilophodon* **had strong, sturdy claws.** This small plant eater, 2 metres long, probably used them to scrabble and dig in soil for seeds and roots.

133 *Deinonychus* **had long, sharp, hooked claws on its hands.** This meat eater, about 3 metres long, would grab a victim and tear at its skin and flesh.

134 *Deinonychus* **had a huge hooked claw, as big as your hand, on the second toe of each foot.** This claw could kick out and flick down like a pointed knife to slash pieces out of the prey.

Deinonychus

135 *Baryonyx* **also had a large claw but this was on the thumb of each hand.** It may have worked as a fish-hook to snatch fish from water. This is another clue that *Baryonyx* probably ate fish.

◄ These giant arms of the dinosaur *Deinocheirus* were found in Mongolia. Each one was bigger than a human, but nothing else of the skeleton has yet been found.

136 *Iguanodon* had claws on its feet. But these were rounded and blunt and looked more like hooves.

Iguanodon

137 *Iguanodon* also had stubby claws on its hands. However its thumb claw was longer and shaped like a spike, perhaps for stabbing enemies.

138 Giant sauropod dinosaurs had almost flat claws. Dinosaurs like *Apatosaurus* looked like they had toenails on their huge feet!

Deadly meat eaters

139 **The biggest meat-eating dinosaurs were the largest predators (hunters) ever to walk the Earth.** Different types came and went during the Age of Dinosaurs. *Allosaurus* was from the middle of this time span. One of the last dinosaurs was also one of the largest predators – *Tyrannosaurus rex*. An earlier hunting dinosaur from South America was even bigger –*Giganotosaurus*.

▼ A group of *Tyrannosaurus rex*.

Giganotosaurus

140 These great predators were well equipped for hunting large prey – including other dinosaurs. They all had massive mouths armed with long sharp teeth in powerful jaws. They had long, strong back legs for fast running, and enormous toe claws for kicking and holding down victims.

141 Meat-eating dinosaurs probably caught their food in various ways. They may have lurked behind rocks or trees and rushed out to surprise a victim. They may have raced as fast as possible after prey that ran away or plodded steadily for a great time to tire out their meal. They might even have scavenged - feasted on the bodies of creatures that were dead or dying.

Allosaurus was 11 metres long and weighed 2 tonnes. It came from North America

Albertosaurus was from North America. It was 9 metres long and weighed one tonne

Spinosaurus came from Africa. It was 14 metres long and weighed 4 tonnes

Carnotaurus from South America was 7.5 metres long and weighed one tonne

The famous *Tyrannosaurus rex* was over 12 metres long and weighed 5 tonnes. It lived in North America.

The biggest carnivore was *Giganotosaurus*. It was over 13 metres long and weighed over 6 tonnes

Look! Listen! Sniff!

142 Like the reptiles of today, dinosaurs could see, hear and smell the world around them. We know this from fossils. The preserved fossil skulls have spaces for eyes, ears and nostrils.

143 Some dinosaurs, like *Troodon*, had very big eyes. There are large, bowl-shaped hollows in their fossil skulls. Today's animals with big eyes can see well in the dark, like mice, owls and night-time lizards. Perhaps *Troodon* prowled through the forest at night, peering in the gloom, looking for small creatures to eat.

Ear
Eye
Nostril

144 There are also spaces on the sides of the head where *Troodon* had its ears. Dinosaur ears were round and flat, like the ears of other reptiles. *Troodon* could hear the tiny noises of little animals moving about in the dark.

◄ *Troodon* was about 2 metres long and lived in North America 70 million years ago. You can see here the large eye sockets.

145 The nostrils of *Troodon* were two holes at the front of its snout. With its delicate sense of smell, *Troodon* could sniff out its prey of insects, worms, little reptiles such as lizards, and small shrew-like mammals.

▲ *Corythosaurus* had a bony plate on its head, instead of a tube like *Parasaurolophus*.

146 Dinosaurs used their eyes, ears and noses not only to find food, but also to detect enemies — and each other. *Parasaurolophus* had a long, hollow, tube-like crest on its head. Perhaps it blew air along this to make a noise like a trumpet, as an elephant does today with its trunk.

▶ *Parasaurolophus* was a 'duck-billed' dinosaur or hadrosaur. It was about 10 metres long and lived 80 million years ago in North America.

BIGGER EYES, BETTER SIGHT

You will need:

stiff card   elastic   safe scissors

Make a *Troodon* mask from card. Carefully cut out the shape as shown, with two small eye holes, each just one cm across. Attach elastic so you can wear the mask and find out how little you can see. Carefully make the eye holes as large as the eyes of the real *Troodon*. Now you can have a much bigger, clearer view of the world!

147 Dinosaurs like *Parasaurolophus* may have made noises to send messages to other members of their group or herd. Different messages could tell the others about finding food or warn them about enemies.

Fastest and slowest

148 Dinosaurs walked and ran at different speeds, according to their size and shape. In the world today, cheetahs and ostriches are slim with long legs and run very fast. Elephants and hippos are massive heavyweights and plod slowly. Dinosaurs were similar. Some were big, heavy and slow. Others were slim, light and speedy.

▼ *Coelophysis* was 3 metres long. It was one of the earliest dinosaurs, living about 220 million years ago.

▲ *Struthiomimus* lived about 75 million years ago in north-west North America.

149 *Struthiomimus* was one of the fastest of all the dinosaurs. It was more than 2 metres tall and 4 metres long. It had very long back legs and large clawed feet, like an ostrich. It also had a horny beak-shaped mouth for pecking food, like an ostrich. This is why it is also called an 'ostrich-dinosaur'. It could probably run at more than 70 kilometres per hour.

150 *Muttaburrasaurus* was a huge ornithopod type of dinosaur, a cousin of *Iguanodon*. It probably walked about as fast as you, around 4–5 kilometres per hour. It might have been able to gallop along at a top speed of 15 kilometres per hour, making the ground shake with its 4-tonne weight!

▲ *Muttaburrasaurus* lived about 110 million years ago in south-east Australia.

151 *Coelophysis* was a slim, lightweight dinosaur. It could probably trot, jump, leap and dart about with great agility. Sometimes it ran upright on its two back legs. Or it could bound along on all fours like a dog at more than 30 kilometres per hour.

QUIZ

Put these dinosaurs and today's animals in order of top running speed, from slowest to fastest.

Human (40 km/h)

Cheetah (100-plus km/h)

Struthiomimus (70 km/h)

Muttaburrasaurus (15 km/h)

Sloth (0.2 km/h)

Coelophysis (30 km/h)

Answer:
Sloth, *Muttaburrasaurus*, *Coelophysis*,
Human, *Struthiomimus*, Cheetah

Dinosaur tanks

152 Some dinosaurs had body defences against predators. These might be large horns and spikes, or thick hard lumps of bonelike armour-plating. Most armoured dinosaurs were plant eaters. They had to defend themselves against big meat-eating dinosaurs such as *Tyrannosaurus rex*.

153 *Triceratops* had three horns, one on its nose and two much longer ones above its eyes. It also had a wide shield-like piece of bone over its neck and shoulders. The horns and neck frill made *Triceratops* look very fearsome. But most of the time it quietly ate plants. If it was attacked, *Triceratops* could charge at the enemy and jab with its horns, like a rhino does today.

▲ *Triceratops* was 9 metres long and weighed over 5 tonnes. It lived 65 million years ago in North America.

154 *Euoplocephalus* was a well-armoured dinosaur. It had bands of thick, leathery skin across its back. Big, hard, pointed lumps of bone were set into this skin like studs on a leather belt. *Euoplocephalus* also had a great lump of bone on its tail. It measured almost one metre across and looked like a massive hammer or club. *Euoplocephalus* could swing it at predators to injure them or break their legs.

DESIGN A DINOSAUR!

Make an imaginary dinosaur! It might have the body armour and tail club of *Euoplocephalus*, or the head horns and neck frill of *Triceratops*. You can draw your dinosaur, or make it out of pieces of card or from modelling clay. You can give it a made-up name, like Euoplo-ceratops or Tri-cephalus. How well protected is your dinosaur? How does it compare to some well-armoured creatures of today, such as a tortoise, armadillo or porcupine?

Styracosaurus

Euoplocephalus

Protoceratops

Dinosaur eggs and nests

155 Like most reptiles today, dinosaurs produced young by laying eggs. These hatched out into baby dinosaurs, which gradually grew into adults. Fossils have been found of eggs with developing dinosaurs inside, as well as fossils of just-hatched baby dinosaurs.

▼ A female *Protoceratops* with her eggs.

156 Many kinds of dinosaur eggs have been found. *Protoceratops* was a pig-sized dinosaur that lived 85 million years ago in what is now the Gobi Desert of Asia.

Protoceratops' egg

157 A *Protoceratops* female arranged her eggs. The eggs were carefully positioned in a spiral shape, or in circles one within the other. They would normally lay around 20 eggs.

158 *Protoceratops* scraped a bowl-shaped nest about one metre across in the dry soil. Probably the female did this. Today, only female reptiles make nests and some care for the eggs or babies. Male reptiles take no part.

Hadrosaur egg

QUIZ

1. How long was *Triceratops*?
2. How many horns did *Triceratops* have?
3. How many eggs did a female *Protoceratops* lay?
4. Did dinosaurs lay hard eggs like birds do, or bendy eggs?
5. How long was a *Tyrannosaurus rex* egg?

Answers:
1. 9 metres 2. Three
3. About 20 eggs 4. They laid bendy, leathery eggs 5. 40 centimetres

159 The eggs probably hatched after a few weeks. The eggshell was slightly leathery and bendy, like most reptile eggshells today, and not brittle or hard like a bird's.

160 Fossils of baby *Protoceratops* show that they looked very much like their parents. But the neck frill of the baby *Protoceratops* was not as large compared to the rest of the body, as in the adult. As the youngster grew, the frill grew faster than the rest of the body.

▶ This shows part of a *Tyrannosaurus rex* egg.

161 Other dinosaurs laid different sizes and shapes of eggs. Huge sauropod dinosaurs like *Brachiosaurus* probably laid rounded eggs as big as basketballs. Eggs of big meat-eaters, like *Tyrannosaurus rex*, were more sausage-shaped, 40 centimetres long and 15 centimetres wide.

162 Most dinosaurs simply laid their eggs in a nest or buried in soil, and left them to hatch on their own. The baby dinosaurs had to find their own food and defend themselves against enemies. But some dinosaurs looked after their babies.

Dinosaur babies

163 Some dinosaur parents looked after their babies and even brought them food in the nest. Fossils of the hadrosaur dinosaur *Maiasaura* include nests, eggs, babies after hatching, and broken eggshells. Some fossils are of unhatched eggs but broken into many small parts, as though squashed by the babies which had already come out of their eggs.

164 The newly hatched *Maiasaura* babies had to stay in the nest. They could not run away because their leg bones had not yet become strong and hard. The nest was a mound of mud about 2 metres across, and up to 20 babies lived in it.

▲ A full-grown *Maiasaura* was about 9 metres long and weighed around 3 tonnes. A newly-hatched *Maiasaura* baby was only 30–40 centimetres long. *Maiasaura* lived about 75 million years ago in North America.

▶ Hundreds of fossil *Maiasaura* nests have been found close together, showing that these dinosaurs bred in groups or colonies. The nests show signs of being dug out and repaired year after year, which suggests the dinosaurs kept coming back to the same place to breed.

165 Fossils of *Maiasaura* nests also contain fossilised twigs, berries and other bits of plants. *Maiasaura* was a plant-eating dinosaur, and it seems that one or both parents brought food to the nest for their babies to eat. The tiny teeth of the babies already had slight scratches and other marks where they had been worn while eating food. This supports the idea that parent *Maiasaura* brought food to their babies in the nest.

I DON'T BELIEVE IT!

Baby dinosaurs grew up to five times faster than human babies! A baby sauropod dinosaur like *Diplodocus* was already one metre long and 30 kilograms in weight when it came out of its egg!

The end for the dinosaurs

166 **All dinosaurs on Earth died out by 65 million years ago.** There are dinosaur fossils in the rocks up to this time, but there are none after. However, there are fossils of other creatures like fish, insects, birds and mammals. What happened to wipe out some of the biggest, most numerous and most successful animals the world has ever seen? There are many ideas. It could have been one disaster, or a combination of several.

167 **The dinosaurs may have been killed by a giant lump of rock, a meteorite.** This would have come from outer space and smashed into the Earth. A meteorite would have thrown up vast clouds of water, rocks, ash and dust that blotted out the Sun for many years. Lack of sunlight would mean that plants could not grow, so plant-eating dinosaurs died out. Meat-eating dinosaurs had no food so they died as well.

▼ A giant meteorite from space may have killed off not only the dinosaurs, but many other kinds of animals and plants too.

170 It might be that dinosaur eggs were eaten by a plague of animals. Small, shrew-like mammals were around at the time. They may have eaten the eggs at night as the dinosaurs slept.

168 Many volcanoes around the Earth could have erupted all at the same time. This would have thrown out red-hot rocks, ash, dust and clouds of poison gas. Dinosaurs would have choked and died in the gloom.

169 Dinosaurs might have been killed by a disease. This could have gradually spread among all the dinosaurs and killed them off.

METEORITE SMASH!

You will need:

plastic bowl   large pebble
flour   desk light

Ask an adult for help. Put the flour in the bowl. This is Earth's surface. Place the desk light so it shines over the top of the bowl. This is the Sun. The pebble is the meteorite from space. WHAM! Drop the pebble into the bowl. See how the tiny bits of flour float in the air like a mist, making the 'Sun' dimmer. A real meteorite smash may have been the beginning of the end for the dinosaurs.

Myths and mistakes

171 As far as we can tell from the clues we have, some of the ideas which have grown up about dinosaurs are not true. For example, dinosaurs are shown in different colours such as brown or green. Some have patches or stripes. But no one knows the true colours of dinosaurs.

There are a few fossils of dinosaur skin. But being fossils, these have turned to stone and so they are the colour of stone. They are no longer the colour of the original dinosaur skin.

◄ We really have no idea what colour the dinosaurs were. We can guess by looking at reptiles today, but they could have been any colour!

◄ This is a fossil of the skin of *Edmontosaurus*. You can see the texture of the skin, but the only colour is of the rock.

172 Similarly, for many years people thought that all dinosaurs were slow and stupid animals. But they were not. Some dinosaurs were quick and agile. Also some, like *Troodon*, had big brains for their body size. They may have been quite 'clever'.

▲ *Troodon* had a large brain for its body size, almost the same as a monkey of today.

173 Scientists began to study fossils of dinosaurs about 160 years ago, in the 19th century. The first dinosaurs to be studied were very big, such as *Megalosaurus*, *Iguanodon* and *Plateosaurus*. So the idea grew up that all dinosaurs were huge. But they were not. *Compsognathus*, one of the smallest dinosaurs, was only 75 centimetres long – about as big as a pet cat of today.

◄ *Compsognathus* weighed only 3 kilograms and lived 155 million years ago in Europe.

◄ Its name means 'elegant jaw'. Its teeth were small and spaced apart from each other. This makes it likely that *Compsognathus* ate small reptiles and insects, rather than attacking large prey.

▲ These *Wannanosaurus* are using their bony skull caps to fight over territory, food or a mate. The battle is fierce, but *Wannanosaurus* was only about 60 centimetres long! It lived in Asia about 85 million years ago.

I DON'T BELIEVE IT!

One dinosaur's thumb was put on its nose! When scientists first dug up fossils of *Iguanodon*, they found a bone shaped like a horn, as if for *Iguanodon*'s nose. Most scientists now believe that the bone was a thumb-claw.

174 Another idea grew up that early cave people had to fight against dinosaurs and kill them – or the other way around. But they did not. There was a very long gap, more than 60 million years, between the very last of the dinosaurs and the earliest people.

175 Some people believe that dinosaurs may survive today in remote, faraway places on Earth, such as thick jungle or ocean islands. But most of the Earth has now been visited and explored, and no living dinosaurs have been seen.

How do we know?

176 We know about dinosaurs mainly from their fossils. Fossils took thousands or millions of years to form. Most fossils form on the bottoms of lakes, rivers or seas, where sand and mud can quickly cover them over and begin to preserve them. If the animal is on dry land, they are more likely to be eaten, or simply to rot away to nothing.

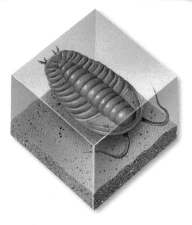

▲ Fossils take millions of years to form. Firstly, an animal, like this trilobite dies. Trilobites lived in the sea about 600 million years ago, long before the first dinosaurs.

▼ *Stegoceras* was a pachycephalosaur or 'bone-head' dinosaur. It was 2 metres long and we can tell from its teeth that it was a herbivore, or plant eater. Studies show it lived 70 million years ago, on the west coast of what is now North America. Like many plant eaters, it probably lived in a large herd.

177 The body parts most likely to fossilize were the hardest ones, which rot away most slowly after death. These included animal parts such as bones, teeth, horns, claws and shells, and plant parts such as bark, seeds and cones.

Stegoceras had long hind legs, with four toes on each foot. Its front legs were much shorter, and had five toes.

178 Very rarely, a dinosaur or other living thing was buried soon after it died. Then a few of the softer body parts also became fossils, such as bits of skin or the remains of the last meal in the stomach.

1. The soft parts rot away.

2. The remaining shell is buried in mud.

3. The mud turns to rock, which turns the shell to rock, and makes a fossil.

The skull of *Stegoceras* was dome-shaped. The thickest part of the bony plate was 6 centimetres thick, and it protected the brain. Its name means 'horny roof'!

▼ *Stegoceras* may have had head-butting contests with rivals at breeding time, like male sheep and goats do today.

180 Dinosaur droppings also formed fossils! They have broken bits of food inside, showing what the dinosaur ate. Some dinosaur droppings are as big as a TV set!

179 Not all dinosaur fossils are from the actual bodies of dinosaurs. Some are the signs, traces or remains that they left while alive. These include eggshells, nests, tunnels, footprints, and claw and teeth marks on food.

QUIZ

Which body parts of a dinosaur were most likely to become fossils? Remember, fossils form from the hardest, toughest bits that last long enough to become buried in the rocks and turned to stone.

Skull bone	Blood
Muscle	Claws
Leg bone	Eye
Scaly skin	Teeth

Answers:
Skull bone, leg bone, teeth and claws are most likely to form fossils

Digging up dinosaurs

181 Every year, thousands of dinosaur fossils are discovered. Most of them are from dinosaurs already known to scientists. But five or ten might be from new kinds of dinosaurs. From the fossils, scientists try to work out what the dinosaur looked like and how it lived, all those millions of years ago.

182 Most dinosaur fossils are found by hard work. Fossil experts called paleontologists study the rocks in a region and decide where fossils are most likely to occur. They spend weeks chipping and digging the rock. They look closely at every tiny piece to see if it is part of a fossil. However some dinosaur fossils are found by luck. People out walking in the countryside come across a fossil tooth or bone by chance. What a discovery!

183 Finding all the fossils of a single dinosaur, neatly in position as in life, is very rare indeed. Usually only a few fossil parts are found from each dinosaur. These are nearly always jumbled up and broken.

▼ These are paleontologists, scientists that look for and study dinosaur bones, uncovering a new skeleton.

People dig carefully into the rock with hammers, picks and brushes.

Scientists make notes, sketches and photographs, to record every stage of the fossil 'dig'.

184 The fossils are taken back to the paleontology laboratory. They are cleaned and laid out to see which parts are which. It is like trying to put together a  jigsaw, with most of the pieces missing. Even those which remain are bent and torn. The fossils are put back together, then soft body parts that did not form fossils, such as skin, are added. Scientists use clues from similar animals alive today, such as crocodiles, to help 'rebuild' the dinosaur.

Cleaning fossils

Laying out fossils

▲ A rebuilt skeleton is displayed in a museum.

Fossils are solid rock and very heavy, but also brittle and easy to crack. So they may need to be wrapped in a strong casing such as plaster-of-paris or glass-fibre.

QUIZ

1. What do we call a scientist that studies fossils?

2. How is a fossil 'dig' recorded?

3. How are fossils packed to protect them?

4. What animals can scientists compare dinosaurs fossils with?

Answers:
1. A Paleontologist 2. Notes, sketches and photographs 3. They are put in plaster-of-paris or glass-fibre 4. Crocodiles

Finding new dinosaurs

185 The first fossils of dinosaurs to be studied by scientists came from Europe and North America. However, since those early discoveries in the 1830s and 1840s, dinosaur fossils have been found all over the world.

186 Some of the most exciting fossils from recent years are being found in China. They include *Caudipteryx*, *Protoarchaeopteryx* and *Sinosauropteryx*. Tiny details of the fossils show that these strange creatures may have had feathers. Today, any creature with feathers is a bird. So were they birds? Or were they dinosaurs with feathers? Nobody knows yet!

◀ Dinosaur fossils have been found all over the world.

NORTH AMERICA

EUROPE

ASIA

CHINA

AFRICA

SOUTH AMERICA

AUSTRALIA

Sinosauropteryx

Caudipteryx

187 Many more exciting finds are being made in Australia, Africa and South America. The small plant eater *Leaellynasaura*, about 2 metres long and one metre tall, lived in Australia 110 million years ago. It may have slept through a cold, snowy winter. Fossils of giant sauropod dinosaurs such as *Jobaria* and *Janenschia* have been uncovered in Africa. In South America there are fossil finds of the biggest plant eaters and meat eaters, such as *Argentinosaurus* and *Giganotosaurus*.

Protoarchaeopteryx

▶ *Jobaria* and *Janenschia* are two giant sauropod dinosaurs from Africa.

188 Some people believe that one day, dinosaurs may be brought back to life. This has already happened – but only in stories, such as the *Jurassic Park* films. However scientists are trying to obtain genetic material, the chemical called DNA, from fossils. The genetic material may contain the 'instructions' for how a dinosaur grew and lived.

189 Dinosaurs lived and died long, long ago. Their world has been and gone, and cannot alter. But what is changing is our knowledge of the dinosaurs. Every year we know more about them. One sure thing about dinosaurs is that what we know now will change in the future.

▲ *Leaellynasaura* was discovered in 1989, in a place called 'Dinosaur Cove' near Melbourne, Australia. The scientists who found its fossils were Pat and Thomas Rich.

I DON'T BELIEVE IT!

One dinosaur is named after a young girl! *Leaellynasaura* was named after the daughter of the scientists who found its fossils!

190 Almost everyone has heard of *Tyrannosaurus rex*. Wasn't it the biggest dinosaur of all time, the greatest meat eater with a mouth big enough to swallow a car and teeth as long as swords? Not one of these 'facts' is true. Certainly *Tyrannosaurus rex* is one of the world's most famous animals. Even though it died out 65 million years ago, it 'lives on' in movies, toys and games, as statues and works of art, and in music and songs. However, *Tyrannosaurus rex* is also the subject of many mistaken beliefs.

▶ A scene from the 2005 movie *King Kong*. With a mighty roar *Tyrannosaurus rex* bares its huge mouth filled with sharp teeth and prepares to attack. Images like this are familiar — but are they correct? For example, did *T rex* really roar loudly?

Terror of its age

▲ The last dinosaurs of the Late Cretaceous Period ranged from small, speedy hunters such as *Avimimus* to giant plant eaters, three horned *Triceratops*, spiky *Edmontonia*, hadrosaurs or 'duckbilled' dinosaurs with strange head crests, and of course *T rex*.

KEY
1. *Tyrannosaurus rex*   5. *Parasaurolophus*   9. *Struthiomimus*
2. *Triceratops*   6. *Lambeosaurus*   10. *Albertosaurus*
3. *Stegoceras*   7. *Avimimus*   11. *Therizinosaurus*
4. *Edmontonia*   8. *Corythosaurus*   12. *Euoplocephalus*

191 *T rex's* full name is *Tyrannosaurus rex,* which means 'king of the tyrant lizards'. However, it wasn't a lizard. It was a large carnivorous, or meat-eating, animal in the reptile group known as the dinosaurs.

192 Dinosaurs, or 'terrible lizards', lived during a time called the Mesozoic Era (251–65 million years ago). The first dinosaurs appeared about 230 million years ago and all had died out, or become extinct, by 65 million years ago.

193 There were hundreds of kinds of dinosaurs. *Plateosaurus* was a bus-sized herbivore (plant eater) from 210 million years ago. *Brachiosaurus* was a giant herbivore from 150 million years ago. *Deinonychus* was a fierce hunter from about 110 million years ago, and was about the size of an adult human.

194 *Tyrannosaurus rex* lived well after all of these dinosaurs. Its time was the last part of the Mesozoic Era, known as the Cretaceous Period (145–65 million years ago), from about 68 to 65 million years ago. *T rex* was one of the very last dinosaurs.

ERA	PERIOD	MYA (Million years ago)
MESOZOIC	CRETACEOUS 145–65 MYA	70, 80, 90, 100, 110, 120, 130, 140, 150
	JURASSIC 200–145 MYA	160, 170, 180, 190, 200
	TRIASSIC 251–200 MYA	210, 220, 230, 240, 250

Jurassic Period: *Allosaurus* was a big meat-eating dinosaur

Triassic Period: *Herrerasaurus* was one of the first dinosaurs

◀ Dinosaurs ruled the land for 160 million years – longer than any other animal group.

A giant predator

195 The size of big, fierce animals such as great white sharks, tigers and crocodiles can be exaggerated (made bigger). People often think *T rex* was bigger than it really was.

196 A full-grown *T rex* was over 12 metres long and more than 3 metres high at the hips. It could rear up and raise its head to more than 5 metres above the ground.

▼ *Tyrannosaurus rex* may have been big, but it was smaller than all the other creatures shown here.

Brachiosaurus
13 metres tall
25 metres nose to tail
40-plus tonnes in weight

197 *Tyrannosaurus rex* was not such a giant compared to some plant-eating animals. It was about the same weight as today's African bush elephant, half the size of the extinct imperial mammoth, and one-tenth as heavy as some of the biggest plant-eating dinosaurs.

Imperial mammoth
4.5 metres tall
12 metres nose to tail
10 tonnes in weight

T rex
3–4 metres tall
11–12 metres nose to tail
5 tonnes in weight

Sperm whale
20 metres nose to tail
50 tonnes in weight

198 Compared to today's biggest meat-eating land animals, *Tyrannosaurus rex* was huge. The largest land carnivores today are polar and grizzly bears, up to 3 metres tall and over 600 kilograms. However that's only one-tenth of the weight of *T rex*.

199 Compared to other extinct meat eaters, *Tyrannosaurus rex* was large. The wolf-like *Andrewsarchus* from 40 million years ago was one of the biggest mammal land carnivores. It stood 2 metres tall, was 4 metres long from nose to tail, and weighed more than one tonne.

200 *Tyrannosaurus rex* is sometimes called 'the biggest predator of all time'. However, it was only one-tenth the size of the sperm whale living in today's oceans, which hunts giant squid. It was also smaller than prehistoric ocean predators such as the pliosaurs *Liopleurodon* and *Kronosaurus* (10 tonnes or more) and the ichthyosaur *Shonisaurus* (more than 20 tonnes).

Compare huge hunters

You will need:

pens   large sheet of paper   animal books

In books or on the Internet, find side-on pictures of *T rex*, a sperm whale, a killer whale and *Andrewsarchus*. Draw them on one sheet of paper to see how they compare:

Sperm whale as long as the paper

T rex nose to tail two-thirds as long as the sperm whale

Killer whale half as long as the sperm whale

Andrewsarchus one-fifth as long as the sperm whale

Profile of *T rex*

201 Fossil experts can work out what an extinct animal such a *Tyrannosaurus rex* looked like when it was alive. They study the size, shape, length, thickness and other details of its fossil bones, teeth, claws and other parts.

202 The tail of *T rex* was almost half its total length. It had a wide, muscular base and was thick and strong almost to the tip, quite unlike the long, thin, whip-like tails of other dinosaurs such as *Diplodocus*.

Backbones (vertebrae) were large, especially at the base of the tail

Massive muscles could bend the tail base with great power, perhaps to swipe at enemies

▼ Dinosaurs are divided into two groups, ornithischians (bird-hipped) and saurischians (lizard-hipped). Meat eaters, including *T rex*, were lizard-hipped. Bird-hipped dinosaurs were plant eaters.

In lizard-hipped dinosaurs, the lower front part of the hip bone angled down and forwards

In bird-hipped dinosaurs, the lower front part of the hip bone angled down and rearwards

Long foot bones meant that the ankle bones were part way up the leg

I DON'T BELIEVE IT!

Tyrannosaurus rex's tail was not very bendy or flexible — it stuck out straight behind the body. This is why its group of dinosaurs is called tetanurans or 'stiff-tails'.

203 The fossil bones of *T rex* show that it was a large, heavily built, powerful dinosaur. It had a huge skull, so its head and mouth were massive. There were holes in the skull for the eyes, ears and nasal openings or nostrils. There were also smaller holes in the bones for blood vessels and nerves.

▼ A cutaway *T rex* shows the thick, strong bones of its skeleton, which have been found preserved in many different fossil remains.

Head was long and low with eyebrow ridges and a large snout

Ribs curved around to protect the soft inner organs

Lungs took in air as the dinosaur breathed in and out

204 The main body of *T rex* was strong and sturdy, with a broad chest and a short but powerful neck. As in other reptiles, the upper body contained the heart, and the lungs for breathing. The lower body contained the stomach, guts and other soft parts.

Guts digested high-nutrient meaty meals, so were smaller in comparison to the guts of plant-eating dinosaurs

Front view shows the narrow body

Long, strong toe bones were tipped with big, sharp claws

205 One of the amazing features of *Tyrannosaurus rex* was its tiny arms (front legs), compared to the massive, pillar-like back legs. Almost no other dinosaur had front limbs that were so different in size from its back limbs.

Was T rex clever?

▼ Many dinosaurs had eyes on the sides of their heads, giving good all-round vision but not a detailed front view. T rex had forward-facing eyes.

View from forward-facing eyes

View from sideways-facing eyes

▶ T rex probably used its long tongue to lick and taste meat before it started to eat.

206 The skull of T rex is well known from several good fossils. They show that the large eyes were set at an angle so they looked forwards rather than to the sides. This allowed T rex to see an object in front with both eyes and judge its distance well.

207 As far as we know dinosaurs, like other reptiles, lacked ear flaps. Instead, they had eardrums of thin skin on the sides of their heads so they could hear.

Brain

Nasal openings (nares)

▲ The braincase of *T rex* was small compared to the size of the whole skull. Nerves connected the brain to the eyes, nose, ears and other body parts.

208 *T rex*'s big nasal openings were at the top of its snout. They opened into a very large chamber inside the skull, which detected smells floating in the air. *T rex*'s sense of smell, like its eyesight, was very good.

209 Some fossils even show the size and shape of *T rex*'s brain! The brain was in a casing called the cranium in the upper rear of the skull. This can be seen in well-preserved skulls. The space inside shows the brain's shape.

I DON'T BELIEVE IT!

The eyeballs of *Tyrannosaurus rex* were up to 8 centimetres across – but those of today's giant squid are almost 30 centimetres!

210 *Tyrannosaurus rex* had the biggest brain of almost any dinosaur. The parts dealing with the sense of smell, called the olfactory lobes, were especially large. So *T rex* had keen senses of sight, hearing and especially smell. It certainly wasn't stupid!

What big teeth!

211 **Teeth are very hard and make good fossils.** The preserved teeth, jaws and skulls of *T rex* tell us about the kinds of food it ate.

212 The skull of a full-grown *T rex* was up to 1.5 metres long, almost the size of a bathtub. Like the skulls of other dinosaurs and reptiles, it was made up of more than 20 bones firmly joined together.

213 *T rex* had 50–60 teeth of different shapes and sizes. They were up to 30 centimetres long, but part of this was the root fixed into the jaw. Teeth were bigger in the upper jaw than the lower. They were also slightly smaller and sharper at the front of the mouth. The back teeth were not especially sharp, and are nicknamed 'deadly big bananas'.

▼ Most of the roughened part of each *T rex* tooth was fixed into the jawbone, with only the smooth part showing.

▲ *T rex* would have used its huge teeth to crunch through bone.

214 _T rex_ grew new teeth regularly to replace those that wore away or broke off. This happened in different parts of the mouth at different times. So each _T rex_ had a mixture of big older teeth and smaller newer teeth.

T rex

Alligator

215 The jaw joints of _Tyrannosaurus rex_ were right at the back of its skull. This allowed the dinosaur to open its jaws wide to take a massive mouthful of food – or perhaps to bite a chunk from a much larger victim.

Hyaena

▶ Because of its huge teeth and jaw muscles, _T rex_ probably had a stronger bite than these living animals.

Snapping turtle

216 Scientists' experiments and calculations have compared the bite strength of _T rex_ with other creatures alive today. In bite force units, _Tyrannosaurus rex_ usually comes out top!

T rex 3100 (estimated)   Great white shark 650
Alligator 2200   Wolf 400
Hyaena 1050   Hyacinth macaw 355
Snapping turtle 1000   Labrador dog 150
Lion 950   Human 120

Great white shark

Tiny arms, big legs

217 *Tyrannosaurus rex's* strangest features were its tiny arms. In fact, they were about the same size as the arms of an adult human, even though *T rex* was more than 50 times bigger than a person. Yet the arms were not weak. They had powerful muscles and two strong clawed fingers.

▶ *T rex's* arms were so small, they could not even be used for passing food to the mouth.

218 What did *Tyrannosaurus rex* use its mini-arms for? There have been many suggestions such as holding onto a victim while biting, pushing itself off the ground if it fell over, and holding onto a partner at breeding time. Perhaps we will never know the true reason.

▶ Bird feet, such as this ostrich's, have many similarities to the feet of *T rex* and similar dinosaurs, such as walking almost on tip-toe.

Ostrich foot

Long foot bones were held above the ground

T rex foot

Large curved claw at tip of toe bone

219 Each of *T rex*'s feet had three great toes with big strong claws. This type of foot was typical of the dinosaur group to which *Tyrannosaurus rex* belonged – the theropods or 'bird feet'. The foot design is similar to the feet of birds, although much bigger.

▲ As *T rex* ran it probably kept its head, neck, main body and tail in a line, almost horizontal or level with the ground.

220 The big, heavy back legs of *Tyrannosaurus rex* show that the dinosaur could make long strides as it walked and ran. The three parts of the leg – the thigh, shin and foot – were all about the same length.

221 Trackways are fossil footprints in mud and sand that give clues to how an animal moved. There are some trackways that could have been made by *Tyrannosaurus rex* or similar dinosaurs. They help to show how fast it walked and ran (see page 109).

What did *T rex* eat?

222 *Tyrannosaurus rex* was a huge hunter, so it probably ate big prey. Other large dinosaurs of its time and place were plant eaters. They included three-horned *Triceratops* and its cousins, and various 'duckbilled' dinosaurs (hadrosaurs) such as *Parasaurolophus* and *Edmontosaurus*.

▼ The giant pterosaur (flying reptile) *Quetzalcoatlus* lived at about the same time as *T rex*. It may have pecked at the remains of a *T rex* kill after the dinosaur had finished feasting.

223 *T rex* could have used its huge mouth, strong teeth and powerful jaw muscles to attack these big plant eaters. It may have lunged at a victim with one massive bite to cause a slashing wound. Then it would retreat a short distance and wait for the prey to weaken from blood loss before moving in to feed.

◀ An adult *Triceratops* would be a fierce foe for *T rex* to tackle. However young, sick and old *Triceratops* might have been easier to kill.

▶ The hadrosaur *Parasaurolophus* might have made loud trumpeting noises through its hollow tube-like head crest, to warn others in its herd that *T rex* was near.

224 One fossil of *Triceratops* has scratch-like gouge marks on its large, bony neck frill. These could have been made by *Tyrannosaurus rex* teeth. The marks are about the correct distance apart, matching the spacing of *T rex* teeth.

▶ Coprolites can be broken apart or sawn through to study the bits of bone, teeth and other items inside.

225 Coprolites are preserved lumps of animal dung or droppings, fossilized into hard stone. Several large coprolites have been found that could be from *Tyrannosaurus rex*. They show many jumbled fragments of bone from its victims, including young *Edmontosaurus* and *Triceratops*.

226 In some dinosaurs, several fossil skeletons have been found preserved together, suggesting they lived as a pack or herd. The remains of several *Tyrannosaurus rex* have also been found in this way, which might suggest a family or a pack-hunting group. Some experts say that more evidence is needed for this idea.

▶ Armoured dinosaurs like *Euoplocephalus* may have defended themselves against *T rex* by swinging their heavy, clubbed tails.

Long live the king!

227 Was *T rex* an active hunter that chased after its victims? Was it an ambush predator that hid in wait to rush out at prey? Was it a scavenger that ate any dead or dying dinosaurs it found? Or did it chase other dinosaurs from their kills and steal the meal for itself?

228 To be an active pursuit hunter, *T rex* must have been able to run fast. Scientists have tried to work out its running speed using models and computers, and by comparisons with other animals.

Who does what?

Research these animals living today and find out if they are mainly fast hunters, sneaky ambushers or scavengers.
Tiger Cheetah Hyaena
Crocodile Vulture
African wild dog

▶ *Tyrannosaurus rex* may have run down smaller dinosaurs such as these *Prenocephale*, perhaps rushing out from its hiding place in a clump of trees.

▲ When scavenging, *T rex* might sniff out a dinosaur that had died from illness or injury.

▲ When hunting, *T rex* would be at risk from injury, such as from the horns of *Triceratops*.

229 Some estimates for the running speed of *T rex* are as fast as 50 kilometres an hour, others as slow as 15 kilometres an hour. Most give a speed of between 20 and 30 kilometres an hour. This is slightly slower than a human sprinter, but probably faster than typical *T rex* prey such as *Triceratops*.

231 Several *T rex* fossils show injuries to body parts such as shins, ribs, neck and jaws. These could have been made by victims fighting back, suggesting that *T rex* hunted live prey.

▶ *T rex* would tear and rip flesh from large prey, gulp in lumps and swallow them whole.

230 Evidence that *T rex* was a scavenger includes its very well developed sense of smell for sniffing out dead, rotting bodies. Also, its powerful teeth could not chew food repeatedly like we do, but they could crush bones at first bite to get at the nutritious jelly-like marrow inside. Maybe a hungry *Tyrannosaurus* rex simply ate anything it could catch or find, so it was a hunter, ambusher and scavenger all in one.

Terror of its age

232 **Did *T rex* live in groups?** Most of its fossils are of lone individuals. Some were found near other specimens of *T rex*. These could have been preserved near each other by chance, or they could have been a group that all died together.

Embryo   Yolk

▲ A baby dinosaur developed as an embryo in its egg, fed by nutrients from the yolk.

▶ The baby probably hatched out by biting through the tough shell, which was flexible like leather.

233 **Living reptiles lay eggs that hatch into young, and dinosaurs such as *T rex* probably did the same.** Many fossil dinosaur eggs have been discovered, but none are known for certain to be from *T rex*. Some dinosaurs laid eggs in nests and looked after their young, but again there are no fossils like this for *T rex*.

▶ Young *T rex* may have killed small prey such as birds, lizards and newly hatched dinosaurs.

235 **It seems that *T rex* grew slowly for about 12–14 years.** Then suddenly it grew very fast, putting on about 2 kilograms every day as a teenager. By 20 years it was full-grown.

234 **Fossils of individual *T rex* are of different sizes and ages, showing how this dinosaur grew up.** Some of the fossil bones are so well preserved that they have 'growth rings', almost like a tree trunk, showing growth speed.

236 Can we tell apart female and male *Tyrannosaurus rex* from their fossils? Some scientists thought that females were bigger, with stronger, thicker bones than the males. However the latest evidence makes this less clear.

▶ In many reptiles today, the adults keep growing with age. However their growth rate gradually reduces, so they get bigger more slowly. It is not certain if dinosaurs such as *T rex* grew like this.

237 The biggest *T rex* found, 'Sue', was about 28 years old when it died. No one knows for certain if *Tyrannosaurus rex* could live longer. As with many of these questions, more fossil finds will help to fill in the details.

Where in the world?

238 *T rex* was one kind, or species, of dinosaur in a group of species known as the genus *Tyrannosaurus*. Were there any other members of this genus?

239 After *T rex* fossils were discovered and named over 100 years ago, fossil-hunters began to find the remains of many similar huge predators. Some were given their own names in the genus *Tyrannosaurus*, but most have now been renamed *Tyrannosaurus rex*.

240 *Tarbosaurus*, 'terrifying lizard', was very similar to *T rex*, almost as big, and it lived at the same time. However its fossils come from Asia – Mongolia and China – rather than North America. Some experts consider it to be another species of *Tyrannosaurus*, called *Tyrannosaurus bataar*. Others think that it's so similar to *T rex* that it should be called *Tyrannosaurus rex*.

241 Fossils of smaller dinosaurs similar to *T rex* have been found in Europe. They include 6-metre-long *Eotyrannus*, from more than 100 million years ago, from the Isle of Wight, southern England. Fossils of *Aviatyrannis* from Portugal are even older, from the Jurassic Period.

◀ *Tarbosaurus* had big teeth, tiny arms and many other features similar to *T rex*. It was named by Russian fossil expert Evgeny Maleev in 1955, exactly 50 years after *T rex* was named.

KEY
- Tyrannosaurus
- Tarbosaurus
- Alioramus
- Daspletosaurus
- Albertosaurus
- Dilong
- Guanlong

▲ Fossils of *T rex* and its close cousins (some shown on the following page) are mainly from North America and Central and East Asia.

242 In 1979, Chinese expert Dong Zhiming named the remains of a big Asian meat-eating dinosaur as *Tyrannosaurus luanchuanensis*, in the same genus as *Tyrannosaurus rex*. After much discussion another name was suggested – *Jenghizkhan*. However some scientists say that like *Tarbosaurus*, *Jenghizkhan* is so similar to *T rex* that it should be called *Tyrannosaurus*.

I DON'T BELIEVE IT!
A fossil skull found in 1942 was named *Nanotyrannus*, 'tiny tyrant'. Like 'Jane' (page 127) it may be a separate kind of small tyrannosaur – or simply a young *T rex*. Experts are undecided.

Tyrannosaur group

243 **What kind of dinosaur was** *Tyrannosaurus rex*? It belonged to the group called tyrannosaurs, known scientifically as the family *Tyrannosauridae*. These dinosaurs had bones, joints and other features that were different from other predatory dinosaurs. They were part of an even bigger group, the tyrannosauroids.

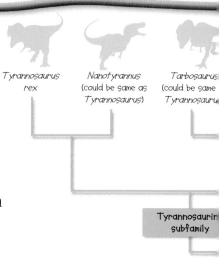

Tyrannosaurus rex

Nanotyrannus (could be same as *Tyrannosaurus*)

Tarbosaurus (could be same *Tyrannosauru*

Tyrannosaurir subfamily

244 **One of the first tyrannosauroids was** *Guanlong,* **'crown dragon'.** Its fossils were discovered in China in 2006 and are about 160 million years old – nearly 100 million years before *Tyrannosaurus rex*. It was 3 metres long and had a strange horn-like plate of bone on its nose.

▲ *Guanlong* may have shown off the crest of thin bone on its head to possible partners at breeding time.

▼ The 'feathers' of *Dilong* were similar to fur and may have kept its body warm.

245 **Another early cousin of** *T rex* **was** *Dilong,* **'emperor dragon', also from China.** Its fossils date to 130 million years ago. *Dilong* was about 2 metres long when fully grown. It had traces of hair-like feathers on the head and tail. As shown later, some experts suggest *Tyrannosaurus rex* itself may have had some kind of feathers.

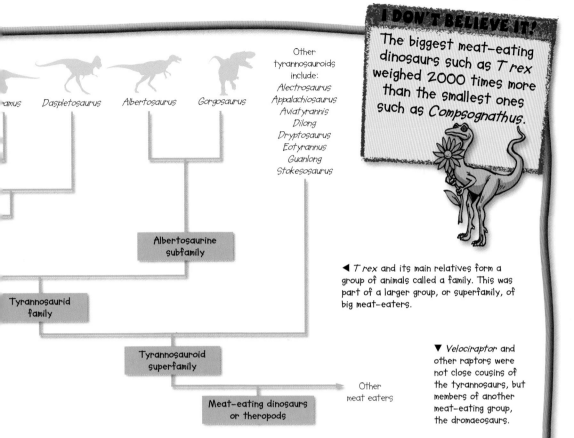

Other
tyrannosauroids
include:
Alectrosaurus
Appalachiosaurus
Aviatyrannis
Dilong
Dryptosaurus
Eotyrannus
Guanlong
Stokesosaurus

...amus   *Daspletosaurus*   *Albertosaurus*   *Gorgosaurus*

I DON'T BELIEVE IT!

The biggest meat-eating dinosaurs such as *T rex* weighed 2000 times more than the smallest ones such as *Compsognathus*.

Albertosaurine
subfamily

◀ *T rex* and its main relatives form a group of animals called a family. This was part of a larger group, or superfamily, of big meat-eaters.

Tyrannosaurid
family

▼ *Velociraptor* and other raptors were not close cousins of the tyrannosaurs, but members of another meat-eating group, the dromaeosaurs.

Tyrannosauroid
superfamily

Other
meat eaters

Meat-eating dinosaurs
or theropods

246 The tyrannosaurs were not the only meat-eating dinosaurs. Others include *Allosaurus*, which was almost as big as *T rex*. It also lived in North America, but 80 million years earlier. *Compsognathus* was a tiny meat eater at just one metre long, and it lived about 150 million years ago. Medium-sized meat-eaters called 'raptors' include *Velociraptor*, from 75 million years ago, and *Deinonychus* dating back 110 million years. Raptors varied in size from about 2–5 metres long. All these meat eaters were in the main dinosaur group called the theropods, or 'bird feet'.

◀ *Compsognathus* chased small prey such as lizards and bugs.

Close cousins

247 In the tyrannosaur group with *T rex* were several of its closest relatives. They were big, fierce dinosaurs, but most lived before *T rex* and were not quite as large.

▲ There are many fossil remains of *Gorgosaurus*, making it one of the best known of all the tyrannosaurs. It had a small horn–like crest above each eye.

248 Fossils of *Gorgosaurus*, 'fierce lizard', come mainly from Alberta, Canada and are 75–70 million years old. *Gorgosaurus* was very similar to *Albertosaurus*, although slightly smaller at 8–9 metres long. Like all tyrannosaurs, it had hollow bones and openings in its skull that helped to reduce its weight. Some experts think that *Gorgosaurus* was really a kind of *Albertosaurus* and that its name should be changed.

▲ *Daspletosaurus* weighed about 2.5 tonnes and had a skull more than one metre long.

249 *Daspletosaurus*, 'frightful lizard', was another dinosaur from Alberta, 80–75 million years ago. Its fossils are also known from other regions of North America, as far south as New Mexico, USA. It was about 8 metres long with especially large jaws and teeth. Its arms were small, but not quite so tiny compared to its body as those of *Tyrannosaurus rex*.

▼ *Alectrosaurus* from Mongolia, Asia was one of the smaller tyrannosaurs, some 5 metres in total length.

▶ *Appalachiosaurus* fossils come from Alabama, USA, which is an area where few other tyrannosaurs have been found. Only one 7-metre-long skeleton has been found, but it was probably not fully grown.

250 *Albertosaurus*, 'Alberta lizard', dates from about 75–70 million years ago. Its fossils were first found in Alberta, Canada. It looked similar to *T rex*, with a huge mouth and sharp teeth, small arms and powerful legs, but it was smaller, at 9–10 metres and around 1.5 tonnes. At one site the remains of over 20 *Albertosaurus* were found, from adults to teenagers to youngsters. This could have been a mixed pack out hunting.

Discovering *T rex*

251 The first fossils of *T rex* were found in the 1870s by Arthur Lakes and John Bell Hatcher, in Wyoming, USA. However these were not recognized as *T rex* until years later. In 1892, fossil expert Edward Drinker Cope, found remains of a big meat-eater and named them *Manospondylus*. Over 100 years later these remains were restudied and renamed as *T rex*.

▲ Edward Drinker Cope (1840–97) named many other kinds of dinosaurs in addition to *T rex*, including *Camarasaurus*, *Amphicoelias*, *Coelophysis*, *Hadrosaurus* and *Monoclonius*.

▶ The fossil bones of big dinosaurs such as *T rex* are solid stone and very heavy. Many years ago, horses dragged them from rocky, remote areas to the nearest road or railway.

252 In 1900, again in Wyoming, leading fossil collector Barnum Brown found the first partial skeleton of *Tyrannosaurus rex*, rather than scattered single bones and teeth. At first the fossils were named as *Dynamosaurus* by Henry Fairfield Osborn of the American Museum of Natural History in New York.

255 *T rex* fossils have always been greatly prized by museums, exhibitions and private collectors. In 1941, the fossils that Brown found in 1902 were sold to the Carnegie Museum of Natural History in Pittsburgh, Pennsylvania, for a huge sum of money. Searching for, selling and buying *T rex* fossils continues today.

▼ Barnum Brown was the most famous fossil-hunter of his time. He sometimes wore a thick fur coat — even when digging for fossils in the scorching sun.

253 Barnum Brown discovered parts of another *Tyrannosaurus rex* fossil skeleton at Hell Creek, Montana, in 1902. In 1905, Osborn wrote a scientific description of these remains and called them *Tyrannosaurus rex*. This was the first time the official name was used. In a way, it was when *T rex* was 'born'.

BARNUM BROWN — DINOSAUR DETECTIVE

Barnum Brown (1873-1963) collected not only dinosaur fossils, but fossils of all kinds, and other scientific treasures such as crystals. He and his teams worked for the American Museum of Natural History in New York. They travelled to remote places, and if there were rivers but no roads, they used a large raft as a floating base camp. They worked fast too, often blasting apart rocks with dynamite. Brown also made a living by informing oil companies about the best places to drill for oil.

254 In 1906, Brown found an even better part-skeleton of *Tyrannosaurus rex* in Montana. The same year, Osborn realized that the *Dynamosaurus* fossils were extremely similar to *Tyrannosaurus rex*, so he renamed those, too, as *Tyrannosaurus rex*. The public began to hear about this huge, fierce, meat-eating monster from long ago, and soon its fame was growing fast.

Working with fossils

▼ There are several stages to the fossilization process, which can take many millions of years.

1. A dinosaur dies and falls into a lake or river, where it sinks to the bottom. The flesh and other soft body parts rot away or are eaten by water-dwelling creatures.

2. The bones and teeth are buried under layers of mud and sand. Silica and other minerals from the rock seep into the bones, filling any available gaps.

3. Over a period of millions of years, minerals replace the original dinosaur bones entirely, but preserve their shape and form. The bones have become fossils.

4. If the rock containing the fossils is pushed up and eroded (worn away), the fossils become exposed. They may then be discovered by a scientist so they can be excavated.

256 Like all animal fossils, those of *T rex* are of the harder parts of the body. They have been preserved in rocks and, over many millions of years, gradually turned to stone.

257 For dinosaurs, the body parts that form fossils are mainly bones, teeth, claws, horns, and less often, skin. There are also fossilized eggs, footprints or trackways, coprolites (droppings) and other clues.

258 Like many other prehistoric creatures, most *T rex* fossils are broken scraps, squashed bits and crushed pieces. They are often very difficult to put together, and scientists have trouble identifying the original animals.

I DON'T BELIEVE IT!

Some *T rex* fossils show injuries that may have been caused by the teeth of other *T rex*. Perhaps they were fighting over food, territory, or breeding partners, or who was boss.

▶ *Archaeopteryx*, the earliest known bird, lived about 80 million years before *T rex*. Its bones show many similarities to small meat-eating dinosaurs.

259 Reptiles today are cold-blooded, but were *T rex* and some other dinosaurs warm-blooded, like mammals and birds? Fossils show that *T rex*'s bone structure and growth rate were similar to mammals and birds. There is also evidence that the chemical make-up of its preserved bones resembles birds. But there is no complete proof one way or the other.

▶ A palaeontologist working at a *T rex* dig site. A variety of tools and special equipment is needed to help remove the fossils from the ground.

260 In 2008, 68-million-year-old fossils of *T rex* (named 'B rex' by palaeontologists) were unearthed in Montana, USA. Examining these very well-preserved bones with a microscope showed they were similar to those of living female birds. So 'B rex' may well have been a female *T rex* producing eggs inside her body when she died aged 15–20 years.

Rebuilding *T rex*

261 Fossil experts use preserved bones and other parts of *T rex* to show what it looked like when alive. The bones are also compared to those of similar animals alive today, known as comparative anatomy. For *T rex*, similar living animals include crocodiles, lizards – and birds.

262 Some fossil bones have patches, grooves and ridges called 'muscle scars'. They show where the animal's muscles were joined to the bones in life. This helps experts work out how the muscles pulled the bones and how *T rex* moved when it was alive.

263 As with other extinct creatures, there are no remains of *T rex*'s soft body parts such as the stomach, guts, heart and lungs. These were eaten by scavengers soon after death or rotted away. However experts can use comparative anatomy with living creatures to imagine what *T rex*'s soft body parts looked like.

▼ Fossil dinosaur skin has a scaly surface, similar to many of today's reptiles.

264 Skin and scales of dinosaurs sometimes form fossils. However they are the colour of the rocks that make the fossils, not the colour of the original skin and scales. So we have no way of knowing *T rex*'s true colour in life.

◄ Close cousins of *T rex* have been preserved with simple hair–like feathers on their skin. It may be possible that *T rex* also had feathers.

▲ This reconstruction of *T rex* shows the modern idea of its body position, with tail held straight out behind. When the skull is moved from the trolley to the front end of the neck bones, it will be positioned low, not high as previously thought.

▶ For many years, *T rex* was thought to hold its head up high and drag its tail along the ground.

265 The first reconstructions of *T rex* showed it standing almost upright like a kangaroo. However from its bone and joint shapes, most experts now think that it held its head and body level with the ground, balanced over its big back legs by its long, heavy tail.

The story of Sue

266 The biggest *Tyrannosaurus rex* found so far is 'Sue'. Its official code number is FMNH PR2081, from the Field Museum of Natural History in Chicago, USA.

267 'Sue' is named after its discoverer, Sue Hendrickson. She was working at a fossil dig in 1990 near the town of Faith, in South Dakota, USA, when she uncovered parts of a massive *T rex*. An entire team of people helped to dig up and clean the remains.

268 'Sue' is amazingly complete for a fossil animal, with about four-fifths of its teeth, bones and other parts preserved. The dinosaur was probably covered with mud soon after it died, which prevented scavenging animals from cracking open or carrying away its bones.

269 'Sue' dates from between 67 and 65.5 million years ago. It measures 12.8 metres from nose to tail-tip and 4 metres tall at the hips. The weight of 'Sue' when alive was probably between 5.5 and 6.5 tonnes.

◀ Sue Hendrickson with the fossil foot of 'Sue'. As well as finding 'Sue' the *T rex*, Sue Hendrickson is an expert diver and has explored shipwrecks and sunken cities.

◄ In May 2000, 'Sue' went on display at the Field Museum of Chicago and has been the star attraction ever since.

270 **After 'Sue' was discovered, there was a dispute about who owned the fossils.** Various people claimed them, including the landowner, the dig team, the organizers of the excavation and the local authorities. After a legal battle, 'Sue' was sold at auction in 1997 in New York. The Field Museum of Chicago paid $8.39 million.

Stan, Jane and the rest

271 Apart from 'Sue', there are more than 30 other sets of *T rex* fossils. Some are just a few bones and teeth, while others are well preserved, fairly complete skeletons.

273 'Wankel rex', specimen MOR 555, was found by Kathy Wankel in 1988. It was excavated by a team from the Museum of the Rockies and is now on show at that museum in Bozeman, Montana.

274 'Tinker', also called 'Kid Rex', was a young *Tyrannosaurus rex*. About two-thirds adult size, it was found in 1998 in South Dakota and named after the leader of the fossil-hunting team, Ron 'Tinker' Frithiof.

272 'Stan' is named after its discoverer Stan Sacrisen. Code numbered BHI 3033, it was dug up near Buffalo, South Dakota, USA in 1992 by a team from the Black Hills Institute. 'Stan' was about 12.2 metres long and 3 tonnes in weight, with 199 bones and 58 teeth. Some bones show signs of injuries that had healed, including broken ribs, a damaged neck and a tooth wound in the skull.

▶ 'Stan' is now at the Black Hills Museum in Hill City, South Dakota.

275 'Jane' is specimen BMRP 2002.4.1 at the Burpee Museum of Natural History, Rockford, Illinois, USA. Found in Montana, it's smaller than a full grown *Tyrannosaurus rex*, at 6.5 metres long and 650–700 kilograms. Some experts believe it is a part-grown youngster, probably 10–12 years old when it died. Others say it is a similar but smaller kind of dinosaur named *Nanotyrannus*.

▶ The fossils of 'Jane' from Montana's Hell Creek took more than four years to dig out, clean up and put together for display.

A new name for T rex

You will need:

pictures of *T rex* in different poses
pen   paper

Copy some pictures of *T rex* onto your paper. Imagine you and your friends have discovered their fossils and given them nicknames. Write these next to your drawings. Perhaps *T rex* should be named after you?

Bigger than the 'king'

276 Until the 1990s, *Tyrannosaurus rex* was famous as the biggest predatory land creature of all time. But the past few years have seen discoveries of even bigger meat-eating or carnivorous dinosaurs.

277 Fossils of *Giganotosaurus*, 'southern giant reptile', were uncovered in 1993 in Patagonia, Argentina. This huge hunter was slightly bigger than *T rex*, at more than 13 metres long and weighing over 6 tonnes. *Giganotosaurus* lived earlier than *T rex*, about 95–90 million years ago.

278 Fossils of *Spinosaurus* were first found in Egypt in 1912. This predator lived 100–95 million years ago, and had long, bony rods sticking up from its back that may have held up a 'sail' of skin. The original remains suggested a big predator, but not as big as *T rex*. However recent finds indicate that *Spinosaurus* may have been larger, maybe 16 metres long and 7 tonnes in weight.

QUIZ

Put these dinosaurs in order of size, biggest to smallest:
Tyrannosaurus rex   Deinonychus
Brachiosaurus   Spinosaurus
Compsognathus   Giganotosaurus

Answer:
Brachiosaurus, Spinosaurus, Giganotosaurus, Tyrannosaurus rex, Deinonychus, Compsognathus

279 *Carcharodontosaurus*, 'shark tooth lizard', was another massive hunter from North Africa. It was first named in 1931 and lived 100–95 million years ago. Recent discoveries in Morocco and Niger show that it could have been about the same size as *T rex*.

280 Another *T rex*–sized dinosaur was *Mapusaurus*, which lived in Argentina around the same time as *T rex* lived in North America. It was not as heavily built as *T rex*, weighing about 3 tonnes.

▼ This skull of *Carcharodontosaurus* measures more than 1.7 metres in length, with teeth 20 centimetres long. The human skull just in front of it gives an idea of just how big this dinosaur was.

▶ *T rex* and the other meat-eaters were not the biggest dinosaurs by far. Much larger are huge plant eaters such as *Brachiosaurus* and *Argentinosaurus*.

T rex superstar

281 *Tyrannosaurus rex* is far more than a big meat-eating dinosaur. It's a world superstar, alongside such famous creatures as the great white shark, blue whale, gorilla, tiger and golden eagle. If *Tyrannosaurus rex* was alive today and could charge money for using its name, pictures, sponsorships and advertising, it would be mega-rich!

282 Ever since its fossils were discovered, *T rex* has starred in books, plays and movies. It's featured in films such as *The Lost World* (first made in 1925, then again in 1960 and 1992), several *King Kong* movies, the animated *The Land Before Time* (1988), and the *Night at the Museum* movies (2006, 2009).

▼ In *Night at the Museum*, Rexy the *T rex* skeleton looks fierce but is really quite cute and chases bones like a puppy.

I DON'T BELIEVE IT!

T rex was one of the stars of the *Jurassic Park* movies. However it didn't live in the Jurassic Period, it lived 80 million years later at the end of the Cretaceous Period.

Gems & Min

▶ In *T rex: Back to the Cretaceous* (1998), Ally finds a mysterious egg-like rock — which transports her back to the end of the Dinosaur Age.

283 In movies, *Tyrannosaurus rex* is perhaps most famous from the *Jurassic Park* series. These began with *Jurassic Park* itself in 1993, then *The Lost World: Jurassic Park* in 1997, and *Jurassic Park 3* in 2001. *Tyrannosaurus rex is* shown breaking out of its fenced enclosure, attacking people and generally causing havoc – but also looking after and protecting its baby with great care.

284 Toy Story movies, games and other products feature an unusual *Tyrannosaurus rex* toy called 'Rex' who is nervous, weedy and worried. This is very unlike the usual fearsome character given to *T rex*.

▶ The *T rex* of *Jurassic Park* tries to sniff out human prey, but in the end it saves them from being attacked by marauding raptor dinosaurs.

131

What next for T rex?

285 Why did *T rex* die out 65 million years ago, along with all other dinosaurs? The main suggestion is that a huge lump of rock from space, an asteroid, hit Earth and caused worldwide disasters of giant waves, volcanic eruptions and a dust cloud that blotted out the Sun. In this end-of Cretaceous mass extinction no dinosaurs, not even the great *T rex*, could survive.

286 Our ideas about *T rex* do not stand still. As scientists discover more fossils and invent new methods of studying them, we learn more about *T rex* and the other animals and plants of its time.

287 Could *Tyrannosaurus rex* or similar dinosaurs still survive today, in thick jungle or on remote mountains? Most of the world's land has now been explored or photographed from aircraft and satellites. Sadly, there's no sign of *T rex*, or other big unknown animals.

288 Could *T rex* somehow be brought back to life from its fossil remains? Even with the latest scientific methods, this is still a very remote and faraway possibility. Even if it worked, where would *Tyrannosaurus rex* live and what would it eat? Its habitat, with the climate, scenery, plants and animals, is long gone.

◄ A dinosaur fan comes face to face with *T rex* at the *Walking with Dinosaurs* tour, 2009. Animatronic (mechanical model) dinosaurs move and roar, but unlike the real ones, they are harmless.

289 *Tyrannosaurus rex* no longer holds the record as the biggest land predator of all time. But it's such a well-known celebrity around the world that it will probably remain the most famous dinosaur, and one of the most popular creatures, for many years to come.

133

EXTINCT

290 Extinction is when all individuals of one kind of living thing die out forever, so there are no more alive. It usually applies to a whole species (kind) of living thing, not just to one individual. Extinction has happened for billions of years since life on Earth began. Scientists estimate that 999 out of every 1000 kinds of living things that have ever existed have become extinct. Today, the number of extinctions is speeding up because of what people are doing to the natural world.

▼ Giant dragonflies, millipedes as big as dining tables and enormous tree ferns once inhabited forests 300 million years ago. However all of the creatures in this prehistoric swamp have long been extinct.

What is extinction?

291 **Extinction is the dying out of a particular kind, or type, of living thing.** It is gone forever and can never come back (although this may change in the future). Extinction affects plants such as flowers and trees, as well as fungi such as mushrooms and moulds. It also affects tiny worms and bugs, and big creatures such as dinosaurs and mammoths.

▲ The 'terror bird' *Phorusrhacos* lived ten million years ago. Nothing like it survives today.

292 **Extinction is linked to how we classify (group) living things.** It usually applies to a species. A species includes all living things that look similar and breed to produce more of their kind. For instance, all lions belong to one species, which scientists call *Panthera leo*.

293 **One example of an extinct species is the giant elk *Megaloceros giganteus* of the last Ice Age.** The last ones died out almost 8000 years ago. But not all elk species became extinct. A similar but separate species, the elk (moose) *Alces alces*, is still alive today.

136

294 Sometimes extinction affects a subspecies.
This is a group of animals within a species that are
all very similar, and slightly different from others in
the species. All tigers today belong to one species,
Panthera tigris. There were once eight subspecies of
tiger. Two have become extinct in the past 100 years,
the Balinese tiger and the Javan tiger.

▶ All six living
subspecies of
tiger differ
slightly – and all
are threatened
with extinction.

Bengal tiger

South China tiger

Siberian tiger

▲ The last Balinese tiger, the smallest
subspecies, was killed in 1937.

295 Extinction can
also affect a group of
closely related species,
which is called a genus.
There have been about ten
species of mammoths over the
last two million years. They all
belonged to the genus
Mammuthus, including the
woolly mammoth and the
steppe mammoth. All
mammoths have died out,
so the genus is extinct.

Sumatran tiger

Malayan tiger

◀ The Columbian mammoth, one
of the biggest in the genus, died
out around 12,000 years ago.

Indochinese tiger

Extinction and evolution

296 Extinctions have happened through billions of years of prehistory as a natural part of evolution. Evolution is the gradual change in living things, resulting in new species appearing. As this happened, other species could not survive and became extinct.

◀ Today's hagfish differ little from their extinct cousins millions of years ago, but they are a separate species.

297 Evolution occurs as a result of changing conditions. Living things adapt to become better suited to conditions as they change, such as the weather and types of habitats (living places).

▶ Unlike the hagfish, the extinct armoured fish *Hemicyclaspis* from 400 million years ago has no living relatives.

I DON'T BELIEVE IT!

Trilobites were a group of marine creatures that survived for almost 300 million years. Within that time at least 18,000 kinds came and went. The last trilobites died out in a mass extinction 250 million years ago.

Trinucleus
450 million years ago

Angelina
490 million years ago

Kolihapeltis
400 million years ago

▲ Many different kinds of trilobites evolved and died out over millions of years.

298 Scientists know about long-gone extinct species from their fossils. These are remains of body parts such as the bones, teeth, horns, claws and shells of animals, and the bark, roots and leaves of plants, which have been preserved in rocks and turned to stone.

▶ *Stegosaurus* was one of the longest-lasting dinosaur species. Its kind survived for over ten million years.

▼ Magnolias are flowering plants that have successfully evolved from 100 million years ago to today.

299 Studying millions of fossils of thousands of extinct species all around the world shows how different kinds of living things came and went long ago. This 'turnover' of species gives the average rate of extinction. For every one million species, one species would die out about once each year.

▲ Scientists have studied more than one million trilobite fossils.

300 Fossil studies show the typical time for a species or genus to survive before going extinct. A mammal species lasted from one to two million years. For sea-living invertebrates (creatures without backbones) such as crabs, species survived between five and ten million years.

Why does it happen?

301 **There are several reasons for extinction.** Many extinctions are combinations of these reasons. We cannot know for sure why prehistoric species became extinct. But we can see the reasons for extinctions today. These may help us to understand what happened in the past.

302 **One reason for extinction is competition.** A species cannot get enough of its needs, such as food or living space, because other species need them too, and are better at getting them. These competing species may be newly evolved, or may have spread from afar.

303 **A species can be forced to extinction by predators, parasites or diseases.** Again, all of these could be new dangers as a result of evolution.

▼ In Australia, introduced farm animals such as sheep, and also wild rabbits, have been better than local species at gaining food.

▲ Australia's rock wallabies have suffered due to competition from sheep and goats.

304 Another cause is when conditions change rapidly. In the distant past there were many periods of natural global warming, when the world became hot and tropical, and then global cooling, when vast ice sheets covered huge areas. Some species could not evolve fast enough to survive the changing conditions.

▲ The giant ant is known from its 50 million-year-old fossils. It was big and fierce, so why did it die out?

305 Genes are chemical instructions inside living things. They determine how animals and plants grow, live and survive – and they have great effects on extinction. If there are very few members of a species, called a 'gene pool', there may not be enough gene variety for the species to evolve and adapt to new conditions.

306 Another cause of extinction is when one species evolves to become so similar to another that the two species can interbreed. They produce 'halfway' offspring called hybrids. If hybrids become well adapted they may gradually take over, and the original species might disappear.

▼ Interbreeding between species such as the coyote and grey wolf complicates saving the rare red wolf.

Grey wolf

Red wolf

Coyote

141

do we know?

307 How do we know if a species is extinct? The more recent the extinction, the harder it is to say. How long should we wait before saying a species is extinct? It might be found living in a remote area years later.

308 Wildlife experts at the IUCN (International Union for Conservation of Nature) say that a species cannot be declared extinct until 50 years have passed with no real sightings of it, or evidence such as droppings or eggshells.

▲ Leadbeater's possums were restricted to a very small area, as land around was turned into farms.

309 Sometimes, a species thought to be extinct 'comes back from the dead'. Usually it has survived in an unexplored area. It is called a 'Lazarus species' after a man in the Bible who came to life again after he died.

310 One 'Lazarus species' is the squirrel-like Leadbeater's possum of Australia. It was thought to be extinct by the 1930s, but in 1965, a group was found living in highland forests in southeast Australia. Plant 'Lazarus species' include the jellyfish tree and Monte Diablo buckwheat.

311 Some people consider creatures such as the yeti (abominable snowman), bunyip and Bigfoot to be extinct. But most scientists would say that these creatures are only from tales and legends. There is no real scientific proof they ever lived, so they cannot be extinct.

312 Some species are 'extinct in the wild'. This means all surviving members are in zoos, wildlife parks or gardens. One example is the toromiro, a tree that disappeared from Easter Island in the Pacific. Experts saved some at Kew Gardens, London, and it is now being taken back to its original home.

▶ A toromiro flower. The toromiro tree once covered parts of Easter Island, but it was wiped out in the wild.

▲ The huge, hairy yeti of the Himalayas is well known in myths and stories, but no real evidence of its existance has been discovered.

▼ In 1987, only 22 Californian condors were left in the wild. All were captured for breeding and chicks were raised using 'condor parent' puppet gloves.

FAME AT LAST

You will need:
books about Australia
the Internet

Look in books or on the Internet for information about the state of Victoria in Australia. See if you can find the state's animal emblem or symbol, and a picture of it. That's Leadbeater's possum!

Not quite extinct

◀ Pterosaurs (pterodactyls) were flying reptiles that died out with the dinosaurs 65 million years ago.

313 **It's easy to decide if prehistoric species are extinct.** No one has seen living dinosaurs. Some myths and legends say they exist, but there's no scientific proof. So we assume all dinosaurs are extinct.

314 Living species (such as the coelacanth) that are very similar to long-extinct ones are known as 'living fossils'. They help us to understand how evolution works and how the original species may have become extinct.

315 Some 'Lazarus species' lived millions of years ago in prehistoric times, but have been recently rediscovered. Fossils show that the coelacanth fish died out over 60 million years ago. In 1938 one was caught off southeast Africa, with more seen since.

▼ Coelacanth fish of today are not exactly the same species from millions of years ago, but very similar.

▶ The Chacoan peccary is similar to the giant Ice Age peccary that disappeared 10,000 years ago.

316 When a particular species is known to be living, it is called 'extant' rather than 'extinct'. Other examples of extant 'living fossils' include Australia's Wollemi pine tree, the pig-like Chacoan peccary, and the shellfish known as the lampshell.

317 A tree 'living fossil' once thought to be extinct is the dawn redwood. It was known only from fossils dating back ten million years. Then in 1944, examples were found in China. The living species, *Metasequoia glyptostroboides,* is slightly different to the long-extinct species.

◀ Large copper butterflies are still found in mainland Europe, but habitats lost to farming mean they are rare.

▶ The dawn redwood, one of only three redwood species, is now planted in parks and gardens across the world.

318 A particular plant or creature may become extinct in one area but be extant in another. In Europe the large copper butterfly became extinct in Britain in the 1860s, but it still lives in many other places across the region.

Beliefs and ideas

319 The way people view extinction has changed through the ages. Scientists' thoughts can be very different to those of other people. Some people don't believe in extinction, perhaps due to religious ideas.

320 In ancient times, people such as the Greek scientist–naturalist Aristotle (384–322 BC) believed that the natural world had never changed. No new species evolved and no old ones became extinct.

321 As people began to study fossils, they realized that they were from living things that were no longer around. Some experts said these plants and animals survived somewhere remote and undiscovered. Others began to suggest that extinction really did happen.

322 Fossil expert Georges Cuvier (1769–1832) was one of the first scientists to say that there probably were extinctions. Due to his religious beliefs, he explained them as happening in the Great Floods described in the Bible.

▼ Baron Georges Cuvier admitted that the fossil elephants he studied had become extinct.

GOOD AND BAD EXTINCTIONS

Make a list of animals that can cause problems such as spreading diseases, eating farmers' crops and damaging trees. Ask your family and friends: If you could make some extinct, which ones would you choose and why? Does everyone have the same answers? Here's a few to get you started: Houseflies, fleas, rats, squirrels, pigeons, foxes, deer.

▲ By altering the malaria-carrying mosquito's genes, scientists may be able to wipe out the disease malaria.

▼ In South America, Darwin studied fossils of the giant armadillo-like *Glyptodon* and wondered why it no longer survived.

324 Modern views continue to change about extinction. Scientists can now identify separate species by studying their genes, rather than what they look like or how they breed. What was thought to be one species could, with genetic information, be two or more. For endangered plants and animals, it might not be one species threatened with extinction, but several.

323 In 1859, extinction became an important topic. Naturalist Charles Darwin described the theory of evolution in his book *On the Origin of Species by Means of Natural Selection*. In it Darwin explained the idea of 'survival of the fittest', and how new species evolved while other species less equipped to deal with their environment died out.

▶ A scene from the 2009 movie *Creation*. Darwin's ideas about evolution shaped modern scientific views on extinction.

Long, long ago

325 The history of life on Earth dates back over three billion years, and extinction has been happening since then. Millions of plants and animals have died out over this time, called the geological timescale.

326 Fossil evidence shows that even 500 million years ago, there was an enormous variety of life with many species becoming extinct. The idea that long ago there were just a few species, which gradually increased through to today, with new ones evolving but very few dying out, is not accurate.

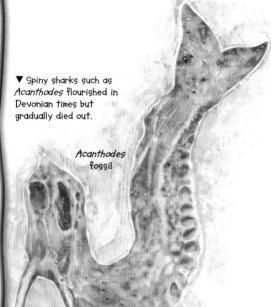

▼ Spiny sharks such as *Acanthodes* flourished in Devonian times but gradually died out.

Acanthodes fossil

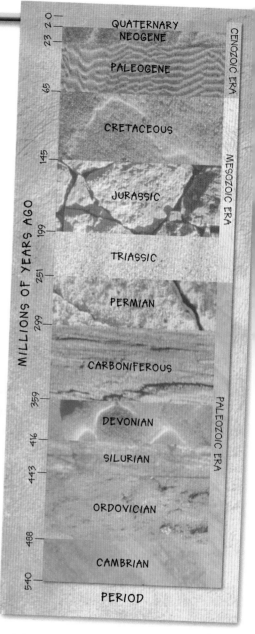

MILLIONS OF YEARS AGO

PERIOD	ERA
QUATERNARY / NEOGENE (2.0, 23)	CENOZOIC ERA
PALEOGENE (65)	
CRETACEOUS (145)	MESOZOIC ERA
JURASSIC (199)	
TRIASSIC (251)	
PERMIAN (299)	PALEOZOIC ERA
CARBONIFEROUS (359)	
DEVONIAN (416)	
SILURIAN (443)	
ORDOVICIAN (488)	
CAMBRIAN (540)	

▲ The geological timescale spans the history of the Earth. This vast amount of time is broken down into eras, and then into time periods. By studying fossils from different periods we can see how abundant life was through prehistory.

327 As we find more fossils, the gaps or 'missing links' in the history of life are filled, and we identify more and more extinctions. Fossils show how whole groups of prehistoric living things started, spread and became common, then faded away. For example, there are many kinds of reptiles alive today, such as crocodiles, snakes, lizards and turtles. But other reptiles, such as dinosaurs, pterosaurs and ichthyosaurs, are long extinct.

Glossopteris fossil

▲ *Glossopteris* or Gondwana tree once covered huge areas, but disappeared.

▼ Ichthyosaurs became extinct with the dinosaurs, 65 million years ago.

Ichthyosaur fossil

QUIZ

Match these extinct animals with their descriptions:
1. Pterosaur 2. Ichthyosaur 3. Early amphibian
A. Dolphin-shaped sea reptile
B. Four-legged swamp-dweller with a fishy tail C. Flying creature with long, thin jaws and claws on its wings and feet

Answers:
1C 2A 3B

328 Fossils also reveal that during some time periods, life was very varied, with lots of new species appearing and others dying out. At other times, plants and animals were less numerous and varied, with fewer new species evolving and lower numbers of extinctions.

▼ *Acanthostega* was one of the first four-legged land creatures.

Acanthostega fossil

◄ The extinct fish *Tiktaalik* shows a link between fish and land animals.

Tiktaalik fossil

Mass extinctions

329 At times in the Earth's history there have been mass extinctions, also called extinction events. Huge numbers of living things died out in a short time, usually less than a few thousand years. In some cases over half of all animals and plants disappeared.

▶ These are just a few of the millions of animals and plants that died out during mass extinctions.

ORDOVICIAN-SILURIAN
450–443 million years ago

Endoceras:
A type of mollusc

CAMBRIAN-ORDOVICIAN
488 million years ago

Pikaia:
An eel-like creature with a
rod-like spinal column

330 The Cambrian–Ordovician mass extinction was 488 million years ago. It marked the change from the time span called the Cambrian Period to the next one, the Ordovician Period. Among the victims were many kinds of trilobites and lampshells, a kind of shellfish.

331 The Ordovician–Silurian mass extinction happened 450–443 million years ago, in two bursts. All life was in the sea at that time. Many types of shellfish, echinoderms (starfish, sea urchins and relatives) and corals died out.

▶ Mass extinctions show as dips in the variety of living things throughout prehistoric time.

Cambrian–Ordovician

Ordovician–Silurian

600   500   400   Time (million years ago)

332 The Late Devonian mass extinction included several bursts 365–359 million years ago. Corals, trilobites and several groups of fish disappeared. It was the end of the 'Age of Fishes'.

Triceratops:
One of the last dinosaurs

LATE DEVONIAN
365–359 million years ago

TRIASSIC-JURASSIC
200 million years ago

Placodus:
A marine reptile

Dunkleosteus:
armoured fish

333 The Triassic–Jurassic mass extinction occurred 200 million years ago. The main groups affected included many sea creatures, amphibians, and certain types of reptiles, including some early dinosaurs.

334 The Cretaceous–Tertiary mass extinction, 65 million years ago, is the most famous. It saw the extinction of the dinosaurs, as well as many other animals and plants. More than two-thirds of all species died out. The cause may have been a meteorite that smashed into Earth, setting off earthquakes, tsunamis and volcanoes, and causing rapid climate change.

Late Devonian

Triassic–Jurassic

Cretaceous–Tertiary

Number of families

800

0

200

100

0

The biggest of all

335 **The most massive of all mass extinctions was the Permian-Triassic or end-of Permian event, 251 million years ago.** Also known as the 'Great Dying', it saw vast losses with more than four-fifths of all Earth's species wiped out.

336 **The 'Great Dying' was probably caused by the same combination of reasons as several other mass extinctions.** These included volcanic eruptions, earthquakes and tsunamis. They were probably set off by the continents drifting into new positions, with accompanying changes in sea levels, ocean currents, wind patterns, rainfall and temperature.

▶ At the end of the Permian Period, the world was rocked by a series of great changes that killed off most kinds of life on Earth.

337 **The changes that probably caused mass extinctions were very complicated because of the way species depend on each other.** If a particular plant could not cope with the changes and died out, then the animals that fed on it were also affected, as were the predators that fed on them. The balance of nature was upset and extinctions followed.

Acanthodian fish

Crinoids

Placoderms

338 Mass extinctions upset some habitats more than others. In many of these events, including the Permian-Triassic one, most losses were marine life. Especially affected were tiny sea plants and creatures that formed the floating 'soup' of life known as plankton.

Diictodon

Lystrosaurus

Gorgonops

339 Mass extinctions were not total disasters. Afterwards, fewer species meant less competition. So there were chances and opportunities for a surge of evolution and new species. Just 20 million years after the Permian-Triassic 'Great Dying', the first dinosaurs were prowling the land while early pterosaurs flapped through the skies.

Corals

Trilobites

Ages of ice

340 Over the past few million years there have been several extinctions linked to more than a dozen ice ages. The first of these started around 2.6 million years ago and the last one faded just 15,000–10,000 years ago. These cold times are called glaciations, and the warmer periods between – like the one today – are interglacials.

341 An example of an extinct ice age species is the sabre-tooth cat *Smilodon*. There were perhaps five species of *Smilodon* starting around 2.5 million years ago. The last one, dying out only 10,000 years ago, was *Smilodon fatalis*.

▲ Last of the ice age sabre-tooth cats, *Smilodon* lived in the Americas and was as big as the largest big cat of today, the Siberian tiger.

342 Hundreds of other ice age animals have died out in the past 25,000 years. They include the woolly rhino, woolly mammoth, cave bear, dire wolf, and various kinds of horses, deer, camels, llamas, beavers, ground sloths, and even mice and rats.

345 **The second reason is the spread of humans.** As the climate warmed, ice sheets and glaciers melted, and people moved north into new areas. Big animals such as mammoths were hunted for food, as shown in Stone Age cave paintings. Others, such as cave bears, were killed because they were dangerous.

343 **Many of these large animals disappeared during a fairly short time period of 15,000–10,000 years ago.** This happened especially across northern lands in North America, Europe and Asia. What was the cause of such widespread losses?

▼ Low sea levels during ice ages allowed people to spread from eastern Asia to North America.

344 **Two main reasons have been suggested for the recent ice age extinctions.** One is rapid natural climate change. As the weather warmed up, some big animals could not evolve fast enough or travel to cooler areas. The woolly mammoth and woolly rhino, for example, may have overheated.

▶ Stone Age people probably trapped and killed mammoths, which would have provided them with food for weeks.

Keeping a record

346 In ancient times, people travelled little and did not record details of nature, so extinctions were hard to identify. From the 1500s, people began to explore the world, study living things and discover new species. They then hunted, shot, ate or collected them – some to extinction.

▲ People exploring remote areas brought back tales of fanciful beasts – perhaps the result of several real creatures that explorers mixed up.

347 Spectacular examples of historical extinction are the elephant birds of Madagascar. There were several species of these giant, flightless birds, similar to ostriches but larger. The biggest stood 3 metres tall and weighed more than 450 kilograms.

348 All elephant birds were extinct by the 1500s. People not only hunted them, but also collected and cooked their huge eggs, more than 35 centimetres in length.

▼ Elephant birds evolved on the island of Madagascar with no big predators to threaten them – until humans arrived.

Steller's sea cow was 8 metres long

Great auks once numbered millions

▲ Extinctions of large creatures continued through recent centuries.

Bluebuck lived in small herds

349 There is a long list of other animal species that went extinct even before 1900. They include the tall New Zealand ground birds called moas (by 1500), the huge European cow known as the auroch (probably 1630s), the North Pacific Steller's sea cow (1760s), the Southern African bluebuck antelope (around 1800) and the Atlantic penguin-like great auk (1850s).

I DON'T BELIEVE IT!

The huge moa of New Zealand was 4 metres tall. It was hunted by the enormous Haast's eagle, the biggest known eagle, which became extinct by 1400.

350 Many plants are also recorded as going extinct during this time. They include the Rio myrtle tree from South America (about 1820s), the string tree from the Atlantic island of St Helena (1860s) and the Indian kerala tree (1880s).

◄ St Helena ebony is a shrub that is being rescued from the brink of extinction.

Gathering pace

351 Over the last 100 years, the rate of extinction has speeded up greatly. More kinds of living things are disappearing than ever before. This is due mainly to human activity such as cutting down forests, habitat loss as natural areas are changed for farmland and houses, hunting, collecting rare species, and releasing chemicals into the environment.

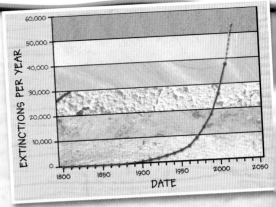

▲ The estimated extinction rate is rocketing as we find out about more threatened species every year.

▶ The spectacled bear of South America's Andes Mountains faces many threats, including the logging of its forest home.

352 One of the first extinctions to receive lots of publicity around the world was the Caribbean monk seal in the 1950s. It was hunted for its oil and meat, and to stop it eating the fish that people wanted to catch. From 2003, expeditions tried to find it again but gave up after five years.

▲ The last confirmed sightings of Caribbean monk seals were southeast of the island of Jamaica in 1952.

Thylacine

353 Other animal extinctions of the last 100 years include the thylacine and the Japanese sea lion. The last thylacine died of neglect in a zoo in Hobart, Tasmania in 1936, while the last Japanese sea lion was seen in 1974. Many plant species have also died out in the last 100 years, including the Cuban holly (1950s), the cry violet or cry pansy in France (1950s) and the woolly begonia of Malaysia (1960s).

354 With each passing year scientists explore, identify and record more living species in greater detail than ever before. As we study and list all of these new plants and animals, we have a better chance of discovering when one goes extinct.

▼ The Bosavi silky cuscus is a rarity — a new species discovered in Papua New Guinea.

FIND THAT SEAL!

You will need:
paper   pens

Imagine you are on an expedition to search for the Caribbean monk seal. Make a list of the equipment you would need. Binoculars, cameras, sketch pad, sound recorder…
You need evidence, so don't forget specimen bottles for some of the seal's hair, or its urine or droppings!

Too many to disappear

355 **The passenger pigeon was once extremely common.** Flocks of millions flew around North America, darkening the skies as they passed. Before Europeans arrived in North America, native people caught the pigeons for their meat and feathers. This was on a small scale and happened for centuries without affecting the overall number of birds.

356 With the arrival of Europeans, especially from about 1700, came many changes. The new settlers altered the land from natural habitats to farms, roads and towns. Habitat loss soon gathered pace, and people also began to catch the pigeons for a cheap supply of food.

▼ Today, birds such as these city starlings seem too numerous to vanish. But we cannot be sure how they will fare in the future.

▶ Passenger pigeons became big business, with hunters shooting and trappers netting the birds to sell their meat in cities.

358 By 1900, the passenger pigeon had just about disappeared in the wild. The last one in captivity, Martha, died in Cincinnati Zoo, Ohio, USA in 1914. With her went one of the most numerous birds that ever existed.

◄ Famous hunter, naturalist and artist John James Audobon painted passenger pigeons. He once said one flock was 'still passing in undiminished numbers... for three days'.

357 By the 1850s, the hunters and trappers noticed that passenger pigeon numbers had started to fall. But the killing continued. Some people tried to raise the pigeons in captivity, but the birds could only breed and thrive in very large flocks. Kept in small groups, they did not eat well or breed. They may have also suffered from a bird illness called Newcastle disease.

I DON'T BELIEVE IT!

Martha, the last passenger pigeon, was named after Martha Washington, wife of the first US president George Washington. There are several statues and memorials to Martha (the pigeon), including one at Cincinnati Zoo.

▲ Passenger pigeons did not survive well in captivity. When the last one died in 1914, it was mounted or 'stuffed' at the Smithsonian Institute.

Island extinctions

Hawaii

▼ Tiny islands in vast oceans around the world are 'hotbeds' of extinctions.

CUBA

Galapagos Islands

Cuban solenodon – this shrew-like creature has not been seen since 2008

Hawaiian black mamo – gone by the 1920s

PACIFIC OCEAN

Galapagos damselfish – became extinct during the 1980s

SOUTHERN ATLANTIC OCEAN

359 **In the past few centuries, more than two-thirds of living things becoming extinct have lived on islands.** Islands can support only small numbers of a particular species, so there is a higher risk of dying out. Each island also has its own particular conditions, to which species adapt over thousands of years. If conditions change, for example, when people arrive, the local wild species may be threatened.

360 **Island plants and animals are also at great risk from introduced species – those brought by people.** These introduced species include sheep, goats, cows, foxes, stoats, mice, rats, cats and dogs. They start to compete with the local species for food, or prey on them, or steal their nest sites, or give them diseases – or all of these.

PACIFIC OCEAN

MAURITIUS

Lesser bilby – not seen on
the island continent of
Australia since the 1950s

AUSTRALIA

INDIAN OCEAN

Mauritius dodo
– disappeared
by the 1690s

THE DODO LIVES AGAIN!

You will need:
sheet of card   scissors   coloured pens
sticky tape   elastic

Cut out a face mask in the shape of a
dodo's head and beak and colour it as
shown (left). Find out from books or
the Internet about the noises a dodo
made. Now you can try to bring the
dodo back to life!

361 Perhaps the most famous
example of any extinct animal is
the dodo. This flightless, turkey-
sized bird lived on Mauritius in the
Indian Ocean, ate fruit and nested
on the ground. It had no natural
predators or enemies. Then people
arrived with animals that hunted it,
its eggs and its chicks. By 1700, the
dodo was gone, leading to the
saying 'dead as a dodo'.

362 At least 50 bird species from the
Hawaiian Islands are extinct. This affected
other wildlife. Some of the birds fed on nectar
and carried pollen so that flowers could breed.
Others ate fruits and spread the seeds in their
droppings. Without the birds, some of these
plants become extinct. When one species
disappears, then another that depends on it dies
out, it is known as co-extinction.

What's happening today?

363 In the natural world today, extinction rates are shooting up due to a huge variety of causes. Scientists call this another time of mass extinction.

364 The main cause of today's extinctions is habitat loss and degradation (changing natural habitats for the worse). The number of people in the world is rising fast and they need land for their houses, farms, factories, roads and leisure, leaving less wild areas.

▲ Acid rain from polluting gases taken up by clouds has devastated large areas of forest.

◀ Logging and other forms of deforestation are major threats in tropical areas.

365 Other causes include pollution and hunting for food or trophies. There is also the collecting of species for displays, introduced species, and diseases that spread from domestic animals and farm plants to wild species. As the early signs of global warming and climate change become more marked, these will also have huge effects on habitats and push species towards extinction.

▲ The baiji is probably now extinct. Some people hope it survives in backwaters of the Yangtze and nearby rivers. There are rare sightings, but for the time being, no proof.

366 In 2007, a search in China failed to find any baijis, or Yangtze river dolphins. This species was threatened for many reasons, including dams built across its rivers, pollution, hunting and the overfishing of its natural prey.

▼ Now extinct, golden toads were probably victims of global warming and increased human activity in their natural habitats.

On the brink

367 Every year, wildlife experts make lists of animals and plants that are threatened with extinction. These are known as the IUCN 'Red Lists', and every year, they grow longer.

▶ Symbols indicate if a species is threatened or not, ranging from LC meaning Least Concern, to EX meaning Extinct.

QUIZ

Which of these amphibians is threatened with extinction?
1. Lungless Mexican salamander
2. South African ghost frog
3. Betic midwife toad
4. Chinese giant salamander
5. Darwin frog

Answer:
All of them, plus thousands of others

368 One of the most endangered groups of animals is the rhinos. There are only five rhino species and all are in huge trouble. The black, Javan and Sumatran rhinos are listed as 'critically endangered'. They will become extinct in 20–50 years unless massive efforts are made to save them.

Sumatran rhino

▼ All rhinos need action to save them. Most numerous is the white rhino, with less than 20,000.

White rhino

Javan rhino

Black rhino

166

369 **A larger group, with many species at risk of extinction, is the amphibians.** More than half of the 6000-plus species are threatened. A terrible problem is the new fungus infection called chytrid disease. Recent amphibian extinctions include the gastric-brooding frog of Australia, which swallowed its eggs so the tadpoles could grow in its stomach. It died out in the 1980s.

▲ Baby gastric-brooding frogs emerged from their mother's mouth. Many other species of frogs, toads and newts are also under threat.

370 **You cannot get closer to extinction than only one remaining individual.** The café marron bush grew on the island of Rodrigues in the Indian Ocean, but finally only one bush was left. Scientists at Kew Gardens, London took cuttings from it in the 1980s and grew them into bushes. Now some are being taken back to Rodrigues.

▲ The world's largest flower, rafflesia, is now extremely rare.

Indian rhino

371 **Coral reefs are among the world's richest places for wildlife.** But these whole habitats may become extinct in the next 100–200 years. They are in great danger from threats such as global warming, pollution, water cloudiness and acidity upsetting the delicate natural balance between their species.

▶ Due to global warming, coral reefs may become 'bleached' and die.

Saved just in time

372 **To save an almost extinct species takes time, effort and money.** This means studying it and its habitat, its contact with other species and finding out how many are left. Scientists assess its needs through field studies – in the wild – and also captive studies. They establish what it eats, where it nests or which soil it likes, so that places can be put aside.

Female

Male

▲ Through a huge conservation effort, the numbers of ladybird spiders in Great Britain have risen.

373 **Rescuing a threatened animal or plant from extinction also means saving its habitat.** Without somewhere natural and safe to live, the species cannot thrive in the wild. Otherwise, even if it is saved, it will always be limited to a park, zoo or similar place, and be extinct in the wild.

▼ In North America, movements of very rare black-footed ferrets are studied by radio transmitter collars.

374 It's less use people coming to an area from far away, and trying to save a species, than local people getting involved. The locals need to have input into the rescue effort. Through ecotourism, visitors can see rare wildlife without damaging it or the habitat and pay money, which is put towards conservation efforts.

◄ Elephant safaris allow paying tourists to get close to rare rhinos without disturbing them too much.

375 Saving one 'flagship' or 'headline' species from extinction can help to save whole habitats. Such species usually appeal to the public because they are big and powerful, like tigers and mountain gorillas, or cute and fluffy, like giant pandas and golden lion tamarins.

▼ Setting up wildlife parks and nature reserves helps not only the headline species, such as these gorillas, but all the plants and animals living there.

169

Should we care?

376 Why should we care if a species goes extinct? Especially if it is some small bug in a remote forest, or a worm on the seabed. Does it really matter or affect us in any way?

377 Many people think that all animals and plants have a right to be here on Earth. We should not destroy nature for little reason. If we let species die out, it shows we do not care for our surroundings and the natural world. These types of reasons are known as moral and ethical arguments.

378 There are medical reasons for saving species. Researchers may discover that a particular type of plant or animal is the source of a new wonder drug to cure illness. If it had gone extinct, we would never know this. Other species can be used for medical research into diseases such as cancers.

379 Scientific reasons to prevent species dying out are also important. Extinction reduces biodiversity, which is the variety of living things necessary for the balance of nature. The genes in certain animals or plants could be used in GM, genetic modification, perhaps to improve our farm crops and make our farm animals healthier.

380 There are also traditional and cultural reasons for caring about extinction. Some endangered species are important to ethnic groups and tribes for their history, ceremonies, myths and special foods. People should not come to an area from afar with new ways of living and cause habitat loss, introduce new animals, plants and diseases and kill off local species.

▲ The Florida panther is an extremely rare subspecies of cougar, or mountain lion. If it dies out, there will still be other cougars elsewhere. So would its disappearance matter?

I DON'T BELIEVE IT!

In the 1800s, European explorers in Australia captured now-extinct creatures including pig-footed bandicoots. But when the explorers got lost and hungry, they ate the bandicoots.

Gone forever?

381 People once thought that extinction is forever, but future science may change this view. The idea of bringing extinct animals or plants back to life can be seen through films such as *Jurassic Park*. Scientists use a species' eggs, its genes or its genetic material such as DNA (de-oxyribonucleic acid).

▲ In the *Jurassic Park* stories, dinosaurs were recreated from their preserved genes and hatched in egg incubators.

▼ Why the Pyrenean ibex died out is unclear, but it may have been the result of infectious diseases.

382 In 2009, a baby Pyrenean ibex, a subspecies of the goat-like Spanish ibex, was born. Its mother was a goat but its genes came from one of the last Pyrenean ibexes, which had died out by 2000. The young ibex was a genetic copy. It died after birth, but it showed what might be possible in the future.

QUIZ

Put these species in order of when they became extinct, from longest ago to most recent.
1. Quagga
2. Dodo
3. Neanderthal humans
4. Baiji (Yangtze river dolphin)
5. Woolly mammoth

Answers:
3. About 30,000 years ago 5. Around 10,000 years ago 2. By 1700 1. 1883 4. By 2007 (probably)

383 To revive extinct species, there are many problems to solve in genetic engineering, altering DNA, cloning and similar methods. However, scientists are taking samples of DNA and other material from all kinds of sources, such as frozen mammoths, dodo bones, the dead seeds of extinct plants, and even long-gone humans, to carry out experiments and see what can be done.

▲ The Barbary lion of North Africa was thought to be extinct from the 1920s, but genetic tests have revealed several living in zoos.

▼ The Quagga Project selects and breeds the most quagga-like zebras over many generations.

384 The quagga, which went extinct in 1883, was a subspecies of the plains zebra of southern Africa. It had zebra stripes on its front half but was plain brown at the rear. The Quagga Project aims to 'breed back' quaggas. This is done by choosing plains zebras that look most like quaggas, and allowing them to mate. Gradually, after several generations, the young of plains zebras should look more and more like quaggas.

Looking to the future

385 In the future, living things will continue to go extinct, with or without human meddling — because that is the nature of life and how it evolves. The damage we are doing to the world, especially with habitat loss and climate change, means that the rate of extinction will only increase.

Ardipithecus ramidus
Extinct: 4.5 million years ago

Australopithecus afarensis
Extinct: 3.5 million years ago

Homo ergaster
Extinct: 1.9 million years ago

Homo erectus
Extinct: 1.7 million years ago

386 What about our own kind, human beings? Over the past four million years there have probably been more than 20 different species of humans and their close cousins on Earth. Only one is left now – ourselves, modern humans, known as *Homo sapiens*. All others have gone extinct.

▲ There have been many different species of human throughout history. Despite advances such as stone tools and controlling fire, they all became extinct.

387 A recent human extinction is the Neanderthal people, *Homo neanderthalensis*. They lived about 250,000 years ago across northern Europe and Asia. As modern humans spread from Africa into Europe and Asia, Neanderthals died out. Whether modern people killed them, or were better at finding food and shelter, is not clear.

I DON'T BELIEVE IT!

Recent surveys indicate that 1 in 8 bird species are at risk of extinction, and within 100 years this could rise to 1 in 4. And birds are a lot less threatened than many other animal groups.

388 Surviving even later than the Neanderthals, but still becoming extinct, were the 'hobbit people' on the island of Flores, Southeast Asia. Known as *Homo floresiensis*, they were only about one metre tall. They may have survived until less than 15,000 years ago.

▶ The remains of *Homo floresiensis* were discovered in 2003. It may be a new species of extinct human.

Homo floresiensis
Extinct: 15,000 years ago

Homo heidelbergensis
Extinct: 600,000 years ago

Homo neanderthalensis
Extinct: 100,000 years ago

389 In the distant future, will humans become extinct? Our knowledge of the natural world, and the harm we are doing it, suggests that our species will not last forever. But humans have shown great skill at surviving all kinds of problems, and are likely to carry on for a very long time yet.

▶ Can modern humans use their wit and intelligence to survive – whilst also saving wild species?

Homo sapiens
Still alive today

ENDANGERED ANIMALS

390 Around the world, wild animals, plants and the places they live in are disappearing fast. From the creatures of the rainforests to the animals that live in mountains, deserts, polar lands, and even in the oceans, countless numbers are under threat. Some animals have become so rare, they will die out forever. The main problem is that people are causing huge amounts of damage to the natural world. It is up to us to change our ways and save animals in danger.

▶ The biggest cat in the Americas, the jaguar is threatened by loss of its habitat. It is also shot or trapped by people in case it attacks their farm animals, their pets — or themselves.

Gone long ago

391 In one sense, animals and plants have always been under threat. It's part of nature's 'struggle for existence'. Creatures must find food, shelter and other needs, and avoid predators and dangers. This has been happening for millions of years, as old types of living things died out, or became extinct, and new ones took over.

Saltasaurus

392 About 65 million years ago, the dinosaurs died out, along with many other animals and plants. This was a mass extinction, but it had nothing to do with people, because there were no humans then. Scientists are not sure why it happened, but the causes were natural. A huge asteroid may have smashed into the Earth. There have been many mass extinctions in the Earth's long history.

▲ The huge *Saltasaurus*, 12 metres long and weighing 8 tonnes, was one of the last dinosaurs. About 65 million years ago, it may have watched as a massive meteorite was about to smash into the Earth and cause the death of millions of animals and plants.

I DON'T BELIEVE IT!

More than 99 out of 100 kinds of animals that ever lived are now extinct — died out and gone forever.

Pteranodon

394 Many other large creatures have died out in the past few thousand years. These include cave bears, woolly rhinos, dire wolves and giant deer. Some of these extinctions happened as people spread around the world.

393 Now there are humans on Earth, animals are becoming extinct at a faster rate than before. Woolly mammoths died out within the past 10,000 years. This may have been partly due to the end of the Ice Age, since they could not cope with warmer weather. However, being hunted by ancient people did not help.

Huge meteorite or asteroid

Herd of *Edmontosaurus*

395 As the centuries passed, from ancient history to medieval times, more animals came under threat. The auroch was a huge wild cow, from which today's farm cattle were bred. It was hunted by people until it disappeared. The last auroch died in 1627, in a Polish forest.

◄ Woolly rhinos were well adapted to the cold with their long coats. Perhaps they could not cope as the Ice Age faded and the world warmed up. They too became extinct.

179

Too late to save

396 **In the last few hundred years, many kinds of animals have become endangered, and dozens have died out.** They include fish, frogs, snakes, birds and mammals. Studying why these extinctions happened can help to save today's endangered animals.

397 **Being very common is no safeguard against human threats.** Five hundred years ago there were perhaps 5000 million passenger pigeons. They were shot and trapped by people for their meat, and their natural habitats were taken over by crops and farm animals. The last passenger pigeon, 'Martha', died in Cincinnati Zoo in 1914.

398 **A creature that went from discovery to extinction in less than 30 years was Steller's sea cow.** It was a huge, 3-tonne cousin of the manatee and dugong, and lived in the Arctic region. It was first described by scientists in 1741. So many were killed in a short space of time, that Steller's sea cow had died out by 1768.

QUIZ

What died out when? Put these animals' extinctions in order, from most long ago to most recent.
A. Dodo
B. Blue antelope
C. Thylacine
D. Passenger pigeon
E. Steller's sea cow

Answers:
A E B D C

► The dodo has become a world symbol of extinction. Only a few bones, feathers and bits of skin remain.

▲ Steller's sea cow was 8 metres long and almost as heavy as an elephant. However size was no protection, as its herds were slaughtered by sailors for meat, blubber and hides.

400 The dodo, a turkey-sized bird with tiny wings that could not fly, was found on the island of Mauritius in the Indian Ocean. Sailors that stopped at the island captured dodos as fresh food. So many were killed that all dodos were extinct by 1700. This has led to the saying 'as dead as a dodo'.

▼ Every 7 September, Australia holds National Threatened Species Day. The day is in memory of the last thylacine that died on this date in 1936 at Hobart Zoo, in the state of Tasmania.

399 Many animals have become endangered, and died out forever. They include the blue antelope of Southern Africa (around 1800), the flightless seabird known as the great auk (1850s), the dog-like marsupial (pouched mammal) known as the thylacine or Tasmanian tiger (1936), and the Caribbean monk seal (1950s). The list is very long, and very sad.

How we know

401 How do we know which animals are endangered and need our help? Explorers and travellers bring back stories of rare and strange creatures. Sometimes they add bits to their tales to make them more exciting. Scientific studies and surveys are needed to find out which creatures are in trouble, and how serious the threats are.

▼ This lion, put to sleep briefly by a tranquillizer dart, is being tracked by its radio collar. Each lion has its own pattern of whisker spots, like a fingerprint, to help identify it.

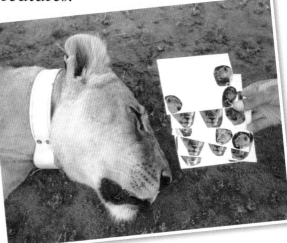

▼ Rangers guard incredibly rare mountain gorillas, which soon get used to having them around. The rangers become well acquainted with the habits of the gorillas, which helps scientists carry out important research.

402 Firing a dart containing a knock-out chemical makes a creature, such as a lion, sleep for a short time. Scientists then work fast to take blood samples, check for diseases, measure and weigh, and gather other useful information, before the animal wakes up.

403 Scientists need to know more than just how many individual animals are left in an endangered species. They try to find out the animals' ages, what they eat, how often they breed, how they move about or migrate, and how long they live. This all helps to build up knowledge of the species, and work out the best ways to take action.

▼ Aerial films and photographs can be studied to count big animals such as elephants, estimate their age and work out if they are male or female.

404 Big animals in open habitats, such as elephants on the African savanna (grassland), are surveyed from the air. Planes, helicopters and even balloons carry people who count the herds and take photographs.

405 It is extremely helpful to capture, tag and release animals. Rare birds such as albatrosses are carefully caught in nets, and small rings are put on their legs. This helps scientists to identify each albatross every time it is seen. Tags in the ears of rhinos can work in the same way.

I DON'T BELIEVE IT!

When studying an endangered animal, one of the best things to have is — its poo! Droppings or dung contain much information about what a creature eats, how healthy it is, and any diseases it may have.

406 Some animals are big enough to attach a radio beacon to, which sends signals up to a satellite. Whales, sea turtles, seals and other sea creatures can be tracked as they swim across the vast oceans.

How endangered?

407 We might suspect an animal is at risk, but how serious is the threat? The scientific organization called the IUCN, World Conservation Union, produces a 'Red List' of threatened species of animals and plants. Each species is given a two-letter description to show its plight.

▲ The leafy sea dragon is threatened as it is caught by exotic fish collectors. It is also killed, dried and powdered for the traditional medicine trade.

408 NT is Near Threatened. A species could be in trouble soon, but not quite yet. An example is the leafy sea dragon, a type of fish, whose flaps of skin make it look like swaying seaweed.

409 VU is Vulnerable. The species is already under threat, and help is needed over the coming years. An example is the northern fur seal, of the northern Pacific region.

◄ The northern fur seal was killed in large numbers for its thick, soft, warm fur, once used for coats.

► Cheetahs once lived across most of Africa and the Middle East, and were even partly tamed and kept as pets by royalty. They may disappear before long.

410 **EN is Endangered.** The species faces big problems and the risk of extinction over the coming years is high. An example is the cheetah, the fastest runner on Earth.

411 **CR is Critically Endangered.** This is the most serious group. Unless there is a huge conservation effort, extinction is just around the corner. An example is the vaquita, the smallest kind of porpoise, from the northern Gulf of California.

▲ Polluted water, drilling for oil and gas, and being caught in fishing nets are all deadly dangers for the 1.5-metre-long vaquita.

▼ Hawaiian crows are only found in captivity. Attempts to breed and release them have so far failed.

MATCH UP

Can you place these threatened creatures in their correct animal groups?

A. Whale shark   1. Bird
B. Spix macaw   2. Fish
C. Vaquita   3. Amphibian
D. Caiman   4. Mammal
E. Olm   5. Reptile

Answers:
A2 B1 C4 D5 E3

412 **EW is Extinct in the Wild.** The species has disappeared in nature, although there may be a few surviving in zoos and wildlife parks. An example is the Hawaiian crow. The last two wild birds disappeared in 2002, although some live in cages. EX is Extinct, or gone forever. Usually this means the animal has not been seen for 50 years.

On the critical list

413 The most threatened animals in the world are CR, Critically Endangered. One of the most famous CR mammals is the mountain gorilla. There are just a few hundred left in the high peaks of Central Africa. They suffer from loss of their natural habitat, being killed for meat and trophies, and from catching human diseases.

▲ Smallest of the rhinos, at about 700 kilograms, the Sumatran rhino is poached for its horns. These are powdered for use in traditional so-called 'medicines'.

414 The most threatened group of big mammals is the rhinos. Of the five species, three are CR – the Javan and Sumatran rhinos of Southeast Asia, and the black rhino of Africa. The Indian rhino is endangered, EN. They all suffer from loss of natural living areas and being killed for their horns.

▼ Although more numerous than their mountain cousins, lowland gorillas face the same threats – loss of habitat and poaching being the two most dangerous.

MAKE A RHINO NOSE

You will need:
large sheet of card   sticky tape

A rhino's nose horn may be more than one metre long! Make your own by rolling some card into a cone shape and taping it firmly. Hold the 'horn' angled up from your own nose. How do rhinos see where they are going?

415 The kouprey or
Cambodian forest ox is
another critical mammal. It has
big horns and weighs more than one
tonne, but there are probably fewer than
250 left in Southeast Asia. Apart from
losing its natural habitat, the kouprey is
hunted by local people and it catches
diseases from farm cattle. It is also killed for
food by soldiers who fight for local warlords
and hide in the forest.

▲ The kouprey
grazes on grasses
by night and hides
in the thick forest
during the day.

▼ Right whales are
slow swimmers and
stay near the
surface, which made
them easy targets
for whalers.

416 The northern right whale
has never recovered from being
slaughtered during the mass killing of
whales in the last century. There are
now probably less than 600 left. These
whales breed so slowly that they may
never increase in numbers.

417 Apart from big,
well-known mammals, many other
smaller mammal species are on
the critical list. They include
the hispid hare (Assam rabbit)
and dwarf blue sheep of the
Himalaya Mountains,
and the northern hairy-
nosed wombat of
northeast Australia.

All kinds under threat

418 Mammals such as pandas, whales and tigers are not the only endangered animals – there are many other threatened species from all animal groups. Among the birds is the Bermuda petrel, the national seabird of the island of Bermuda. Only about 250 survive and the islanders are making a huge conservation effort to help them.

▲ The young Bermuda petrel stays at sea for about five years before it comes back to land to breed.

419 A critical reptile is the Batagur baska (river turtle or terrapin) of India and Southeast Asia. One reason for its rarity was that people collected its eggs, especially in Cambodia, to give as presents to the king. King Norodom Sihamoni of Cambodia has now given orders to protect the baska.

▼ The batagur 'royal turtle' grows to more than one metre long and 30 kilograms in weight. It eats all kinds of foods, from plants to fish and crabs.

420 An endangered amphibian is Hamilton's frog of New Zealand. It is perhaps the rarest frog in the world. Hamilton's frog does not croak, does not have webbed feet, and hatches from its egg not as a tadpole, but as a fully formed froglet.

▼ The Devil's Hole pupfish is one of several very rare fish, each found in one small pool.

▲ Hamilton's frog is less than 5 cm long. There may be as few as 300 left in the wild.

421 A fish that is vulnerable (VU) is the Devil's Hole pupfish. It lives naturally in just one warm pool, Devil's Hole, in a limestone cave in the desert near Death Valley, USA. There are usually around 200–400 pupfish there, but after problems with floods and droughts, the number by 2006 was less than 50.

422 One of the rarest insects is the Queen Alexandra's birdwing butterfly. It lives in a small area on the island of Papua New Guinea. In 1950, a nearby volcano erupted and destroyed much of the butterfly's forest habitat, so it is now endangered (EN).

Male

▶ Like many tropical butterflies, the female and male Queen Alexandra's birdwing look quite different from each other.

I DON'T BELIEVE IT!

The Bermuda petrel was thought to be extinct for over 300 years until a breeding group was discovered on some coastal rocks in 1951.

Female

189

The greatest threat

423 **Endangered animals face dozens of different threats, but the greatest problem for most of them is habitat loss.** This means the wild places or natural habitats where they live are being changed or destroyed, so animals, plants and other wildlife can no longer survive there.

424 **Today, habitat loss is happening at a terrifying rate, especially for tropical forests.** These forests are 'hot spots' that have the richest range of wildlife, known as biodiversity. They occur mainly in Central and South America, West Africa and Southeast Asia – and this is where most endangered animals live.

▶ Tropical forests are chopped down for their valuable hardwoods such as teak and mahogany. What remains is burnt and the land cleared for crops.

425 **Habitat loss is not a new threat – it has been happening for thousands of years.** Across much of Europe, farmland for crops and livestock gradually replaced once-great woods and forests. This meant the disappearance from Britain of forest animals such as bears, wild boars, wolves and beavers.

426 **The muriquis or woolly spider monkeys of Brazil are critically endangered.** Trees in their tropical forests have been chopped down for logs and the timber trade. Then the land is cleared for farm animals and crops. The monkeys, along with thousands of other forest species, have fewer places to live.

427 **In Borneo, animals from pygmy elephants to orang-utans are under threat as their forests are cleared for oil palm trees and other crops.** Oil palm plantations are one of the main reasons for habitat loss across the tropics. The vegetable oil from the fleshy fruits is used for cooking, to make margarine and prepared meals, and for a vehicle fuel known as biodiesel.

191

Too many people

428 Many animals no longer live in their natural habitats because people now live there. The number of people in the world increases by about 150 every minute. They need houses, land for farms, shops, schools, factories and roads. More people means less places for wildlife.

429 Animals living in lakes, rivers, marshes and swamps are some of the most endangered. Their habitats are drained and cleared for towns, ports and waterside holiday centres. Tourist areas along rivers and coastlines endanger all kinds of animals.

▼ Across the world, cities spread into nearby natural habitats, such as this shanty town in Colombia, South America.

QUIZ

Can you name the major threats these animals face?
1. Mediterranean monk seal
2. Red panda
3. Black-necked crane
4. Golden bamboo lemur

Answers:
1. Spread of holiday areas along the Mediterranean 2. Loss of bamboo 3. Tourists 4. Loss of trees in Madagascar due to spreading villages and farms

430 The Mediterranean monk seal has suffered greatly from the spread of tourism. Its breeding and resting areas have been taken over for holiday villages, sunbathing beaches and water sports. This seal has also been hunted by fishermen, who believe it 'steals' their fish, and affected by pollution. It is now critical, with fewer than 600 left.

▲ The shy Mediterranean monk seal is frightened by boats and divers, and tries to hide in underwater caves.

432 The black-necked crane lives in the highlands around the Himalayas in Asia. It faces several threats. One is the development of tourism in a region known as the Ladakh Valley in India. People come to gaze at the marvellous scenery and watch the wildlife, but they disturb the cranes, who are shy and less likely to breed.

► Black-necked cranes are sometimes poisoned by pesticide chemicals used by farmers.

431 The giant panda is a famous rare animal, and its distant cousin, the red panda, is also under threat. This tree-dwelling bamboo-eater from South and East Asia has fewer places to live, as towns and villages spread quickly. It's also hunted for its fur, especially its bushy tail, which is used to make hats and good luck wedding charms.

► The red panda is fully protected by law, but hunting continues for its fur.

Pollution problems

433 Pollution is a threat to all wildlife, as the wastes and chemicals we make get into the air, soil and water. Like many dangers to animals, pollution is often combined with other threats, such as habitat loss and climate change. Sometimes it is difficult to separate these dangers, since one is part of another.

▲ This Atlantic croaker fish has become blind with misty eyes, or cataracts, due to chemicals in the water.

434 Harmful chemicals spread quickly through water to affect streams, rivers, lakes and even the open ocean. Caspian seals live in the landlocked Caspian Sea, a vast lake in West Asia. Industries and factories around the lake shore pollute its waters. The seals suffer from sores and fur loss, and are less resistant to diseases.

◄ Oil spillages are a devastating form of pollution. This beaver is covered in oil, which it tries to lick from its coat. By doing so it swallows poisonous chemicals that may kill it.

435 **The largest amphibians in the world are Chinese and Japanese giant salamanders.** They are in danger from pollution of their cool, fast-flowing, highland streams. There are few factories there, but the clouds and rains carry polluting chemicals from the smoke and fumes of factory chimneys far away.

POLLUTION HAZARDS

Next time you are in the park or countryside, look out for types of pollution. Find out how they could harm animals, and how we can reduce them. Look for examples such as:

Litter in ponds • Plastic bags in bushes and hedges • Pools of oil or fuel from vehicles Broken glass • Pipes carrying poisonous liquids into ditches, streams or rivers • Metal wire, plastic tags and similar objects

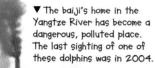

▼ The baiji's home in the Yangtze River has become a dangerous, polluted place. The last sighting of one of these dolphins was in 2004.

436 **A survey in 2006 failed to find any baijis, or Chinese river dolphins.** One of the threats to this dolphin is pollution of its main river, the Yangtze or Chang Jiang, by factories along its banks, and by farm chemicals seeping into the water from fields. The pollution has harmed not only the baiji but also the fish and other animals that it eats. Further threats include hunting by people for its meat, the building of dams, drowning in fishing nets and being hit by boats.

Baiji (Chinese river dolphin)

ange in the weather

The whole world faces climate change, which could endanger many animal species. The weather is gradually becoming warmer because our atmosphere (the layer of air around Earth) is being altered by 'greenhouse gases'. These come mainly from burning fuels such as petrol, diesel, wood, coal and natural gas. They make the Earth trap heat from the Sun, and so the planet gets hotter.

438 In the far north, polar bears are threatened because ice floes (big lumps of ice) are melting faster. The bears use the ice floes to hunt seals from and to rest on. There used to be plenty of floes, but now polar bears can swim for hours before finding one. Some bears even drown, exhausted in the open sea.

439 In the far south, penguins have trouble finding icebergs to rest on. As in the north, the icebergs melt faster due to global warming. Like the polar bears, the penguins cannot get out of the water for a rest, and because they cannot fly, they may drown.

▶ Fewer, smaller ice floes spell terrible trouble for polar bears.

▼ Penguins become tired after feeding in the water for several hours, and need to rest on the shore or an iceberg. Global warming means that the ice is melting and penguins' resting places are disappearing.

440
Global warming is changing the seasons, which may affect huge numbers of animals. An earlier spring means that insects in Europe breed a week or two before they used to. However, migrating birds from Africa, such as pied flycatchers, swallows and swifts, might arrive too late to catch the insects for their chicks. Scientists call this 'uncoupling' of the natural links between animals and their seasonal food.

441
The huge Asian fish, the beluga sturgeon, is already endangered. It is poached for the female's eggs, which are sold as the expensive food caviar. However, as global warming continues, the sturgeon's rivers and lakes will be affected, which could push the fish to extinction even more quickly.

I DON'T BELIEVE IT!
Scientists studying 40,000 tree swallows say that the birds now lay their eggs nine days earlier than they did 40 years ago, probably as a result of global warming.

▲ Beluga sturgeons used to grow to more than 5 metres long, but most of them are now caught and killed before they reach such a great size.

Poaching and souvenirs

Weight for weight, rhino horn can be worth more than gems such as rubies and pearls.

443 The main reason that rhinos are so endangered is because of poaching for their horns. The horns are carved into decorative objects such as dagger handles, or ground down to make traditional Chinese medicine. The most common use is to bring down fevers – although there is little scientific proof this works.

442 Some animals are endangered because they are hunted for trophies, souvenirs, and body parts. Poaching is the illegal killing of animals for their body parts, such as elephants for their ivory tusks.

MATCH UP

Can you match the animals with the products they are killed or captured for?

A. Tiger
B. Elephant
C. Giant clam
D. Rhino

1. Dagger handle
2. Tourist souvenir
3. Bones
4. Ivory

Answers:
A3 B4 C2 D1

444 Rhinos are not the only victims of traditional medicines. In parts of Asia and South America, tiger bones are ground into powders for making pills, blood from sea turtles is drunk fresh, and horns of rare antelopes and gazelles are mashed into soup.

▼ This bonfire of seized elephant ivory was built in Kenya in 1989. Huge piles of tusks were burnt to try and stop the trade in ivory, but it did not succeed.

445 On holiday, some people buy souvenirs — some of which are made from endangered animals. The souvenir trade threatens shellfish such as conches and giant clams, starfish, sea urchins, and unusual fish such as seahorses. People can buy items carved from the ivory of elephants and walruses, deer antlers and antelope horns. People should avoid all animal souvenirs (and rare plants too).

446 The trade in animal body parts and products is controlled by national and international rules. Most countries have signed the agreement called CITES, the Convention on International Trade in Endangered Species. However, in thick jungles and remote places, it's difficult to stop poaching, while smugglers always invent new tricks to get illegal items from place to place.

▶ Buying tourist souvenirs such as dried seahorses simply supports the catching and killing of them.

199

Kill or be killed

447 Some animals are endangered because of the threat they pose to people – at least, that is the belief. Big, powerful predators are seen as dangerous to people, pets and farm animals. The risk of possible attack leads to persecution and revenge killing of the animal species. Hunters become the hunted.

448 In Central and South America, the jaguar, a spotted big cat, is often killed because of the risk that it might attack farm animals. Large areas of forest are cleared for cattle grazing, and some ranchers hire professional jaguar hunters who shoot the big cats on sight. Jaguars used to be killed for another reason – their beautiful fur coats. However, trade in jaguar fur and other body parts is now illegal.

◄ In parts of South America, hunters kill small crocodiles called caimans to sell their skins and flesh, even though it's against the law.

449 Crocodiles and alligators are shot because of the threats they pose to people and their animals. The endangered Cuban crocodile lives in only a small region of rivers and swamps on the Caribbean island of Cuba. It is a small crocodile, about 2 to 2.5 metres long. However, it has long been hunted because of the danger of attack, as well as for its meat and skin.

▲ Great white sharks can be lured to their death by baits.

450 The great white shark is one of the most feared of all animals. People hunt and kill it just in case it attacks swimmers. This shark is now rare enough to be on the Red List of threatened species as VU, vulnerable.

I DON'T BELIEVE IT!

About 100 years ago there were probably more than 100,000 tigers. Now there are probably fewer than 5000 in the wild.

451 Tigers face many threats, especially habitat loss, poaching and being killed in case they become 'man-eaters'. As villages and farms spread, tigers have less natural prey, and they are also more likely to wander near people and farm livestock. Another major threat is being poached for their body parts, such as their bones, teeth and bile (liver fluid) to put in traditional medicines. This fate probably affects one tiger every day.

▶ Like any hungry predator, a tiger will take advantage of a weak farm animal such as a sheep.

Eaten to extinction?

452 **The bushmeat trade – hunting wild animals for food – is a growing threat to many species.** People have always ventured into the forest to kill wild animals to eat. However, modern rifles, traps and other weapons mean that more animals can be caught, and sold at market. This growing trade in commercial bushmeat has become a huge problem.

▲ Bushmeat is sold at many local markets such as this one in West Africa. Once the animals have been skinned and cut up, it's difficult to identify if they are protected.

453 **In Africa, the drill and mandrill are the world's largest monkeys, and both are in huge danger from the bushmeat trade.** Killing one of these animals and selling most of its meat provides enough money to buy a week's food for a family.

▼ For thousands of years, local people have caught and eaten animals, such as this monkey, from the forests around them.

I DON'T BELIEVE IT!

The blackbuck antelope is protected in India. It was introduced to the US, and it breeds so well on ranches that numbers have to be reduced. So it's eaten in restaurants, and spare blackbucks are sent back to India to keep up the numbers.

▶ Near Lake Turkana in East Africa, villagers have caught and killed a hippo — bushmeat hunting can be very dangerous for people, too.

454 In West Africa, the pygmy hippo is endangered due to hunting for its meat. This small hippo lives in thick forests and travels along regular tracks to and from its feeding areas. If hunters find a track, they lie in wait for their prey. Fewer than 3000 pygmy hippos are left in the wild.

▶ In West Africa, logging vehicles leaving the forest are checked for animals captured for the bushmeat trade.

455 Mainly in India, and through most of Southeast Asia, bushmeat hunting is affecting more animals. The thamin, or Eld's deer, is listed as VU, vulnerable. In some places they have so little forest left that they eat farm crops. Local people kill them to stop the crop damage — and to have a meal.

456 In South America, the Brazilian tapir's flesh is considered a delicacy, so it is a prize target for bushmeat hunters. It is VU, vulnerable, but its cousin, the mountain tapir, is even more at risk. There are less than 2500 in the wild and better protection is needed.

457 Some animals are endangered because they are caught from the wild to become pets or captives. There is a thriving illegal trade in supplying rare animals as pets, and to personal collectors and private zoos. It is not only illegal but also cruel and wasteful. Many of the animals suffer and die on the long journeys to their new homes.

▼ Criminals dig up and steal the eggs of the Komodo dragon, which fetch large sums of money in the illegal collecting trade.

▲ Exotic pets, such as this macaw, often travel in terrible conditions, cramped and dirty, with little or no food and water. They end up in cages where they often die.

458 The world's biggest lizard, the endangered Komodo dragon, has its eggs stolen from the wild by thieves. These are sold to egg collectors, reptile breeders and lizard fanciers. This is illegal, but some people cannot resist the thrill of having such a rare egg, even if they must keep it secret.

459 Colourful, clever birds such as parrots and macaws are sometimes caught for the caged bird trade, rather than being bred in captivity. Rare species such as the hyacinth macaw, the biggest of all the parrots, and the green-winged macaw, are taken from the wild. It is against the law, but bird collectors pay huge amounts for them.

QUIZ

1. What is the world's biggest lizard?
2. Why is this lizard endangered?
3. What is the world's biggest parrot?
4. What is the world's biggest frog?

Answers:
1. Komodo dragon 2. Because people steal its eggs to sell 3. Hyacinth macaw 4. Goliath frog

◀ This tilapia cichlid fish has a been caught from the wild and placed in an aquarium. It has a burn mark on its back from resting too near to the aquarium lights.

461 Various tropical fish are caught from rivers and lakes for the aquarium trade. Some of the rarest are the tilapia cichlid fishes of the African Rift Valley lakes. Responsible aquarium suppliers and respected pet stores know about threatened species and do not accept those caught in the wild.

460 The world's biggest frog, the Goliath frog of Africa, is taken from the wild and sold to amphibian fanciers and private collectors. Its head and body are 30 centimetres long, and it can leap 6 metres in one jump. Being so large, this frog is also a good catch for the bushmeat trade.

▶ In West Africa, Goliath frogs – classed as endangered, EN – are caught in nets or traps. Their numbers are thought to have halved in the past 20 years.

Island problems

462 Many threatened animals live on islands. Here, the creatures and plants have lived together for many years. They have changed, or evolved, to become specialized to their unique habitat. The small size of many islands means less animals, and the unique habitat is easily upset when people arrive.

Mangrove finch

▲ Each type of Galapagos Island finch, including this mangrove finch, has evolved a beak shape suited to eating certain kinds of food.

463 The mangrove finch, which lives on the Galapagos Islands in the Pacific Ocean, is critically endangered. It is one of Darwin's finches – the birds that helped English naturalist Charles Darwin (1809–1882) work out his theory of evolution, which is so important to science.

464 Also on the Galapagos, giant tortoises are under threat, partly due to a common island problem – introduced species. People have taken many animals to islands, such as cats, rats, rabbits and dogs. These new arrivals destroy the natural habitat, prey on some local species, and compete for food and shelter.

▶ 'Lonesome George' is the last of his kind – a Pinta Island giant Galapagos tortoise. When he dies, the species will no longer exist.

465 **The island of Madagascar has amazing and unique wildlife, but much of it is in danger.** Lemurs, such as the ring-tailed lemur, are found nowhere else in the wild. However, many Madagascan species are threatened by a mixture of habitat loss, hunting for food, capture for the illegal pet trade, and the problem of introduced species.

◀ Ring-tailed lemurs are popular in wildlife parks and zoos, but are becoming rarer on their island home of Madagascar.

467 There have been more than 700 known animal extinctions in the last 400 years – and about half of these were on islands. In the Hawaiian islands alone about 25 kinds of birds, 70 types of snails, 80 kinds of insects and more than 100 plants have disappeared in the past 200 years.

466 **On islands, not just exciting species such as giant tortoises and colourful birds are threatened.** There are less glamorous species, such as the partula snails of the South Pacific islands. They were eaten by a predatory snail called Euglandina, which was introduced to provide food for local people.

▶ Some species of partula snails now survive only in zoos or science laboratories.

Stop the slaughter

468 For more than 50 years there has been a growing awareness of endangered animals and how we can save them. 'Headline' species such as pandas, whales, tigers and gorillas grab the interest of people and help to raise money for conservation. This conservation work can then protect natural habitats and so save many other species as well.

▲ The Born Free Foundation is an international wildlife charity working around the world to protect threatened species in the wild.

469 In the 1960s, the giant panda of China became famous as the symbol of the World Wildlife Fund, WWF (now World Wide Fund for Nature). Huge conservation efforts mean the giant panda is now off the critical list, with some 2000 in the wild, although it is still listed as EN, endangered.

◀ Pandas eat almost nothing but particular kinds of bamboo, so they rely heavily on their specialized habitat.

I DON'T BELIEVE IT!

The giant panda was chosen as a symbol of conservation partly because of its black-and-white colours. These make its image easier to photocopy without the need for any colours.

470 In the 1970s, people started to protest against the commercial hunting of great whales, which was threatening many whale species. 'Save the Whale' campaigns and marches became popular. Eventually in 1980 there was a world ban on the mass hunting of large whales.

471 In the 1990s, the terrible crisis facing the tiger became clear. Save the Tiger Fund was founded in 1995 to fight the many dangers facing the biggest of big cats. However, it is too late for some varieties, or subspecies, of tiger. The Balinese tiger from the island of Bali became extinct in the 1930s, and the Javan tiger followed in the 1980s.

▶ Great whales, such as these blue whales, are now fairly safe from mass slaughter. However, they breed very slowly and their numbers will take many years to start rising again.

472 In the 1980s, there were many anti-fur campaigns, to stop the killing of wild cats and other animals for their fur coats. This helped to reduce one of the threats to many beautiful cat species, not only big cats, but also medium and small species such as the ocelot and margay. Sadly, fur is becoming a popular fashion item once more.

A place to live

473 The main way to save threatened animals is to stop or reverse the process of habitat loss, and give them a place to live. In a handful of cases, breeding endangered species in zoos and small parks can help, but in the end, animals need their natural habitats – not only for themselves, but for many other kinds of animals and plants living in their habitat.

▲ Bison were just saved from extinction and now roam freely in Yellowstone, Wood Buffalo and other North American parks.

▼ The Great Barrier Reef Marine Park has gradually been extended over the years, with limited tourism in some areas and complete protection in others.

474 Natural places are preserved by setting aside large areas as national parks, nature reserves and wildlife sanctuaries. In 1872, Yellowstone National Park in the USA became the world's first national park. As in other protected areas, there are laws preventing people from damaging the animals, plants or habitat. Yellowstone's animals include the American bison or 'buffalo', which used to roam the prairies in millions. It almost became extinct in the 1880s but was just saved.

475 Some of the most important and precious wild areas are given the title of World Heritage Site. In Ethiopia, East Africa, the Simien National Park is home to extremely rare animals such as the gelada baboon, the Ethiopian wolf (Simien fox or jackal), and a type of wild goat called the Walia ibex, of which there are only 500 left.

▲ The 500 surviving Ethiopian wolves are found in only a few areas, such as the Bale Mountains and Simien National Park in Ethiopia.

476 One of the world's biggest protected ocean areas is Australia's Great Barrier Reef Marine Park, home to amazing animals from tiny coral creatures to huge sharks. In 2006 the US set up the even bigger NorthWest Hawaiian Island National Monument. This reserve is home to more than 7000 animal species including the threatened Hawaiian monk seal, green turtle and Laysan albatross.

QUIZ

Where would you find these rare animals?

1. Ethiopian wolf
2. American bison
3. Hawaiian monk seal
4. Green turtle

Answers:
1. Simien National Park, Ethiopia 2. Yellowstone National Park, USA 3. NorthWest Hawaiian Island National Monument 4. Great Barrier Reef, Australia

Captive breeding

477 Zoos, wildlife parks and breeding centres may play an important role in saving animals. Some animals are kept and encouraged to breed and build up their numbers, hopefully for release back into the wild. This method needs expert knowledge about the species, so the zoo keepers can look after the animals well. However, it can only be used in selected cases.

478 Not only big exciting animals are bred in captivity – one of the smallest is the Chatham Island black robin. By the early 1980s, only five remained, with just one female, 'Old Blue'. Careful captive breeding involved taking away her first batch of eggs, so she would lay a second clutch, while keepers cared for the first batch so they hatched. There are now more than 250 black robins.

▼ When rare animals such as the giant panda are reared in captivity, scientists can learn much about them.

◄ Pere David's deer have been released back into their home area of China.

479 For many years, Pere David's deer lived only in reserves owned by the emperors of China. Gradually the deer disappeared – many were eaten. However, a few were taken to Woburn animal park in the UK, where they bred. In the 1980s, some Pere David's deer were released back into the wild in China, where they are still CR, critically endangered.

480 The critically endangered Grand Cayman Blue Iguana was down to fewer than 15 lizards. Since 1996, captive-bred lizards have been released into protected areas on the island of Grand Cayman, and more reserves and releases are planned.

▼ Blue Iguanas are tagged so they can be closely monitored in their protected areas.

▼ Tigers breed well in some zoos, but release into the wild is virtually impossible. Captive tigers lose their instinct to kill, so may starve to death.

481 There are many problems when releasing captive-bred animals back into the wild, especially for apes such as orang-utans. Young apes learn from their parents about how to find food and avoid danger. If they are brought up in captivity they may need to be taught by people how to become wild again.

Conservation ups and downs

482 Many endangered animals face a variety of threats, so helping them needs a variety of actions, all organized into a conservation programme. For example, it is little use providing a wildlife park for a rare bird if the park is overrun with rats that will eat the bird's eggs.

▶ The Arabian oryx seemed to be recovering its numbers, but these are falling again.

483 By 1972 the last wild Arabian oryx, a gazelle from the Middle East, had been killed. However, some oryx had been captured and bred, especially in Phoenix Zoo, USA. A reserve was set up in Oman in the Middle East and 10 captive-bred oryx were released there in 1981. Their numbers rose. However in 2007, Oman reduced the reserve's size. Oryx numbers have since fallen from over 400 to less than 70.

MAKE A CONDOR PUPPET!

You will need:
old sock   paints and paintbrush

A Californian condor chick takes food from its parent. So conservation workers 'trick the chick' by making parent look-alike puppets. Paint an old sock with the colours shown to make a pretend condor head. Would you take food from it?

▶ Pygmy hogs are about 30 centimetres tall and weigh just 10 kilograms. They were once widespread along the southern foothills of the Himalaya Mountains, in marshes and swamps with tall grasses.

484 The Californian condor is a huge bird of prey from southwest North America. Its numbers fell over many years due to habitat loss, poaching, poisoning from eating animals killed by lead shot from guns or pesticide chemicals, and even crashing into power lines. In 1987, all 22 known condors were captured for breeding at Los Angeles Zoo and San Diego Wild Animal Park. Gradually numbers increased. By the mid 2000s there were more than 250 birds, including more than 100 back in the wild.

485 The pygmy hog of the Indian region is CR, critically endangered. There are probably less than 200 left, mainly due to loss of their natural habitat for farming, and also being killed for food. One of their last areas is the Manas Tiger Reserve in the Assam region. In 1995, the Pygmy Hog Conservation Programme was founded to help this unusual type of pig to survive.

◀ Californian condors are big enough to carry radio tracking devices, so scientists can study how far they fly, and where they feed and nest.

Future help

486 Saving threatened animals is not just for wildlife organizations and governments – everyone can help. You could volunteer for a conservation group, or set up a wildlife club in your school or neighbourhood. You might raise awareness by telling family and friends about threatened species, or have a 'rare animals' birthday party.

487 Local zoos and wildlife parks often have lots of information about endangered animals and their conservation. You can visit, write or email them, to ask if they are involved in conservation. Find out how zoos share information about their rare animals, so suitable individuals can be brought together for breeding. Wildlife conservation organizations often offer animal adoptions so you can sponsor a rare animal, maybe as a birthday present or a gift.

488 Saving threatened animals cannot be done without saving their habitats – and taking into account people. The people who live in the same area as a rare species may be very poor and very hungry. They see lots of time and money being spent on the endangered animal, but nothing for themselves.

216

489 Countries and governments must take into account their people, animals, plants and habitats, for a long-term and sustainable result. For example, wildlife can help to raise money by encouraging environmentally responsible tourism. This is when people pay to see rare creatures, such as gorillas, whales and tigers, under careful, monitored conditions. Then the money is used for local conservation that helps people as well as wildlife. Only in this way can people and endangered animals live together for the future.

▶ A close-up view of a tiger can encourage tourists to support campaigns to save these beautiful animals, and thereby protect large areas of their habitat for other creatures and plants.

490 Imagine standing in a forest as the sun goes down. Listen carefully and you will hear animals stirring and moving in the moonlight. Animals that are most active at night are called 'nocturnal'. From bugs to bears and bats to cats, there are thousands of animals that wait for the day to draw to an end and darkness to fall.

▶ The beautiful ocelot comes out at night to look for food. This cat lives in Central and South America and it hunts for birds, rodents, lizards and bats.

Super senses

491 Nocturnal animals are mainly active at night. This means they need super senses to find their way around in the dark. The darkness offers some protection from predators – animals that may want to eat them – but without great senses they would find it hard to search out food and mates.

▼ This maned wolf is sniffing the air trying to pick up the scent of its prey. Dogs' noses, or muzzles, are filled with smell-detecting cells. The black, leathery end to a dog's nose has two large nostrils, which pass the scents, or odours, over the smell-detecting cells.

492 The five main senses are sight, hearing, smell, touch and taste. Nocturnal animals usually have several or all of their senses heightened. These super senses are what help them to survive.

493 Members of the dog family have an incredible sense of smell. Some of them can detect odours, or smells, up to 50 times better than a human can. Wild dogs, such as wolves, coyotes, foxes and jackals, hunt at night. They use their large sensitive noses, or muzzles, to help them find their prey.

494 Raccoons not only have good eyesight for seeing in the dark, they have sensitive fingertips, too. These mischievous animals paddle in water, feeling under rocks for hiding crayfish, a type of shellfish. They use their long, agile fingers to grab the crunchy creatures before cracking them open to eat.

▲ This smart raccoon knows that it may find some eggs or chicks inside a bird's nesting box.

▲ A Malayan tapir is hard to see in the dark. It feeds on twigs and leaves in the forest.

495 Nocturnal animals may have super senses, but some of them have an extra trick to help them stay hidden from view – camouflage. Dull colours and dappled patterns on their skin or fur help them blend in with their surroundings. Malayan tapirs have distinctive coat patterns with black fur at the front and white at the back. This breaks up their outline and fools tigers – their main predators.

THE TOUCHY-FEELY GAME

Play this game to find out just how useful a sense of touch is.

You will need:
Two pillow cases
Small objects with different textures (rough, smooth, cold, furry, etc)
A friend

1. Each person must secretly place five objects in their pillow case.
2. Swap pillow cases with your friend.
3. Use your fingers to feel each object and work out what it is. No peeking though!

Bright eyes

496 Finding your way in the dark is much easier if you can see well. Human night vision isn't very good and we find it hard to see anything in much detail without light to help us. Many nocturnal animals have astonishing vision and they can see a world of activity that's invisible to us.

497 Most snakes rely on their senses of smell, hearing or touch to detect prey, but nocturnal tree snakes rely on their vision, too. They have narrow faces that allow them to clearly see what's right in front of them. Once a tree snake has spotted its prey, it folds its neck into an S-shape, focuses its eyes and then lunges with lightning speed. Its vision is so sharp, a tree snake can judge the distance to its prey with amazing, deadly accuracy.

▲ A tawny owl can spot tiny prey, such as mice, with ease. Its mottled feathers and dull colours help it to remain hidden as it hunts.

▲ Vine snakes live in trees where they hunt prey such as lizards or passing birds. Their bodies are long and extremely slender and they have excellent eyesight.

498 Tarsiers are odd-looking nocturnal animals that live in the tropical rainforests of Southeast Asia. They have enormous eyes and each eyeball is bigger than the animal's brain! Tarsiers can't move their eyes but they can swivel their heads 180 degrees in each direction, which helps them to hunt insects at night.

◀ Tarsiers dart around the treetops in their forest home. As well as having amazing vision, they have good hearing, too.

499 Cats are well-known for their night-time hunting skills and owe much of their success to their eyesight. They have large eyes that are especially good at helping them to see at night. The pupil of each eye – the black part in the centre – can open up wide to let in more light in dim conditions. The back of the eyeball is coated in a mirror-like layer, which reflects light, making vision even clearer.

I DON'T BELIEVE IT!

Mammals are furry animals and have been around for more than 200 million years. Most were nocturnal until the dinosaurs died out 65 million years ago. With their major predators gone, mammals were finally able to come out in daylight!

500 In an animal's eyes there are two types of cell that help them to see – rods and cones. Rods help eyes to detect light and cones help eyes detect colour. Nocturnal animals are usually colour blind. This is because they have a large number of rods in their eyes, which means there isn't much room left for the colour-detecting cones.

Noises in the dark

501 **Animals need to communicate with each other, and many do this by making noises.** Communicating by sound is especially important to nocturnal creatures as noises carry well at night – a time when vision is not always so useful.

502 **In the wild, night is not a quiet, peaceful time.** The air can be filled with the screeching of owls, booming roars of lions and endless chatter of cicadas and grasshoppers. Animals that live in groups are described as being 'sociable', and nocturnal creatures use a variety of sounds to communicate. Some sounds are made using voices, while others are made by foot stomping and drumming.

◀ Grasshoppers have 'ears' on their legs or bodies rather than their heads. Males rub their wings or legs together to make noises

▼ A lioness roars loudly to scare predators away from her cubs. Lions prefer to hunt in the cool of night.

503 At night, white-tailed deer are on their guard for predators that may be lurking nearby. If they sense danger, the deer use sound to alert their herd. They make snorting noises through their noses and beat the ground with their hooves. Foot-stomping may help to scare predators away, too.

504 Crocodiles and alligators are impressive night-time hunters. They rest in the day, soaking up the sun. At night they become quick-moving creatures whose roars carry far across the still water. Male alligators make loud booming calls to attract females in the dark, but it's also been discovered that they can make rumbling low sounds that we can't hear.

► Bat-eared foxes have huge ears. They mostly eat insects and use their amazing sense of hearing to listen for beetle larvae gnawing through dung balls.

505 Many nocturnal creatures have good hearing. Some have developed very large ears, or ears that can be moved to pinpoint noises better. Sound is 'caught' by the outer ear and then channelled through the ear canal to the hearing organ – the cochlea – inside the head. Sound information is then carried to the brain as electrical messages.

506 Many animals rely on their sense of smell far more than humans do and this is especially true of nocturnal animals. They use their sense of smell to find food, detect predators and find out about the other animals that are in their habitat – animals that may be hidden from view in the darkness.

507 Kiwis are rare, night-active birds from New Zealand and they have the best sense of smell of any bird. These fluffy birds have nostrils at the tips of their beaks and they use them to sniff out worms and other insects in leaf litter. Their eyesight is very poor, but they can hear well.

▼ Kiwis tap the ground with their sensitive beaks to disturb worms and insects. They capture their prey by pushing their beaks into the soil. They also eat snails, spiders and berries.

Brain Teaser

A hungry sloth bear digs up 100 termites in one nest. In the next nest, he gets double that number. In the third nest he greedily gobbles up only half of the original number.

How many termites did the sloth bear eat altogether?

Answer: 350

508 Snakes can 'taste' smells with their tongues and they rely greatly on scents in the darkness. Snakes are able to smell in two ways – with their nostrils, or with their long, forked tongues. A snake flicks its tongue in the air to pick up scent particles, which are transferred to the roof of its mouth. Messages are sent to its brain that tell the snake about any nearby animals. This is especially useful when hunting at night.

Nostril

Jacobson's organ

◀ ▼ A rat snake flicks its tongue in and out to pick up odours and transfer them to the Jacobson's organ, where they are sensed.

▼ Skunks have poor eyesight and can't see much further than a few metres in front of them. They use their excellent sense of smell to find food in the darkness.

509 Skunks are mostly active at twilight. These black-and-white striped animals spend the day in burrows and come out at sunset to look for food. They have a strong sense of smell and use it to sniff out bugs and small creatures such as mice and frogs. If threatened, a skunk sprays a foul-smelling liquid at its attacker – some say it's like a mixture of of rotten eggs, burnt rubber and garlic!

▼ A sloth bear's sucking noises can be heard up to 100 metres away!

510 By night, shaggy-haired sloth bears shuffle noisily through the forests in India. They hunt for termites and other bugs to eat and they find them using their noses. Once they pick up the scent of an ant or termite nest they rip it open using their long claws and suck up the tasty insects like a vacuum cleaner!

Feeling the way

511 Nocturnal animals often need a good sense of touch because it gives them extra information about their dark surroundings. Whiskers, hairy snouts, delicate fingertips and soft skin – there are many ways that animals can feel what's around them in the dark.

Whisker-like feathers

512 Frogs and toads have very sensitive skins and the natterjack toad is no exception. This nocturnal toad spends the day hiding under rocks and stones. At night it emerges to hunt for insects, spiders and worms. If it's disturbed by a predator, a natterjack toad can lighten or darken the colour of its skin to blend in with its surroundings. This helps it to hide from hungry hunters.

▶ Natterjack toads hunt for food at night. They can lighten or darken their skin colour to hide from enemies.

◀ Kakapos grow to a length of around 64 centimetres and they have small, useless wings. When they walk they hold their bristly faces close to the ground to feel their surroundings. Kakapos only breed every two to four years.

◀ A harvest mouse uses its sensitive whiskers to help find its way in the darkness.

513 Kakapos are the only nocturnal, flightless parrots in the world. Like all birds, they are very sensitive to touch, but kakapos have special whisker-like feathers near their beaks that they use to feel around. These, combined with their well-developed sense of smell, help the birds to find food, such as roots, fruit, nectar and fungi, in the twilight. Kakapos also give off a sweet-smelling body odour that may let other birds know they are there.

514 When a harvest mouse creeps quietly through the shadows, it uses its whiskers to feel the way. Whiskers are long, sensitive hairs. If a mouse pokes its head into a narrow space, it can tell by the pressure on its whiskers whether it can squeeze its whole body through.

515 The brushtail possum has a big, bushy tail that is very sensitive. At night when it becomes active, the possum holds its tail in the air and waves it around to feel its surroundings.

Brushtail possums live in Australia and many live in and around cities and towns. During the day they rest in tree hollows or even in house lofts!

I DON'T BELIEVE IT!

There are less than 90 kakapos alive in the entire world and every one of them has been given its own name. They live on four small islands near New Zealand where a team of scientists work hard to save them from extinction.

Fred

▶ The underside of the brushtail possum's tail is hairless, which helps it grip as it climbs trees.

Bugs at night

516 Insects and other bugs are amongst the noisiest nocturnal animals, especially in hot countries. An evening walk in a rainforest is accompanied by a chorus of clicks, buzzing, humming and chattering. These are some of the sounds made by millions of insects, which are invertebrates – animals without backbones.

▲ Common earwigs are insects that measure 8 to 18 millimetres in length. They are native to Europe, but are found in many countries.

517 Just like bigger creatures, insects and bugs use sound to communicate with each other at night. Cockroaches are leathery-skinned insects that are common throughout the world. Most spend their time scuttling silently through the leaf litter and twigs on the forest floor. However, the Madagascan hissing cockraoch can hiss if it's disturbed by pushing air out through its abdomen.

518 They may look menacing, but earwigs are completely harmless. By day they hide under leaves or in cracks and crevices. At night they come out to eat rotting plant and animal matter. They have pincers on the ends of their tails, which they use to scare predators away.

◄ Cockroaches can feel movement through their feet, which warns them to dash under cover to avoid predators.

▲ Feathery moth antennae can detect tiny scent particles.

519 Moths have special organs on the front of their heads called **antennae.** These long, slender or feathery structures detect smells and moths use them to find food and mates. These sensitive organs also help moths find their way in the dark. Moths with damaged antennae can't fly in straight lines – they crash into walls or fly backwards!

▲ Female moon moths produce a chemical that tells males they are ready to mate. Males use their antennae to pick up the scent of the female moths from several hundred metres away.

520 Moths are some of the most elegant and beautiful nocturnal insects. They have decorative patterns that help to camouflage, or hide, them. Members of the tiger moth family are often brightly coloured to tell predators that they are poisonous. Tiger moths also make high-pitched clicks to deter bats, which hunt by sound not sight. Once a bat has tried to eat one nasty-tasting tiger moth, it knows to avoid all clicking moths!

◀ There are many different types of tiger moth but most of them have fat bodies and brightly coloured wings. These warn predators that they are poisonous.

BED-SHEET BUGS!

Find out what nocturnal insects share your habitat.

You will need:
large white sheet   torch
notebook and pencil or camera

On a warm evening, hang a sheet up outside and shine a torch onto it. Wait patiently nearby and soon insects will be attracted to the sheet. Take photos or make sketches of all the bugs you see so you can identify them later. Be careful not to touch them though!

Light at night

521 One way for some nocturnal animals to deal with the dark is to turn on the lights! Some of the most striking nocturnal creatures are fireflies and they light up by a process called bioluminescence (bio-loom-in-ess-ens). All sorts of animals can glow in the dark including insects, spiders, fish and worms.

▶ The flashing lights of fireflies are hard to miss, even in a dark, wet woodland. These beetles are also known as lightning bugs.

522 If you're a small, dull nocturnal insect it can be hard to attract a mate. Fireflies, which are actually a type of beetle, overcome this problem by flashing lights at one another. Tropical fireflies gather together and flash lights at the same time, making a spectacular light show. The lights turn on in patterns that vary according to the type of firefly. It's thought that firefly larvae may also use their lights to warn predators not to eat them.

525 Flashlight fish live where sunlight scarcely reaches — in deep water or caves. They have areas under their eyes called 'photophores'. These contain bacteria that produce light. The light helps the fish to see where they are going. It also attracts mates and lures prey in to eat. If a bigger animal comes too close, the fish flicks its light on and off before swimming away.

▲ Flashlight fish use their light to attract shrimps and small fish to eat.

523 Bioluminescence is a chemical process that happens inside an animal's body. Fireflies have special organs on their abdomens that contain these essential chemicals. When they mix with oxygen, a reaction occurs, making a sudden bright flash of light.

I DON'T BELIEVE IT!

Some crafty fireflies flash their lights to grab a bite to eat. They aren't after mates, but they fool other fireflies into thinking that they are. When the curious insect comes to investigate the flashing, they find themselves being attacked — and maybe eaten!

524 Bobtail squids have developed a bright way to forage for food at night and remain invisible to nearby predators. These animals can flash light around themselves, helping to hide their shadows as they swim. This clever trick is achieved with the help of some bioluminescent bacteria and some shiny plates that work like mirrors to reflect the light in lots of directions.

▲ Bobtail squids are small, soft-bodied animals that live in coastal waters, especially around Hawaii.

Coasts and seas

526 In water as on land, some animals choose to stay hidden from view in the daylight hours, but emerge at night. Many sea creatures live in waters so deep that light never reaches them and they live in constant darkness. In shallower water it is bright by day, but as the sun sets, many kinds of fish start their feeding and breeding.

▲ On wet, stormy nights, European eels can survive out of water for several hours.

527 The European eel is an odd-looking fish that can even travel across land. At night these long, snake-like fish may leave the water and slither across damp ground. They do this as they journey back to their breeding grounds to reproduce.

▼ Horseshoe crabs can reach 60 centimetres in length. They live in North America and Southeast Asia.

528 Horseshoe crabs are most active at night, mainly to avoid predators. They are called 'living fossils' because they have barely changed in 300 million years. They live in coastal waters but come to land to mate. These unusual animals wait until sunset before marching up onto the beaches where the females dig holes to lay their eggs – often several thousand each!

Lantern fish live in the deepest, darkest parts of the ocean. They become active at night and swim upwards — covering a distance of around 400 metres — to feed near the surface. Their bodies are so delicate that they die within a few hours if captured.

530 Angel sharks are night-time hunters. Different kinds live all around the world and most grow to one to two metres in length. They were once common in the Atlantic Ocean and Mediterranean Sea, but now some are almost extinct. These flat sharks lie camouflaged on the seafloor during the day. At night, they swim upwards catching small, shelled animals and fish as they go.

▶ With their wide mouths and sharp teeth, moray eels make fearsome predators.

▲ Also known as monkfish, angel sharks are heavily fished for food and many types are endangered.

529 Moray eels are nocturnal predators. They lie in wait for their prey, then ambush it. These long, thick-bodied fish rely on their sense of smell to detect other animals, so they can feed at night just as easily as in the day. They normally hide in cracks and crevices on the sea floor, but will emerge from a hiding place under the cover of darkness.

531 As darkness falls in the ocean, the world's biggest octopus comes out to hunt. The giant Pacific octopus can measure an incredible 7.5 metres from one tentacle tip to another. These extraordinary animals have soft, fleshy bodies and eight tentacles that are covered in large suckers.

▼ Ocean-living molluscs such as this giant Pacific octopus don't have hard shells to protect their soft bodies, so they need some impressive tricks to help them survive.

532 During the day, octopuses sleep in dens on the seabed close to land. They forage for food at night, searching for fish and shelled animals to eat. They kill their prey by biting it or pulling it apart with their tentacles. Sometimes, octopuses pour poisons onto the animal to soften its flesh, ready for eating!

I DON'T BELIEVE IT!

Female giant Pacific octopuses can lay up to 100,000 eggs at a time. They have 280 suckers on each tentacle, making 2240 in total. These monsters can swim to depths of 750 metres and can weigh as much as 180 kilograms!

533 Southern stingrays feed primarily at night. They have flat bodies that are almost invisible when lying on the seafloor. This helps them to hide from their main predators, such as hammerhead sharks. Stingrays have poor eyesight, but good senses of smell and touch, which they use to find crabs, shrimps and small fish when hunting at night.

▲ During the day, stingrays lie hidden from predators. However, should a predator come too close, stingrays have a deadly defence. Tey have tails equipped with sharp spines, which can pierce flesh and inject poison.

534 Cuttlefish use colourful displays to communicate with one another in dimly lit waters. These molluscs are able to change the colour of their skin in seconds, producing a range of beautiful, shimmering and metallic shades. This also creates an effective camouflage – a handy way to avoid being eaten!

◄ Cuttlefish, like squid and octopuses, are molluscs. These are animals without backbones that have soft bodies, and some types are covered with a hard shell. Cuttlefish may look a bit like giant slugs, but they are believed to be very intelligent animals.

Restless reptiles

535 Most reptiles live in hot countries and many of them wait until the coolness of night to become active. Reptiles are animals with scaly skins that lay their eggs on land. There are four main groups of reptile – tortoises and turtles, lizards, snakes, and crocodiles and alligators.

◄ Tokay geckos are one of the largest geckos and they can be aggressive. They will attack other lizards and even bite humans who try to handle them. Tokay geckos can reach up to 35 centimetres in length and are usually brightly patterned.

536 Geckos are small nocturnal lizards that can climb walls and even walk upside down on ceilings. They have large eyes to help them see in the dark and thick toe pads that stick to surfaces. Tokay geckos from Southeast Asia are named after the loud 'to-kay' call males make, and they have unusually big yellow eyes.

537 Nocturnal snakes are superb hunters because their senses are so well adapted to detecting prey in the dark. Some snakes have an extra skill – they can feel the heat from another animal's body. Snakes, such as the western diamond rattlesnake, do this using special heat-detecting pits between their eyes and nostrils. Using this extra sense, the snake can find its prey in the dark and strike with deadly accuracy.

Heat-sensing pit

The snake moves its head from side to side to locate its prey

Body heat emitted from prey

▲ A western diamondback rattlesnake uses its heat-detecting pits to work out the distance and direction of its prey.

538 Some reptiles are huge and fearsome night-time hunters. Black caimans, which are members of the crocodile family, can reach 6 metres in length. They live in South America in freshwater rivers and lakes and at night they come to shallow water or land to hunt. Their dark skin colour means they can creep up on prey, such as deer or large rodents, unnoticed.

▼ Black caimans are nocturnal hunters. They wait for prey to come to the water's edge to drink then pounce with speed. Adult caimans are big enough to drag deer and tapirs into the water.

539 Common kraits are one of the deadliest snakes of Pakistan, India and Sri Lanka, and they are nocturnal. They prey on other snakes and rodents, sometimes straying into buildings to find them. Once they have found their prey, kraits lunge their fangs into it, injecting a lethal venom.

Whoo's there?

540 Owls are nocturnal birds of prey with superb vision and excellent hearing. Their eyes are large and face forwards, which helps them to judge distance. Their hearing is so good, they can locate their prey in total darkness just by listening!

541 The heart-shaped face of a barn owl works like a pair of ears! It helps to direct sound towards the sides of the owl's head, where the ears are situated at different heights. This helps them to pinpoint exactly where a sound is coming from. As they hover in the sky, barn owls can hear the tiny, high-pitched sounds made by small animals hidden in the vegetation below. Barn owls are able to fly almost silently towards their prey.

I DON'T BELIEVE IT!

Barn owls have white undersides, which may not appear to be the best camouflage for a nocturnal animal. This actually helps them to disappear against the sky when seen from below, allowing them to stalk and attack their prey more easily.

542 Barn owls are the most widespread land birds in the world and live on every continent, except Antarctica. They spend the day roosting (resting) in barns, buildings or trees and at night they come out to hunt. They catch rodents, such as rats, voles and mice.

▲ Barn owls have special adaptations that help them to hunt in the dark. Their soft feathers deaden the noise of flapping wings as they descend towards their unsuspecting prey.

543 Barn owls can see twice as well as humans by day and many times better at night. If an owl and a human were looking at the same image at night, the owl would see the image much more brightly. It would also be able to detect the smallest movement, which would be invisible to the human eye.

544 If they feel threatened or scared, owls slap their beaks together loudly making a clapping noise – this can sometimes be heard after dark. Barn owls shriek and hiss, but tawny owls are much more vocal. Their range of different calls can often be heard in the forests of Europe and Asia where they live. Male tawny owls make a loud 'hu-hooo' sound, which carries far in the still darkness. Females make a 'ke-wick' sound in reply. These noisy birds also make soft warbles and ear-piercing screeches!

Night fliers

545 Owls are the best-known nocturnal birds, but there are others that also use the cover of darkness to hunt. Many of them are so well adapted to life spent in the air that they can scarcely walk or hop. They sleep during the day, often roosting in trees, or hidden amongst plants on the ground.

▲ The gaping mouth of a nightjar acts like a net, catching insects as the bird flies.

▼ During the day, the common potoo mimics a branch to avoid the attention of predators.

546 Nightjars are stocky birds with big mouths that fly at night with their beaks wide open to catch insects. During the day, nightjars sleep on the ground or on low branches, without making nests. Their plumage – covering of feathers – is grey and brown, which camouflages them from predators, such as cats and foxes.

547 Potoos are odd-looking nocturnal birds from Central and South America. Their plumage is brown and they have yellow eyes. During the day they perch in trees, staying still with their eyes shut so that they may be mistaken for branches! At night, potoos dart through the sky gobbling up insects.

548 Few birds sing at night, but the nightingale's song can be heard floating through the darkness. The nightingale is known throughout the world for its beautiful song. Only male birds sing regularly after sunset and they use their songs of whistles, chirrups and trills to attract females.

◀ Frogmouths may attack and even kill other birds. They have very short legs and tiny feet.

▲ A nightingale's song is the only sign of this secretive bird's presence. Its dull colours keep it camouflaged.

549 Frogmouths are nocturnal birds from Asia and Australia that hunt on the ground. During the day they perch in trees, camouflaged by grey feathers mottled with dark stripes and blotches. A frogmouth's large, forward-facing eyes help it to spy prey at night, such as insects and small animals. Once prey is in sight, a frogmouth will pounce from its tree perch, capturing the animal in its beak.

HIDE ME, SEE ME!

Many animals are coloured or patterned in a way that helps them hide. This is called camouflage. But does it really work? Test it for yourself.

You will need:
thick, strong paper or card
paints or pens of different colours
scissors

Draw bold outlines of two birds. Colour one using bright, bold colours, but colour the other one in splodges of dull browns, greys and greens. Cut out your bird shapes and take them to a garden, park or woodland and hide them between plants. Which bird is easier to see?

Kangaroos and koalas

550 Kangaroos and koalas are marsupials, or pouched mammals, and most members of this group are nocturnal. There are about 196 types of marsupials living in and around Australia and about 85 types that live on the American continent. They are a strange group of animals that give birth to tiny youngsters that grow in a pouch on their mother's belly.

▼ Red kangaroos have a good sense of smell and they use it to find water in the Australian deserts.

551 Red kangaroos live in the great heat of the Australian outback where it's too hot for most animals to be active during the day. The red kangaroo is the world's largest marsupial. Its body reaches 1.6 metres in length and its tail is another 1.2 metres. It forages at night, nibbling at shoots, tender plants and leaves.

I DON'T BELIEVE IT!

Quolls are catlike marsupials of Australia. They spend the night hunting, but during the day they like to sleep. Quolls find it difficult to nap if there's too much noise, so these clever creatures can fold their ears down to block out sound!

552 Koalas are bear-like marsupials that spend all day sleeping and all night eating. They eat and sleep up in the trees, and eucalyptus leaves are their main food. With stocky bodies, short limbs and leathery noses, koalas are easy to recognize.

553 Virginia opossums forage at night and survive on all sorts of food, including grubs, fruit, eggs and scraps they scavenge from bins. They live in North and Central America and shelter in piles of vegetation or under buildings. Opossums have an unusual skill – if they are scared they drop down and act dead, with their eyes and mouths open. They do this for up to six hours at a time – long enough for a predator to get bored and wander off!

▲ A Tasmanian devil gorges on its meal alone, but other devils may soon come to join in, drawn by the smell of fresh meat.

▼ A female Virginia opossum has up to 18 young in her litter, but she only has teats to feed 13 of them. She protects her young until they are old enough to fend for themselves.

554 In Australia's southern island of Tasmania, a terrible screeching and barking may be heard in the night – a Tasmanian devil. These marsupials are known for their noisy, aggressive behaviour and if they are alarmed, devils screech and bark. They can smell dead animals from far away and have such powerful jaws they can grind and chew bones and gristle.

Quick and curious

555 Leaping between branches in moonlit forests requires excellent eyesight and fast reactions. These are qualities shared by many nocturnal primates. Lemurs, bushbabies, monkeys and apes are primates – intelligent mammals that have grasping hands and eyes that are set on the front of their faces.

▲ Owl, or night, monkeys are the only nocturnal monkeys of the Americas. They can see very well in the dark, thanks to their enormous eyes, but they are colour blind.

556 The only truly nocturnal monkeys are the night, or owl, monkeys, also called douroucoulis. Night monkeys have large owl-like eyes and small rounded heads. They feed on fruit, bugs, seeds and small animals. They howl, hoot and holler to communicate with one another in the darkness.

557 Mouse lemurs are the smallest of all primates and they are nocturnal. Some are only 18 centimetres long and weigh around 30 grams – about the same as four grapes! Mouse lemurs have very soft fur that is grey or orange-brown, with a black-and-white underneath. They live in trees and eat fruit, flowers, insects, spiders and occasionally frogs and lizards.

558 Bushbabies are small, furry animals that have huge eyes and can see well in the dark. They live in trees in the forests of East and central Africa. They run through the branches at night looking for insects, flowers, seeds and eggs to eat. During the day, bushbabies huddle together in hollow trees or sleep in old birds' nests.

559 As the sun sets on the island of Madagascar, the loud calls of ruffed lemurs can be heard across the treetops. These black-and-white, furry primates stay in touch with one another by making strange noises, which sound like someone laughing and screeching at the same time!

▶ Ruffed lemurs are most active at dawn and dusk, rather than through the night.

560 A slender loris uses all of its senses to guide it through the treetops at night. They are small primates that have huge eyes, nimble fingers and pointed noses. They live in India and Sri Lanka and they use stealth to hunt insects. A slender loris creeps up slowly and quietly behind its prey, sniffs its victim and then lunges, grabbing it in its hands.

◀ A slender loris measures no more than 26 centimetres in length and weighs around 300 grams. Its arms and legs are pencil-thin.

Supersonic sounds

561 A flutter of wings and the glimpse of a swooping body in the night sky are often the only clues you'll get that a bat is nearby. Bats are the nocturnal masters of the sky. They are small, furry mammals that are so well adapted to life on the wing that they can pass by almost unnoticed by humans and animals alike.

▲ During the day, bats hang upside down and rest — this is called roosting.

562 Except for the polar regions, bats can be found all over the world. They roost in caves, trees, under logs and in buildings. There are nearly 1000 different types, or species, of bat – the smallest have wingspans of 15 centimetres, and the biggest have wingspans of 1.5 metres or more!

563 Bats are the only mammals that have wings. Their wings have developed from forelimbs and have a thin membrane of skin that stretches over long, bony digits, or fingers. Bats can change direction easily in flight, which helps them chase and catch insects.

I DON'T BELIEVE IT!

Bats can live for a surprisingly long time — often for 10 to 25 years. Some wild bats have been known to live to the ripe old age of 30! This is partly because bats are able to avoid being eaten as few animals can catch them when they dash and dart between trees.

564 Although bats have good eyesight, they depend more on their senses of smell and hearing to find their prey at night. Most types of bat have a special sense called echolocation. They produce very high-pitched sounds – too high for most people to hear – that bounce off objects in front of them. When the sound comes back to a bat's ears, like an echo, they can tell by the way it has changed, how far away the object is and its size.

565 There are two main groups of bat – plant-eating bats and hunting bats. Both groups are mainly nocturnal. However, it is the hunters that use echolocation to find their prey. Most plant eaters don't echolocate and tend to be bigger than hunting bats. Some plant-eating bats, such as the Rodrigues fruit bat, are active in the day. The word 'diurnal' (die-ur-nal) is used to describe creatures that are active during the day.

◀ The word 'sonic' means making sounds, and the high-pitched noises of bats can be described as 'ultrasonic' – too high for us to hear.

566 Oilbirds are unique – they are the world's only fruit-eating nocturnal birds, and they echolocate like bats. Oilbirds live in South America and they spend their days in total darkness, sleeping in pitch-black caves. They wake after sunset and travel up to 75 kilometres in search of food.

Echoes bouncing back off the moth

Sound waves from the bat

◀ Bats make high-pitched sounds, called clicks, using their mouths or noses. The sound hits an insect and bounces back to the bat's ears. The reflected sound gives the bat information about the location and size of the insect.

Insect eaters

567 Since many insects, grubs and worms are active night, so are the mammals that hunt them. Aardvarks are unusual ant-eating animals of Africa that snuffle and snort in the darkness. Their name means 'earth-pig' in Afrikaans, one of many languages spoken in South Africa, and they do look quite like long-nosed pigs with their big, fleshy snouts.

◄ Hedgehogs sleep during the day. At night, they come out to search for insects and worms to eat.

569 If they are scared, hedgehogs roll themselves into a tight ball with only their sharp spines showing. They may be able to defend themselves against foxes, but hedgehogs are no match for a car – thousands of these European mammals are killed on roads every year.

▶ Aardvarks live alone and come out at sunset to forage for food. These long-snouted animals can eat up to 50,000 insects in one night!

568 At night, aardvarks search for termites and ants using their good sense of smell as their eyesight is poor. They rip open nests and lick up the insects with their long tongues. Aardvarks also have large front claws, which they use for digging their burrows where they sleep during the day. They can close their ears and nostrils to stop dirt from getting in them as they dig.

570 Few people ever see pangolins as they are shy and secretive nocturnal creatures. Pangolins are armoured animals that live in Africa and Asia. Their bodies are covered in thick, overlapping scales, which are formed from layers of hardened skin. Pangolins don't have teeth, but lick up ants and termites with their long, sticky tongues.

▲ Pangolins have short legs and bodies measuring up to one metre in length. They can climb trees or dig burrows underground using their long, sharp claws.

571 Shrews are active by night as well as day, since they must eat every few hours to survive. They are mouse-like, furry creatures with long snouts and are some of the smallest mammals in the world. They rely mostly on their sense of smell to find food, but some of them use echolocation – a way of locating objects using sound that is used by bats and oilbirds.

◄ A tiny shrew prepares to devour an earthworm, which looks like a giant in comparison.

Chisellers and chewers

572 Some of the world's commonest mammals are nocturnal rodents such as mice, rats, voles and lemmings. This group of animals can exist in almost any habitat all over the world, except the Antarctic. They have big eyes to see in the dark, furry bodies, and teeth that are perfect for gnawing and chewing. Most also have good hearing, and long whiskers to feel their way in the dark.

573 Rats are active in the day, but more so at night. They are experts in survival – able to live almost anywhere. One of the reasons for their success is that they can eat nearly anything. Rats hunt for food but they are just as likely to scavenge rubbish from bins at night or find morsels in the sewers. These unpopular animals have been known to start eating the flesh of living things and spread deadly diseases.

▼ At night, rats roam around towns scavenging any food and scraps they can find.

574 Giant flying squirrels emerge from their tree holes at night and search for nuts, berries and shoots. They can 'fly' between trees by stretching out thin membranes of skin between their limbs, allowing them to glide through the air.

575 American beavers are large rodents, often measuring more than one metre in length from nose to tail-tip. They spend the day resting in a lodge, which is a nest made from mud and sticks with underwater entrances. Beavers leave their nests as the sun begins to set and they remain busy through much of the night, feeding on plants. They find their way around using their long whiskers to guide them.

▼ Beavers chisel at trees and branches, cutting them up for use in the dams they build on rivers and streams. These dams create wetlands where many types of animal and plant thrive.

576 Edible dormice are small, nocturnal rodents that live in woods, or make their nests near or under buildings. During the late summer and autumn they fatten themselves up with seeds, fruit and nuts to prepare for hibernation – a long winter sleep. The ancient Romans kept edible dormice and overfed them until they were so fat they could hardly move. They were cooked until crisp and crunchy and served at dinners and parties!

Death by stealth

▶ The serval is a member of the cat family that lives in Africa. Its large eyes help it to see prey in the dim light of the setting sun.

577 Hunting at night provides a perfect opportunit for carnivores to pounce on their prey, unseen and undetected. The word 'carnivore' describes meat eating animals, and members of the cat family are amongst the most agile and elegant of them all.

▼ The glow from the eyes of these lions comes from the tapetum – a layer of light-reflecting cells that all cats have in their eyeballs.

578 Wildcats are the ancestors of domestic, or pet, cats. Like domestic cats, wildcats are active at night as well as during the day, but they do most of their hunting at night. They look like large, stocky tabby cats with black-tipped, bushy tails. They eat small rodents, rabbits and birds.

579 Many big cats choose the twilight hours – dawn and dusk – to look for food. Most live in places where the day's heat is too great for stalking and running. Cool nights are more comfortable for most animals, including prey animals such as antelope and deer that gather at waterholes or riversides. Big cats will sometimes lie in wait there – their tawny, stripy or spotty coats helping them to stay hidden in the shadows.

254

580 **Leopards can hunt in the day or at night, but are more likely to be successful when the light is low.** These strong, solitary animals are the most widespread of all big cats. Part of their success is due to their supreme hunting skills and the wide range of food they will eat. One clever leopard tactic is to ambush a group of baboons as they sleep at night – too startled to fight or run, the monkeys make sitting targets.

581 **Wolves are carnivores and, like many other members of the dog family, they are nocturnal.** Using their strong sense of smell wolves are able to detect animals, such as deer, moose, rabbits or beavers, and follow their scent trail for many kilometres. Wolves will always choose the weakest member of a herd to attack and they know to approach their prey from downwind so that it does not smell them!

QUIZ

1. What name is given to animals that are active in the day – diurnal or eternal?
2. What is a carnivore – a meat eater or a plant eater?
3. What name is given to an animal that preys upon, or hunts, others – prefect or predator?

Answers:
1. Diurnal 2. A meat eater 3. Predator

▼ Wolves live in the far north, where night-time can last 20 hours or more during the long, cold winters.

Hungry hippos

582 At dusk on the African grassland, diurnal (daytime) animals visit waterholes before resting for the night, and nocturnal animals become active. Hippopotamuses aren't everyone's idea of nocturnal creatures, but these huge mammals have very sensitive skin that easily burns in the hot sun. They spend the day wallowing in cool pools and come onto land at night to feed.

583 Hippos are plant eaters and spend the night chewing on plants at the waterside. They grunt and snuffle like pigs as they graze, eating up to 40 kilograms of plants and grass every night. Like lots of other nocturnal animals, hippos don't sleep all day, but have active times mixed with long naps.

▼ As the sun disappears behind the horizon, hippos amble onto the shore t graze on grass for most of the night.

584 Rhinos are another animal of the African plains that prefer to feed once the sun has set and it is cool. These enormous plant eaters have poor eyesight and depend on their excellent sense of smell to find food and sense predators. By day they rest in the shade or bathe in mud to keep cool.

▲ At night, rhinoceroses rely on their senses of smell and hearing to stay safe from predators. They mainly eat grass, but will also eat fruit, leaves and crops.

585 Spotted hyenas are night-time hunters of the African grasslands. They are most active after dusk, and spend the day in burrows that they have either dug themselves, or have taken over from aardvarks or warthogs. Hyenas call to one another at night with a whooping noise. These calls show obedience to a senior member of the group.

▶ Hyenas can ambush and kill large animals because they work together in groups. They have excellent senses of sight, hearing and smell.

A new day dawns

586 As night draws to an end, nocturnal creatures head back to their dens and burrows. Smaller animals steal away to hide beneath rocks, in caves or under plants. With their stomachs full it's time to rest and stay safe – and that means remaining hidden from view.

▶ Flying foxes, or fruit bats, are nocturnal plant-eating bats. During the day, they roost, hanging upside down by their feet from tree branches, in groups that sometimes number several thousand.

587 The break of dawn is a time of great activity and noise. Nocturnal animals are gradually replaced by diurnal ones. Birds announce the sunrise with their songs and bats can still be seen flitting around amongst the treetops, snatching insects out of the air. Lions laze around, having spent the night roaming the plains hunting, eating and napping. Cubs play in the cool air and perhaps wander to a waterhole to take a drink, before the whole pride settles down to a morning snooze.

WORD GAME

How many words can you make from the letters in the word NOCTURNAL? You should be able to find the names of three animals that you have read about in this book!

588 Domestic cats are expert hunters and are most active in the twilight hours. Their well-developed senses of sight, hearing, taste and touch make them successful night-time hunters. They often return to their homes with small rodents, birds or insects they have caught in the night. Domestic cats usually spend the day sleeping and lazing around.

589 In rainforests and woodlands, morning dew drips from leaves as owls cease their hooting and foxes fall silent. Rodents scurry out of the light, seeking safety under stones or in cracks in tree trunks, and owls return to their treeholes. Now, diurnal birds of prey, such as eagles and hawks, hover in the sky, on the lookout for small rodents far below.

▼ European badgers snuggle together in their dens, called setts, to keep warm. They spend most of the day asleep.

▼ These young tawny owls have a safe place to hide during daylight hours. In this treehole, they are out of the reach of predators and protected from bad weather.

DEADLY CREATURES

590 **The world is full of animals that are fighting to survive.** There are many reasons why animals may attack one another. Some are called predators and they kill for food. Others only kill to defend themselves, their young or their homes. Whatever the reason for using their claws, jaws, poisons or stings, these creatures are fascinating, but deadly.

▼ To catch its prey, the Nile crocodile lies very still in the water until the gazelle comes close. Then it shoots out of its hiding place, trying to catch the gazelle in its powerful jaws.

Killer carnivores

◀ False vampire bats have very sharp teeth, like the vampire bat. They catch and feed on frogs, mice, birds and other bats.

591 **Animals that eat meat are called carnivores.** Scavengers are carnivores that steal meat from others, or find dead animals to eat. Most carnivores, however, have to hunt and kill. These animals are called predators.

592 **Killer whales are some of the largest predators in the world.** Despite their size, these mighty beasts often hunt in groups called pods. By working together, killer whales can kill large animals, including other whales. However, they usually hunt smaller creatures, such as sea lions and dolphins.

▼ Anacondas are types of boa, and are the heaviest snakes in the world. As they don't have chewing teeth, snakes swallow their prey whole. Anacondas feed on large rodents called capybara, deer, fish and birds.

593 **Vampire bats do not eat meat, but they do feed on other animals.** With their razor-sharp teeth, vampire bats pierce the skin of a sleeping animal, such as a horse or pig, and drink their blood. False vampire bats are bigger, and they eat the flesh of other animals.

594 With their cold eyes and gaping mouths, piranhas are fierce-looking predators. When a shoal, or group, of piranhas attack, they work together like an enormous slicing machine. Within minutes, they can strip a horse to its skeleton using their tiny triangular teeth.

▲ Red piranhas are aggressive, speedy predators. They work together in a group to attack their prey, such as birds.

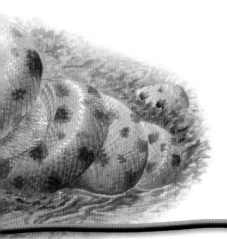

595 Some snakes rely on venom, or poison, to kill their prey, but constrictors squeeze their victims to death. Pythons and boas wrap their enormous bodies around the victim. Every time the captured animal breathes out, the snake squeezes a little tighter, until its prey can no longer breathe.

Lethal weapons

596 Many animals have deadly weapons, including teeth, claws, horns and stings. They are perfect for killing prey, or fighting enemies.

597 Inside the mouth of a meat-eating predator is an impressive collection of deadly daggers — teeth. Different teeth do different jobs. Canines, or fangs, are long and knife-like, and are used to grab prey or pierce skin. Teeth at the front of the mouth are very sharp, and are ideal for cutting and slicing flesh.

◀ Mandrills are part of the same family as monkeys, called primates. Males bare their enormous fangs when they are anxious, or want to scare other males. The fangs may reach up to 7 centimetres in length.

598 Stings are common weapons in the animal world and they are used by creatures such as jellyfish and scorpions. Stings usually contain poison or venom. The stingray, for example, is a fish with a long saw-shaped spine on its tail, which is coated in poison.

599 Elephant and walrus tusks are overgrown teeth that make fearsome weapons when used to stab and lunge at attackers. Males use their tusks to fight one another at mating time, or to scare away predators. An elephant can kill a person with a single thrust from its mighty tusks.

▼ Birds of prey grab hold of their victim with powerful talons, which pierce the flesh with ease.

▼ Cats have sharp claws that can be pulled back into the paws when they are not being used.

601 Some animals fight for mates, or territory (the area they live in). Horned animals, such as deer, are not predators, but they may fight and attack other animals. These animals have been known to harm humans when they are scared.

600 Eagles have huge claws called talons. The bird grasps prey in its feet, killing it by piercing and squeezing with its talons. Eagles and other carnivorous (meat-eating) birds are called birds of prey.

▲ Ibex are wild goats. They use their thick, curved horns to fight for mates or territory. Horns can be used to stab, wound and even kill.

Silent hunters

602 Agile and fast, with sharp teeth and claws, cats are some of the deadliest predators in the world. Most cats hunt alone, but lions works as a team to catch their prey.

603 A group of lions is called a pride, and the females are the hunters. Cubs spend hours play-fighting. This helps them to practise the skills they will need to catch and kill prey when they are older.

604 In Asia, many people are fearful of living near tigers. However, tigers hunt small creatures, such as birds, monkeys and reptiles. They have been known to attack bigger animals, such as rhinos and elephants, but it is rare for them to kill humans.

I DON'T BELIEVE IT!

The Iberian lynx is one of the most endangered wild cats in the world. There are about 250 adults left in the wild, and they are expected to become extinct (die out) in the near future.

605 Cheetahs are the fastest hunters on land, and can reach speeds of more than 100 kilometres an hour. Despite their great speed, cheetahs often fail to catch the animal they are chasing. Although these cats have great spurts of energy, they tire very quickly. If cheetahs have not caught their prey in about 30 seconds, it may escape – this time.

606 Leopards are secretive killers. They live throughout Africa and Asia, but are rarely seen. They are agile climbers and spend much of their time in trees, waiting for unsuspecting animals to wander by. Like most cats, leopards kill prey by sinking their huge teeth into the victim's neck.

▼ Lionesses hunt in a group, which means they can attack big, aggressive animals, such as buffaloes.

267

Big, bold and beastly

▶ Polar bears are meat eaters. They wait by a seal's breathing hole for the seal to appear above the water. With one swift bite, the bear kills its prey, drags it out of the water and begins to feast.

607 Big, white and fluffy, polar bears look cuddly, but they are deadly predators. Occasionally, polar bears travel from the icy Arctic to small towns in search of food. At these times, they are hungry and dangerous, and may attack.

▼ A polar bear's paw is as big as a dinner plate, and is equipped with five big claws, one on each toe.

608 Polar bears use their huge paws to swim with ease underwater. They can hold their breath for several minutes, waiting until the time is right to swim up and grab their prey. On land, these ferocious bears hunt by creeping up on their prey, then pouncing, leaving the victim with no escape.

610 Grizzlies are brown bears of North America. They often come into contact with humans when searching for food and raiding rubbish bins, and are considered to be extremely dangerous. Grizzlies often live in woods and forests. They mainly feed on berries, fruit, bulbs and roots, but also fish for salmon in fast-flowing rivers.

▲ Kodiak bears live in Alaska where they eat fish, grass, plants and berries. They only bare their teeth and roar to defend themselves against predators.

611 Black bears in Asia rarely attack humans, but when they do, the attack is often fatal. Asian black bears are herbivores. This means that they eat plants rather than meat. If they are scared, these shy animals may attack to kill.

609 Brown bears are one of the largest meat eaters in the world, and can stand more than 3 metres tall. They are powerful animals, with long front claws and strong jaws.

▶ Brown bears catch salmon as they leap out of the water. A snap of the jaws is enough to grab the wriggling fish.

Skills to kill

612 Monkeys and apes belong to the same group of animals as humans, called primates. These intelligent creatures have great skills of communication and teamwork. Although monkeys, gorillas and chimps appear to be playful, they can be dangerous.

613 It was once believed that chimps only ate plants and insects. However, it has been discovered that groups of chimps ambush and attack colobus monkeys. Each chimp takes its own role in the hunting team. During the chase, the chimps communicate with each other by screeching and hooting.

614 Chimps also kill each other. Groups of male chimps patrol the forest, looking for males from another area. If they find one, the group may gang up on the stranger and kill him.

▶ Chimps use their great intelligence to organize hunts. Some of them scream, hoot and chase the colobus monkey. Other chimps in the group hide, ready to attack.

615 Baboons live in family groups and eat a wide range of foods, from seeds to antelopes. Young males eventually leave their family, and fight with other males to join a new group and find mates.

616 A mighty gorilla may seem fierce, but it is actually one of the most gentle primates. Large adult males, called silverbacks, only charge to protect their families by scaring other animals, or humans, away. Gorillas can inflict terrible bite wounds with their fearsome fangs.

I DON'T BELIEVE IT!

Chimps are skilled at making and using tools. It is easy for them to hold sticks and rocks in their hands. They use sticks to break open insects' nests and they use rocks to smash nuts.

Canine killers

617 **Wolves, coyotes and African hunting dogs belong to the dog family.** Most live and hunt in groups, or packs. By working together, a pack can attack and kill large prey, such as deer and bison.

◀ When a wolf feels threatened, the fur on its back, called its hackles, stands on end. This makes it look bigger and fiercer.

618 **Wolves have excellent senses of sight, hearing and smell to help them to find their prey.** These strong, agile creatures have been known to travel a distance of 100 kilometres in just one night in search of food.

619 **Coyotes are wild dogs that live in North America.** They normally hunt in pairs or on their own, although they may join together as a group to chase large prey, such as deer.

620 Like wild cats, coyotes hunt by keeping still and watching an animal nearby. They wait for the right moment, then creep towards their prey and pounce, landing on top of the startled victim. Coyotes are swift runners and often chase jackrabbits across rocks and up hills.

BE A WOLF!

1. One person is Mr Wolf and stands with their back to the other players.
2. The players stand 10 paces away and shout, "What's the time, Mr Wolf?".
3. If Mr Wolf shouts, "It's 10 o'clock", the players take 10 steps towards Mr Wolf.
4. Watch out because when Mr Wolf shouts "Dinnertime", he chases the other players and whoever he catches is out of the game!

▼ When African hunting dogs pursue their prey, such as the wildebeest, the chase may go on for several kilometres, but the dogs rarely give up. They wait until their prey tires, then leap in for the kill.

621 African wild dogs are deadly pack hunters. They work as a team to chase and torment their prey. The whole pack shares the meal, tearing at the meat with their sharp teeth.

Ambush and attack

622 Lurking beneath the surface of the water, a deadly hunter waits, ready to pounce. Lying absolutely still, only its eyes and nostrils are visible. With one swift movement, the victim is dragged underwater. This killer is the crocodile, a relative of the dinosaurs.

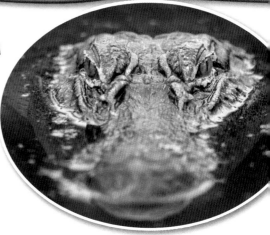

▲ Crocodiles and alligators are well-suited to their aquatic lifestyle. They spend much of their day in water, keeping cool and hidden from view.

Only teeth in the upper jaw are visible

Alligator

▲▼ When a crocodile's mouth is closed, some of the teeth on its lower jaw can be seen. Alligators have wide u-shaped jaws, but the jaws of crocodiles are narrow and v-shaped.

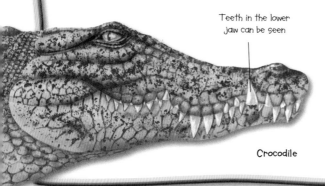

Teeth in the lower jaw can be seen

Crocodile

623 When a crocodile has its prey in sight, it moves at lightning speed. The prey has little chance to escape as the crocodile pulls it underwater. Gripping the victim in its mighty jaws, the crocodile twists and turns in a 'deathspin' until its victim has drowned.

624 The largest crocodiles in the world live in estuaries, where rivers meet the oceans. They are called estuarine crocodiles and can reach a staggering 7 metres in length. These giant predators are often known as man-eating crocodiles, although they are most likely to catch turtles, snakes, monkeys, cows and pigs.

625 Alligators are very strong reptiles with wide jaws and thick, scaly skin on their backs. They live in marshes, ponds and rivers, often close to where people live. Like all crocodiles and alligators, the American alligator will catch and eat anything. They have even been known to attack humans.

▼ Crocodiles and alligators have huge jaws, full of teeth. As well as being used for grabbing and holding prey, they use their teeth to slice pieces from the body of the victim.

I DON'T BELIEVE IT!

Crocodiles and alligators store their uneaten food underwater for several weeks. The remains rot, making it easier for the reptiles to swallow. Yum!

Ravenous raptors

626 Eagles, hawks, kites and ospreys are fearsome predators called birds of prey. Equipped with incredible eyesight, powerful legs, and sharp claws and bills, they hunt during the day, soaring high in the sky as they look for food.

▶ Eagle owls are large, powerful birds. They hunt and capture large animals, including other owls and birds of prey.

628 Birds do not have teeth. They have bills, or beaks, instead. Tearing large pieces of meat is a difficult job using just a bill. Birds of prey use their curved claws, called talons, to hold or rip their food apart, or they just swallow it whole.

627 Birds of prey are also known as raptors, which comes from the Latin word 'rapere', meaning 'to seize'. Once they have captured their prey, such as a mouse, bird or frog, a raptor usually takes it to its nest to start pulling off fur and feathers. Bones are also thrown away, and the ground near a raptor's nest may be strewn with animal remains.

▶ Like most birds of prey, golden eagles have razor-sharp, hooked bills. They use them to tear the body of their prey apart.

629 Little more than the flap of a wing can be heard as an owl swoops down to grab an unsuspecting mouse. Owls hunt at night. They can even see small movements on the ground, thanks to their large eyes and sharp eyesight. When they hunt in total darkness, they rely on their excellent sense of hearing to find food.

QUIZ

The names of raptors have been jumbled up. Can you work out what they are?

1. GELEA
2. ITKE
3. CFALNO
4. LOW
5. PRYESO
6. KAWH

Answers:
1. Eagle 2. Kite 3. Falcon
4. Owl 5. Osprey 6. Hawk

630 Peregrine falcons are the fastest hunters in the world, reaching speeds of up to 230 kilometres an hour as they swoop down to attack other birds. Peregrines hunt on the wing. This means that they catch their prey while in flight. They chase their prey to tire it out, before lashing out with their sharp talons.

▼ Bald eagles live on a diet of fish, which they swipe out of the water using their talons.

631 Ospreys dive, feet-first, into the water from a great height in pursuit of their prey. Fish may be slippery, but ospreys have spiky scales on the underside of the feet so they can grip more easily. Once ospreys have a fish firmly in their grasp, they fly away to find a safe place to eat.

Mighty monsters

632 Not all deadly creatures kill for food. Many of them only attack when they are frightened. Some plant-eating animals fight to protect their young, or when they feel scared.

633 Hippos may appear calm when they are wallowing at the edge of a waterhole, but they kill more people in Africa than any other large animal. These huge creatures fiercely protect their own stretch of water, and females are extremely aggressive when they have calves and feel threatened.

634 African buffaloes can be very aggressive towards other animals and humans. If they become scared, they move quickly and attack with their huge horns. Groups of buffaloes surround a calf or ill member of the herd to protect it. They face outwards to prevent predators getting too close.

635 If an elephant starts flapping its ears and trumpeting, it is giving a warning sign to stay away. However, when an elephant folds its ears back, curls its trunk under its mouth and begins to run – then it really means business. Elephants will attack to keep other animals or humans away from the infants in their herd, and males will fight one another for a mate.

636 With huge bodies and massive horns, rhinos look like fearsome predators. They are actually related to horses and eat a diet of leaves, grass and fruit. Rhinos can become aggressive, however, when they are scared. They have poor eyesight, which may be why they can easily feel confused or threatened, and attack without warning.

◄ Male hippos fight one another using their massive teeth as weapons. Severe injuries can occur, leading to the death of at least one of the hippos.

I DON'T BELIEVE IT!

Adult male elephants are called bulls, and they can become killers. A single stab from an elephant's tusk is enough to cause a fatal wound, and one elephant is strong enough to flip a car over onto its side!

Toxic tools

▶ Marine toads are the largest toads in the world. When they are threatened, venom oozes from the glands in the toad's skin. This poison could kill a small animal in minutes.

637 Some animals rely on teeth and claws to kill prey, but others have an even deadlier weapon called venom. Venom is the name given to any poison that is made by an animal's body. There are lots of different types of venom. Some cause only a painful sting, but others can result in death.

▼ The death stalker scorpion is one of the most dangerous scorpions in the world. It lives in North Africa and the Middle East. One sting can cause paralysis (loss of movement) and heart failure in humans.

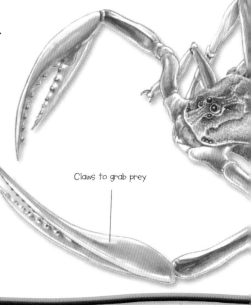

Claws to grab prey

638 The marine toad produces venom from special areas, called glands, behind its eyes. The venom is not used to kill prey, but to protect the toad from being eaten by other animals because it is extremely poisonous if swallowed.

639 Many snakes have venom glands in their mouths. They use their fangs to inject poison straight into their victim's body. Venom is made from saliva mixed with deadly substances. Spitting cobras shoot venom from their mouths. This venom can cause blindness in humans.

640 Scorpions belong to the same group as spiders – arachnids. Instead of producing venom in their fangs, they have stings in their tails. They use venom to kill prey, such as lizards and mice, or to defend themselves. Few scorpions can cause serious injury to humans, but some, such as the death stalker scorpion, are deadly.

A scorpion's stinger is called a telson

Eight legs like a spider

641 Even small insects can harm other animals. Hornets, wasps and bees have stings in their tails that are attached to venom sacs. A single sting causes swelling and pain, and may prove fatal to people who are allergic to the venom.

▶ Hornets, like wasps, usually only sting to defend themselves or to kill their prey.

Sting

Scary snakes

▶ Venomous snakes, such as the rattlesnake, inject venom using their large fangs. Snakes use their venom to paralyze (stop all movement) or kill their prey.

Venom runs down the groove on the outside of the fangs and is then injected into the victim's body

643 Cobras kill more than 10,000 people in India every year. As a warning sign, cobras spread their neck ribs, or hoods, to make them look more fearsome. Then they quickly lunge forwards and sink their fangs into their prey.

642 With unblinking eyes, sharp fangs and flickering tongues, snakes look like menacing killers. Despite their fearsome reputation, snakes only attack people when they feel threatened.

644 The taipan is one of Australia's most venomous snakes. When this snake attacks, it injects large amounts of venom that can kill a person in less than an hour.

645
Carpet vipers are small snakes found throughout many parts of Africa and Asia. They are responsible for hundreds, maybe thousands, of human deaths every year. Carpet viper venom affects the nervous system and the blood, causing the victim to bleed to death.

I DON'T BELIEVE IT!
Snakes can open their jaws so wide that they can swallow their prey whole. Large snakes, such as constrictors, can even swallow antelopes or pigs!

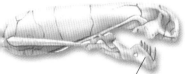

◀ Primitive snakes have a heavy skull with a short lower jaw and few teeth.

Short jaw that cannot open very wide

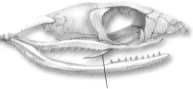

◀ Rear-fanged snakes have fangs in the roof of their mouths.

Fangs are towards the rear of the mouth, below the eye

◀ Some snakes have fangs at the front of their mouths.

The fangs are hollow, and positioned at the front of the mouth

646
Gaboon vipers have the longest fangs of any snake, reaching 5 centimetres in length. They produce large amounts of venom, which they inject deeply into the flesh with dagger-like teeth. Although slow and calm by nature, Gaboon vipers attack with great speed and a single bite can kill a human in less than two hours.

▶ Snakes kill their prey with a lethal bite. Then they swallow the victim, such as a rodent, whole.

Dragons and monsters

▼ Komodo dragons use their powerful jaws to tear the flesh of their victim, and then eat everything, including bones and fur.

647 **Komodo dragons are not really dragons, but lizards.** They can reach 3 metres in length and up to 100 kilograms in weight, making them the largest lizards in the world. They hunt their prey using their sensitive sense of smell.

648 Once the Komodo has caught its prey, it sinks its sharp teeth into the victim's flesh. With a mouth full of poisonous bacteria, one bite is enough to kill an animal with an infection, even if it escapes the Komodo's clutches.

649 There are only two truly poisonous lizards – the Gila monster and the Mexican beaded lizard. Gila monsters live in North America and they have bands of black, pink and yellow on their scaly skin to warn predators to stay away.

▲ Gila monsters use their sense of smell to hunt small animals and find reptile eggs. They can kill their prey with a single bite.

▼ Fire salamanders are amphibians, like frogs. They hunt insects and earthworms, mainly at night.

650 Fire salamanders look like a cross between a lizard and a frog. They have bold patterns on their skin to warn predators that they are poisonous. The poison, or toxin, is on their skin and tastes foul. They squirt the toxin at predators, irritating or even killing them.

Fearsome frogs

651 At first glance, few frogs appear fearsome. They may not have teeth or claws, but frogs and toads produce a deadly substance in their moist skin. This substance may taste foul or even be poisonous. The most poisonous frogs live in the forests of Central and South America. They are called poison-dart frogs.

652 One of the deadliest frogs is the golden poison-dart frog. It lives in rainforests in western Colombia, and its skin produces a very powerful poison – one of the deadliest known substances. A single touch is enough to cause almost instant death.

▼ The strawberry poison-dart frog is also known as the 'blue jeans' frog because of its blue legs.

653 Many poison-dart frogs are becoming rare in the wild. This is because the rainforests where they live are being cut down. Some poison-dart frogs can be kept in captivity, where they gradually become less poisonous. When they are raised in captivity, these frogs are not poisonous at all.

◄ The male green poison-dart frog carries tadpoles on his back. He takes them to a safe place in water where they will grow into adults.

655 People who live in the rainforests of Central and South America use the poison from frogs to catch food. A hunter wipes the tip of a dart on the poisonous frog's back, then carefully puts it in a blowpipe. One puff sends the lethal dart into the body of an unsuspecting monkey or bird.

▼ Poison is wiped off the back of the golden poison-dart frog with a dart. One frog produces enough poison for more than 50 darts.

654 Looking after eggs is the job of male green poison-dart frogs. The female lays her eggs amongst the leaf litter on the forest floor. The male guards them until they hatch into tadpoles, then carries them to water, where they will grow into frogs.

Eight-legged hunters

656 Many people believe that the deadliest spider is the tarantula. These hairy spiders may look like monsters, but they don't really deserve their killer reputation. Tarantulas rarely bite humans, and not all tarantulas are venomous.

▲ After an insect becomes trapped in the spider's web, the spider kills it with a venomous bite. The spider will eat almost every part of its prey.

657 Tarantulas hunt their prey, such as insects, frogs and lizards, rather than spinning webs. They use their large fangs to inject venom into their prey and crush it into a pulp. Digestive juices are poured over the victim until it turns into a liquid and can be sucked up.

658 Black widow spiders are one of the most dangerous spiders in the world, but they only attack if disturbed. A bite from a male is nothing to worry about, but a bite from a female may prove fatal.

◄ Female black widow spiders use their poison not only to catch prey, but also to kill their partners after mating.

659 Spiders belong to a group of animals called arachnids, along with scorpions and ticks. Some ticks can kill without using deadly poison. They attach themselves to the bodies of humans and other animals, and suck their blood. This can spread deadly diseases.

660 There are many types of funnel web spider, and some of them are very venomous. When a funnel web spider is threatened, it stands on its hind legs and rears, showing its huge fangs. These killers bite their prey many times, injecting poison.

▲ The fangs of the funnel web spider are so strong that they can pierce human skin, even fingernails. Its bite can cause death in just 15 minutes.

Clever defenders

661 To survive in a dangerous world, animals need to be able to hide, fight, or appear deadly. When it is threatened, the spiny puffer fish swallows large amounts of water, making its body swell up and its spines stand on end.

662 Spines can be used to pass venom into the victim's body, or used as weapons of defence. The long, sharp spines on the Cape porcupine are called quills, and they stick into an attacker's body, causing painful injuries.

▼▶ The spiny puffer fish stiffens and swells its body, changing from an ordinary-looking fish to a spiky ball.

◀ Tortoises are protected from predators by their tough shell. Even the sharp claws and teeth of lion cubs cannot break it.

663 Some animals hide from their predators using camouflage. This means the colour or pattern of an animal's skin blends in with its surroundings. Lizards called chameleons are masters of camouflage. They can change their skin colour from brown to green so they blend in with their background. They do this to communicate with one another.

664 The bold colours and pattern on the coral snake's skin warns predators that it is poisonous. The milk snake looks almost identical to the coral snake, but it is not venomous. Its colour keeps it safe though, because predators think it is poisonous.

I DON'T BELIEVE IT!

Electric eels have an unusual way of staying safe – they zap prey and predators with electricity! They can produce 600 volts of power at a time, which is enough to kill a human!

▶ The harmless milk snake looks similar to the venomous coral snake, so predators stay away. This life-saving animal trick is called mimicry.

Danger at sea

665 Deep in the ocean lurk some of the deadliest creatures in the world. There are keen-eyed killers, venomous stingers and sharp-toothed hunters, but as few of these animals come into contact with humans, attacks are rare.

▶ The Australian box jellyfish is also known as the sea wasp. Its tentacles can grow more than 3 metres in length and one animal has enough venom to kill 60 people.

666 Barracudas are long, strong, powerful fish. They lunge at their prey, baring dagger-like teeth. Although they prey on other fish, barracudas may mistake swimmers for food and attack them.

667 The box jellyfish is one of the most lethal creatures in the world. A touch from only one tentacle can kill a human. The floating body of a jellyfish is harmless, but danger lies in the many tentacles that drift below. Each tentacle is covered with tiny stingers that shoot venom into the victim.

◀ Barracudas are fierce fish with powerful jaws and sharp teeth.

668 A Portuguese Man o' War may look like a single animal, but actually it is made up of many creatures, called polyps. A gas-filled chamber floats on the water's surface, and long tendrils, each measuring 20 metres or more, hang below. The tendrils have venomous stings that catch food for the whole colony of polyps.

▲ Stingrays have stings in their tails that look like darts. They use them in defence to stab any animal that frightens them.

669 The most dangerous octopus in the world only measures 10 to 20 centimetres in length. The blue-ringed octopus grabs prey with its tentacles and then bites deeply, injecting venom into the victim. The venom can kill a human in just four minutes.

► The tiny blue-ringed octopus has enough venom to kill ten people.

Sharks in the shadows

670 Few animals send a shiver down the spine quite like a great white shark. This huge fish is a skilled hunter. Its bullet-shaped body can slice through the water at lightning speed, powered by huge muscles and a crescent-shaped tail.

671 Sharks are fish, and belong to the same family as rays and skates. Most sharks are predators and feed on fish, squid, seals and other sea creatures. Some sharks hunt with quick spurts of energy as they chase their prey. Others lie in wait for victims to pass by.

672 One of the deadliest sharks can be found in oceans and seas throughout the world. Blue sharks often hunt in packs and circle their prey before attacking. Although these creatures normally eat fish and squid, they will attack humans.

673 Bull sharks are a deadly threat to humans. This is because they live in areas close to human homes. They often swim inland, using the same rivers that people use to bathe and collect water, and may attack.

▲ Great white sharks are fearsome predators. They have rows of ultra-sharp triangular teeth that are perfect for taking large bites out of prey, such as seals, sea lions and dolphins.

674 Grey reef sharks are sleek, swift predators of the Indian and Pacific oceans. Unusually, they give plenty of warning before they attack. If the grey reef shark feels threatened, it drops its fins down, raises its snout and starts weaving and rolling through the water.

Peril at the shore

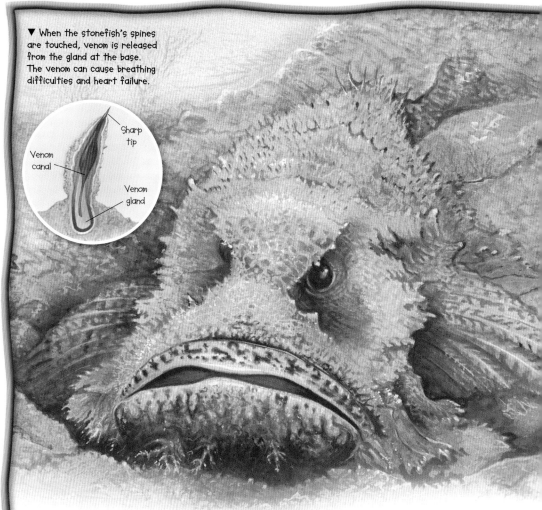

▼ When the stonefish's spines are touched, venom is released from the gland at the base. The venom can cause breathing difficulties and heart failure.

Sharp tip

Venom canal

Venom gland

▲ While hidden amongst rocks, the camouflaged stonefish waits for its prey, such as small fish.

675 The seashore may seem like a quiet place, but danger lies beneath the gently lapping waves. While some predators actively hunt their prey, some creatures just sit and wait.

676 Stonefish may look like a piece of rocky coral, but their cunning disguise hides a deadly surprise. One touch of the sharp spines on the stonefish's back results in an injection of venom, which may be fatal.

DESIGN TIME

You've now read about lots of dangerous animals and the tools they use to kill their prey. Now it's time to draw or paint your own deadly creature.

Will it have claws, fangs, spikes, venom or horns? What will you call it? Perhaps a clawfish or a dragon monkey?

677 Lionfish are graceful swimmers, but the long spines on their fins inject venom as swiftly as a needle. A single injury from one spine causes immediate sickness and great pain, but it is unlikely to prove deadly to a human.

▼ Cone shells use their long proboscis to shoot a poisonous dart into their prey. The venom is very powerful and quickly paralyzes the prey.

678 Sea snakes spend their lives in water. They breathe air, so they need to keep returning to the surface. All sea snakes are poisonous, and although their bites are painless at first, the venom is very powerful and can kill.

679 Seashells are not always as harmless as they appear. Rather than chasing their prey, cone shells attack other animals using a poison that paralyzes the victim so it cannot escape. The venom of fish-eating cone shells can paralyze a fish within seconds. Although their venom can be fatal to humans, it is being used by scientists to develop medicines that reduce pain.

Minibeasts

◀ Although houseflies do not have stings, they are dangerous to humans. They can spread diseases if they land on food.

680 Animals don't have to be big to be beastly. There are many small animals, particularly insects, that are killers. Some of them, such as ants, are predators that hunt to eat. Others, such as locusts, cause destruction that affects humans.

681 Ants are found almost everywhere, except in water. Most ants are harmless to humans, but army ants and driver ants turn tropical forests and woodlands into battlefields. The stings of army ants contain chemicals that dissolve flesh. Once their prey has turned to liquid, the ants can begin to drink it.

▼ Millions of army ants live in a single group, or colony. They hunt together, swarming through leaf litter and attacking anything in their way.

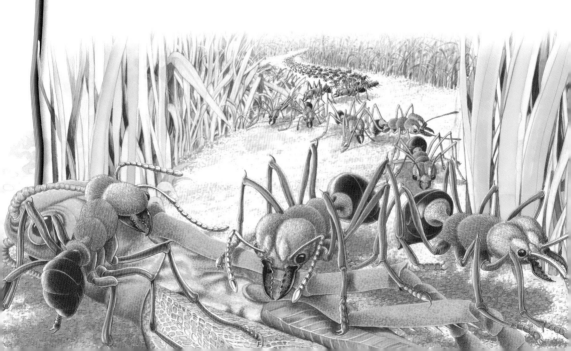

682 Driver ants have large jaws that can slice easily through food. They hunt in large numbers and swarm through forests hunting for prey. Driver ants can kill large animals, such as cows, by biting them to death. They have also been known to strip a chicken down to its skeleton in less than a day.

683 Deadly plagues of locusts have been written about for thousands of years. When they search for food, they travel in swarms of millions, eating all the plants they encounter. This can leave humans without any food.

▲ Killer bees fiercely protect their hive by swarming around it. They will attack anything that approaches the nest.

684 Killer bees are a new type of bee that was created by a scientist. He was hoping to breed bees that made lots of honey, but the bees proved to be extremely aggressive. Killer bees swarm in huge groups and when one bee stings, the others quickly join in. One sting is not deadly, but lots of bee stings can kill a human. It is thought that about 1000 people have been killed by these minibeasts.

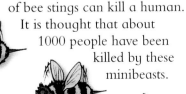

The enemy within

685 Many deadly creatures are too small to be seen. They are parasites, living on or inside the body of humans or animals, causing harm, disease and even death. An animal that is home to a parasite is called a host.

686 Rats are known to spread disease. They carry bacteria on their paws and in their mouths, but they also carry another type of parasite called fleas. Even the fleas can have parasites inside their bodies – plague bacteria.

687 Humans have suffered from plagues for thousands of years. These diseases are spread when rat fleas bite people, spreading the plague bacteria. Plague usually only occurs when people live in dirty conditions where rats and their fleas can breed. Plague can spread quickly, wiping out millions of lives.

▼ The Black Death, or bubonic plague, was spread by rats and it wiped out one-third of Europe's population (25 million people) about 700 years ago.

▼ Tsetse flies feed on blood and spread parasites that cause sleeping sickness. This painful disease is common in developing countries and leads to death if not treated.

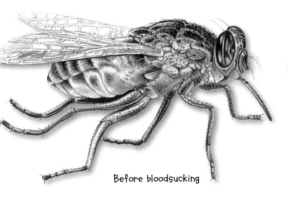

Before bloodsucking

After bloodsucking

689 The mosquito and its tiny parasites are among the deadliest creatures in the world. When mosquitoes suck human and animal blood, they pass parasites into the host's body, including the parasite that causes malaria. Malaria is a disease that mainly affects people living in hot countries in the developing world. It causes about one million deaths a year in Africa.

688 Some of the most common parasites are worms. Tiny threadlike worms called nematodes live inside the bodies of most animals, including some humans. Nematodes can spread disease. Tapeworms belong to a different family of worms called flatworms. They absorb food from their host's intestine.

▶ Mosquitoes pierce the skin of the victim to suck their blood, spreading deadly diseases, such as malaria.

BIRDS OF PREY

690 Birds of prey are magnificent hunters of the sky. They soar through the air using their large wings to keep them aloft, as they scan the ground below for food. Some birds of prey, such as eagles, are hunters and kill to eat. Others, such as vultures, eat carrion (dead animals). Birds of prey are also called raptors, from the Latin *rapere*, meaning to grab or seize, because they kill with their feet.

▼ A long-legged buzzard brings food to its chicks. These birds of prey nest on cliff ledges and feed on small mammals, reptiles and large insects.

Eagle-eyed predators

691 Like all hunters, birds of prey need to be kitted out with tools. They have sharp senses, muscular bodies, tough beaks and grasping feet with sharp talons. They can detect prey from great distances and launch deadly attacks with skill and accuracy. Some can fly at super speeds.

▼ Golden eagles are large birds, measuring about 2 metres from wing tip to wing tip.

Finger–like primary flight feathers at wing tips

Rusty brown feathers

692 Raptors are able to fly high above the ground. The sky not only offers a great view of prey, it is also a safe place for birds as they search. As adults, birds of prey do have natural enemies, but even on land they are usually a match for most other predators due to their size.

693 Good eyesight is essential for raptors. They need to be able to locate prey that is in grass or under cover, often from a great distance. Birds of prey have eyes that are packed with light-detecting cells. The eyes are positioned near the front of the head, which means a bird can see well in front, to the side and partly around to the back.

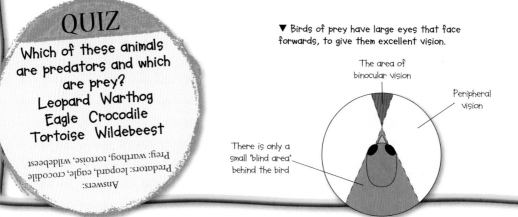

▼ Birds of prey have large eyes that face forwards, to give them excellent vision.

The area of binocular vision

Peripheral vision

There is only a small 'blind area' behind the bird

694 Birds of prey have big, powerful bodies.

This helps them catch and kill food, but means they need more energy to fly. Meat is an energy-packed food, ideal for building muscles. Even the largest birds of prey can swoop and soar, although smaller birds are usually more acrobatic in flight.

Pale feathers on crown

Large bill

Large, broad wings

Large tail

Powerful feet with sharp talons

Birds of prey may carry their food to a safe place to eat it, but others eat their prey where it was killed

White-tailed eagle
Large, heavy bill

▶ Eagles and vultures have big, tough bills, but falcons have smaller, sharp bills. A bird's bill and talons are made of a hard substance called keratin, the same as our nails.

Egyptian vulture
Long, hooked bill

695 Scientists used to think that all birds of prey had a poor sense of smell. The turkey vulture is the only bird of prey known to have a good sense of smell, and probably the only one able to smell out its food. They can detect carrion on the ground while they are flying.

Gyrfalcon
Short bill with a sharp hook

Where do they live?

▲ Steller's sea eagle eats mainly fish, so this bird of prey lives near rivers, lakes and seashores. It only breeds in far eastern Russia.

696 Warm, tropical regions are home to many species (types) of birds of prey. They live on grasslands or in rainforests where there is lots to eat. Away from the tropics there are fewer raptors. Their habitats include forests, wetlands and coastal areas.

▼ Peregrine falcons are one of the world's most common birds of prey and they live on every continent, except Antarctica.

697 Birds of prey live all over the world, except Antarctica. No raptors can survive the freezing conditions of the south polar region, where food is scarce. Some are able to find food and endure the cold of the northern Arctic area. Snowy owls, peregrine falcons and white-tailed eagles can all cope with the cold, but travel to warmer places when the worst weather bites.

▶ Vultures and a jackal fight over the carcass of a zebra on an African grassland.

698 Some birds of prey can live in different habitats in different parts of the world. Ospreys and peregrine falcons are found in the Americas, Africa, Asia, Europe and Australia. Ospreys prefer to live near water, while peregrines like hills, cliffs and even cities.

▶ This family of Harris hawks has made a prickly home out of a cactus. In deserts, trees are scarce.

699 Barn owls live in many parts of the world, but one of their favourite places to build a nest is inside an old building. They frequently choose barns or church steeples to live in, where they are unlikely to be disturbed and can find a good supply of small rodents to eat.

700 Harris hawks hunt in deserts and other dry places. Small animals that live in these places often stay hidden from view and out of the strong sunlight, which makes them hard to find. Smart Harris hawks deal with this problem by living and hunting in groups, which makes it easier for them to seek and kill their fast-moving prey.

Little and large

701 The largest birds of prey are Andean condors. Their wingspan, which is measured from wing tip to wing tip, can be 3 metres in males. Condors have the biggest wings of all birds, which can catch the wind to soar above mountains at incredible heights of 5.5 kilometres.

Andean condor
Body length: 120 centimetres
Average wingspan: 3 metres

▶ These wings are shown to scale. Large birds with big wings are able to soar and travel long distances. Birds with smaller wings are more agile in flight and can hunt at greater speeds.

Black-thighed falconet

702 In Europe, the largest raptors are white-tailed eagles. They are found from Greenland to Turkey, but there are just 10,000 in the wild. These birds came close to extinction after years of shooting and poisoning, but are now protected in many countries. In Australia, the largest raptors are wedge-tailed eagles. They can grow to more than one metre long, with a wingspan of up to 2.3 metres.

◀ Little black-thighed falconets can easily dart through forests to hunt prey because of their small size.

703 The smallest birds of prey are the falconets from Southeast Asia. There are five species and the smallest are the white-fronted falconet and the black-thighed falconet. Falconets are just 14 to 18 centimetres long from bill to tail tip. Most feed on insects, but the pied falconet, which is the largest, can catch small animals.

MEASURING SIZE

Using a measuring tape, discover just how large or small these birds are. If you were standing next to an Eurasian eagle owl, would it reach your waist? If your arms were wings, what would your wingspan measure?

Eurasian eagle owl
Body length: 70 centimetres
Average wingspan: 2 metres

704 Some owls are big birds.
Eurasian eagle owls are about
70 centimetres tall and they are
large enough to hunt deer fawns, although
they also eat beetles, rats and voles. They can
hunt in forests, but they prefer open spaces.

Common buzzard
Body length: 48 centimetres
Average wingspan: 125 centimetres

705 The largest bird of prey that ever lived was probably Haast's eagle.
It lived in New
Zealand until around 500 years ago. Six million years
ago, a giant bird called *Argentavis* flew across
what is now Argentina. It had a body
like a condor, but its wingspan was
similar to that of a small plane!

Black-thighed falconet
Body length: 15 centimetres
Average wingspan:
30 centimetres

Hovering and soaring

706 **Birds of prey have one advantage over most other predators – they can fly.** Flying allows creatures to escape from other animals and stay safe. They can explore new areas easily as they search for food, mates or places to breed.

707 **Birds' bodies are perfectly adapted for flying.** They have light bones that are mostly hollow, but still strong. Their big hearts and lungs can collect lots of oxygen with every breath. This is the gas that animals need to turn their food into energy.

Skull

Narrow, pointed wings

Humerus – similar to our upper arm bone

Metacarpals – form a 'hand'

Keel – where large flight muscles are attached

Wingbeats are stiff and shallow

Ribs

▶ Hovering and flying require lots of energy, so kestrels have light bodies with muscles and powerful wings. Their skeleton is very light and flexible, but also strong and rigid.

The long tail feathers are spread out to keep the bird steady while it is hovering, looking for food

I DON'T BELIEVE IT!

Hobbies are amongst the fastest, most acrobatic fliers of all. They can dive, twist and turn, bombing towards the ground at great speeds, only opening their wings a few metres above the ground.

708 **Kestrels hover and look as if they are hardly moving.** They fly facing the wind, staying in the same spot above the ground. Kestrels spread their tails and the feathers at their wing tips turn up, which helps them to stay steady. As they lower their heads, they get a good view of the ground and any small animals, before launching an attack.

709 Birds of prey with long, broad wings soar through the sky. They also have large, fan-shaped tails that, with their wings, catch the air like a parachute.

Soaring birds, such as eagles and vultures, often wait until the air is warm before they fly. As air is heated by the Sun it rises. Large, soaring birds use these flows of warm air, called thermal uplifts, to get airborne and rise high above the ground.

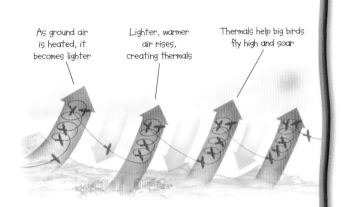

As ground air is heated, it becomes lighter

Lighter, warmer air rises, creating thermals

Thermals help big birds fly high and soar

▲ Thermals are hot air currents that travel upwards. Birds of prey use them to reach greater heights.

710 At breeding time, male birds of prey often perform display flights. These might help to attract females or mark out territory. There are different patterns of display flights, from circling round and round, to dive bombing or swooping up and down.

▶ At mating time, one golden eagle dives towards its mate, which turns its back, and they wrestle one another with their feet.

Nests, eggs and chicks

711 Like all birds, raptors lay eggs, usually in nests. Females may build nests in trees or on cliffs. Some birds of prey use the same nest every year, adding more sticks until it is huge. Golden eagle nests can eventually grow to 6 metres deep and 2 metres wide!

▶ Ospreys often use the same nest, year after year, so their nest becomes massive.

712 Big birds of prey have few natural predators, so only lay one or two eggs a year. Caring for chicks is hard work because they need a lot of food. If large birds of prey had more chicks, they might not be able to find enough food to feed them all and some would die. Smaller birds of prey usually breed earlier in the year and lay more eggs.

713 One egg is laid at a time and the female sits on it to keep it warm. It can take several days before all the eggs are laid. While the female protects the eggs and chicks, the male does most of the hunting and brings food to the nest. When the chicks hatch, they are covered in soft feathers called down.

▼ A peregrine falcon chick hatches from its egg.

▶ At two days old, the chick is fluffy and cheeps for food.

714 If food is scarce, the smallest chicks are not fed and die. Eagle chicks battle with each other and a larger, hungrier chick may push its brother or sister out of the nest or even eat it. It takes just a few weeks for the chicks of a small bird of prey, such as a merlin, to grow adult feathers and be able to fly, but it can take over four months for vulture chicks to reach this stage.

715 Young birds of prey may stay in their parents' care for many months. They have to learn how to hunt before they become independent, and might rely on their parents to bring them food for a whole year after hatching. When they are old enough to mate they may find a partner and stay with them for life.

▼ When it is 28 days old, the young bird is growing its adult plumage (feathers) and the old down is falling out.

▶ Juvenile peregrines have brown feathers. The face markings are paler than in older birds.

Home and away

716 Birds of prey may fly long distances (migrate) in search of food or places to breed. Raptors that live near the Equator don't usually migrate as their tropical homes contain enough food and are warm all year round.

▼ Migrating birds of prey follow certain routes every year. Some of the major migration routes are shown here.

717 Animals of the north struggle to survive in the cold. Many small animals hibernate (sleep) during winter. This leaves some birds of prey hungry, so they travel south to warmer areas. Golden eagles, gyrfalcons and goshawks stay in their northerly homes unless they live in the extreme north.

Hawk Mountain

Veracruz

▼ Every year, people gather to watch birds fly overhead at Hawk Mountain, USA.

718 Migrating birds usually fly over land, not water. Warm air currents that help large birds to soar for long distances develop above continents rather than oceans, so the routes avoid stretches of water. Big groups of birds may fly together over strips of land and crossing points, such as at Gibraltar, where Europe meets Africa, or the Black Sea coast.

Swainson's hawk European kestrel Gryfalcon

▲ The routes taken by these migrating birds are shown in white on the map.

720 No one really knows how migrating birds find their way. They may follow the Sun, but it is likely they use clues, such as landmarks they recognize after using the same routes for years, and the Earth's magnetic field.

719 The largest raptor migrations are over Veracruz, in Mexico. Over five million birds have been seen flying over the area in autumn, including 2.7 million turkey vultures and 2.4 million broad-winged hawks.

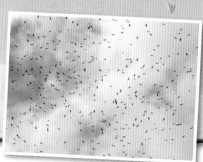

◀ Broad-winged hawks migrate over Veracruz, Mexico in huge flocks.

721 Predators need good senses to find prey, speed to catch it and weapons for killing it. Raptors are equipped with bodies that are ideal for locating and killing, but learning the skills to hunt takes time, patience and practice.

722 The most important weapons are feet and mouths. Raptors' bills are usually hooked, with a pointed tip. Birds that hunt other birds, such as falcons, hawks and owls, often have short, hooked bills. Those raptors that hunt larger animals need long, strong bills.

◀ Tawny owls have soft feathers that muffle noise, so they can take off in silence.

▼ This golden eagle's toes have dagger-like claws (talons) that can pierce flesh with ease.

723 Raptors' feet have talons and they are highly developed for hunting. Each foot has three strong, scaly toes at the front and one at the side or back. When the toes are bent they can grasp like a hand – perfect for holding wriggling prey.

Sharp hooks on an osprey's foot help it to grab and hold slippery fish

When a barn owl grabs its prey, its foot can spread wide to get a good grip

A black vulture does not need very sharp talons, as it usually feeds on carrion

▲ The shape of a bird's talons depends on how it hunts and its type of prey.

725 Feet give clues about how a bird hunts.
Birds of prey with short legs and short feet usually kill on the ground. Birds with long legs, long feet and slender, sharp talons catch and kill their prey in the air. Birds with especially big hind toes grab hold of large animals, such as rabbits or even deer.

► Rapid wingbeats can change the owl's direction easily.

724 Tawny owls mostly hunt at night.
They wait on a perch, looking and listening for small animals that may be moving around nearby. They sometimes beat their wings to startle other perching birds, forcing them into flight. Once the birds are in the air, the owls can follow their movements and prepare to attack. They can even pick birds or bats off their perches or out of nests.

► As they prepare to grab their prey, tawny owls spread their wings to cover it and they kill it instantly with their bill and feet.

Scrounging scavengers

◀ Vultures and marabou storks feast on the carcass of a dead animal.

726 Not all birds of prey hunt live prey. Some eat any meat they can find and are called scavengers, or carrion-eaters. Some birds of prey only scavenge when they cannot find live prey, but others never hunt and only eat leftovers.

727 Vultures are birds of prey that mostly scavenge dead animals. They often have bald heads and necks because feathers would get messy and bloody from delving into dead bodies. Vultures often look for hyenas or lions tucking into a meal, then swoop down to feed when the coast is clear.

King vulture

Lammergeier

Lappet-faced vulture

Adult griffon vultures have white feathers
n their necks, a yellow-white bill and
ellow-brown eyes. Youngsters have darker
eathers, brown bills and eyes.

28 Griffon vultures like
to wash in water after feeding. They
have bare heads and necks for reaching
into carcasses. These birds soar over open
areas, using their long, broad wings,
ooking for carrion. Griffon vultures fly in
groups of up to 40 for hours at a time and
they may frighten other predators away
o get at food.

730 African vultures take turns
to munch through a body. Lappet-
faced vultures have big bills that are
perfect for ripping through skin and fur,
so they often eat first. Hooded vultures
come along later to eat softer meat,
and lammergeiers (bearded
vultures) tackle the leftovers.

◄ Few animals are clever
enough to use tools, but
Egyptian vultures can break
tough eggs with stones.

729 Vultures and other
scavenging birds make the most of any
dining opportunities. Turkey vultures are
often seen flying or perched near roads –
ready to tuck in when animals and cars
collide on the highway. Egyptian vultures
find it difficult to break open eggs with
their bill, so they use stones to crack them
open instead.

◄ Vultures usually have long, thin
necks that help them probe deep
into a carcass to feed. Their bills
are particularly long and strong,
because carrion is tough to eat.

Fussy eaters

731 **Some birds of prey have unusual diets.** Lesser spotted eagles that live around wetlands feast on frogs. Snail kites have curved, hooked bills for extracting snails from their shells. Palm-nut vultures eat the fruits of palm trees.

▲ When ospreys plunge into water, they close their nostrils so the water doesn't shoot up into their nose. They carry their catch back to the nest to eat in peace or feed it to their chicks.

▶ Snail kites live in South American wetlands and eat water snails, turtles and crabs. They also hunt rodents, such as rats and mice.

732 **Plucking a fish out of water takes huge skill.** Yet some birds of prey can achieve this incredible feat. They soar over water, watching for movement at the surface. Once they have spied a fish, the birds dive down and plunge their feet into the water to grab it. This requires sharp eyesight, quick reactions and an agile body.

733 **Ospreys are fish-eaters.** These birds of prey nest near lakes and rivers or by clean, calm coastal areas. They hover up to 30 metres above the water until they spot a fish. Then they dive down with half-closed wings and stretch out their legs and feet just before hitting the water.

734
White-tailed eagles pluck both fish and ducks out of the water. They perch on trees and swoop down to grab prey. Sharp growths, called spicules, on the feet help to grip wet prey and large bills are ideal for ripping and tearing flesh.

735
Lammergeiers eat a diet of bones and scraps left behind by other predators. They pick up large bones with their feet and fly to a height of 80 metres before dropping the bones to the ground to split them. These birds also drop tortoises to get to the soft flesh inside the shell.

FISH EATERS
Penguins are flightless birds that catch fish to eat. Find out where they live and how they catch fish. How are their bodies different to those of birds of prey?

▶ If a bone is dropped from a great height it splits open. The lammergeier can then eat the soft marrow inside.

Snake stampers

Black flight
feathers

Black crest
feathers

736 Secretary birds
are not like other
raptors. They are tall,
elegant and long-legged.
These birds stride through
the long grasses of African
plains, looking for insects and
other animals to eat. When
they find their prey, they stamp
and peck it to death.

Grey plumage
on body

737 Secretary birds eat snakes, even
poisonous ones, such as cobras and adders.
When it spies a snake in the vegetation, a
secretary bird runs towards it and stamps on it, or
inflicts a kick to the head. A sharp peck to the
back of the snake's neck finishes it off. If the prey
proves too tough to kill this way, the bird may
grab it in its beak, take to the skies and drop it
from a great height.

Large feet

Long legs

▶ A male secretary bird can grow to about 1.4 metres
tall. Secretary birds might get their name from the crest
of long, black quill feathers on their heads, which
look like old-fashioned ink pens.

738 Snakes are no match for a secretary bird. These predators run fast during a chase and their legs are covered in thick scales to protect them from bites. If a snake fights back, the secretary bird spreads its wings to form a shield. The flapping wings scare the snake and if it bites a feather, the bird will suffer no harm. They often hunt in pairs and can walk more than 25 kilometres every day in search of food.

739 When they are angry, excited or scared, secretary birds raise their quill feathers. Their body feathers are grey and white, but black feathers at the top of their long legs make them appear as if they are wearing short trousers! Males and females look similar, but females are smaller.

► Short-toed eagles feed dead snakes to their young, which have enormous appetites.

740 Not many birds of prey eat snakes, but short-toed eagles eat almost nothing else. They attack snakes that are nearly 2 metres long and even eat poisonous ones. A family of short-toed eagles needs at least five snakes every day, so the adults spend a lot of time hunting their slithery prey.

Eagles

741 Eagles are large, heavy-bodied birds with strong legs, big bills and feet, and broad wings. They are usually smaller than vultures, but larger than most other birds of prey. There are about 60 types, including fish eagles, snake eagles, harpy eagles and hawk eagles.

742 These birds live in all regions of the world except Antarctica. Golden eagles are one of the most common, widespread types. There may be as many as one million and they live in North America, Europe and Asia, around mountains, forests and cliffs. The Great Nicobar serpent eagle is a rare eagle. It lives on one small island near India, and there may be fewer than 1000.

▼ Large birds of prey, such as eagles, rely on thermals to reach height in the sky.

2. An eagle uses thermals to reach a good height for spotting its prey, and then swoops.

1. Warm air thermals travel upwards.

743 Eagles are not as agile as some other birds of prey. When they hunt, they are more likely to soar and stoop than to hover and dive. Eagles often perch to watch for prey, then swoop in low for the kill.

4. The eagle flies off with its prey held firmly in its feet.

3. As the bird flies towards its prey, it swings its feet forward to grab hold of it.

744 The lowland forests of South America are home to the impressive-looking harpy eagle. These birds of prey are huge and can grow to over one metre long, with wingspans of 2 metres. They have large, two-pointed crests on their heads and their massive feet are the size of a grizzly bear's paw. Harpy eagles hunt tree-dwelling animals, such as monkeys and sloths, which they chase through the branches.

▲ Male harpy eagles have grey feathers on their heads and black plumage on their chests and backs. Females are paler.

745 Bald eagles are the national emblem of the USA. They have white heads and tails and yellow bills, which makes them easy to identify. Youngsters have brown feathers and do not develop their white markings until they are four or five years old. Bald eagles will eat almost anything, from carrion to fish, which they might steal from other birds.

I DON'T BELIEVE IT!

Harpy eagles may be named after winged creatures called harpies, from Greek mythology. Harpies had a woman's face and a vulture's body or were winged spirits that snatched food.

► Male and female bald eagles are almost identical in appearance, although females are usually slightly bigger than their mates.

Kites and buzzards

746 Kites are small raptors with short bills and long, narrow wings and tails. They are elegant fliers that flap their wings slowly. Kites catch small prey, such as insects and rodents. They live throughout the world, mostly in warm places.

◀ Swallow-tailed kites rarely flap their wings while flying, but twist their tails to change direction quickly

747 Black kites are omnivores, which means they will eat almost anything. They even scavenge rubbish. These birds live in Africa, Australia, Europe and parts of Asia, especially in woods, near farmland and water, or where humans are found. Red kites are rarer and only found in parts of Europe. They mostly eat other birds, but will also eat whatever is available.

748 Swallow-tailed kites live in tropical rainforests of South America. They have long, elegant wings and forked tails that give them the appearance of swallows. These birds can swoop, soar and dive, changing direction rapidly to pursue prey. They build their nests at the tops of tall trees.

▶ Red kites hunt over grasslands, lakes and rubbish dumps. They also search roads for roadkill.

749 Buzzards are big-bodied birds with broad wings and large, rounded tails. When they fly, they beat their wings slowly and gracefully. They eat small mammals and insects. Honey buzzards eat wasps and bees. They rip open hives with their talons and bills, then eat the larvae, pupae and adult insects. These birds have slit-like nostrils and bristles instead of feathers between their eyes, which may protect them from stings.

750 In the Americas, buzzards are often called hawks. Swainson's hawk spends summer in the USA and travels to South America for winter. When breeding, they eat mice, squirrels and reptiles, but for the rest of the year they survive mostly on insects, such as grasshoppers and beetles. They often walk along the ground looking for food and sometimes hunt in teams.

◀ A common buzzard feeds during winter. There are nearly 30 species (types) of buzzards and they belong to a group of raptors called Buteos.

QUIZ

1. Which kites have the appearance of swallows?
2. Which buzzards eat wasps and bees?
3. Which hawk sometimes hunts in teams?

Answers:
1. Swallow-tailed kites
2. Honey buzzards
3. Swainson's hawk

327

Fast falcons

▶ A peregrine falcon pursues a swallow. It has recently been discovered that peregrines that live in towns are able to hunt at night, helped by city lights to find their prey.

752 **Peregrines are travellers and have one of the longest migrations of any raptors.** American peregrines have been known to cover 25,000 kilometres in just one year. These raptors are the most widespread of all birds of prey and live on every continent except Antarctica, but they are rare.

751 **A peregrine falcon can move faster than any other animal on Earth.** These birds reach speeds of 100 kilometres an hour when chasing prey. When peregrines stoop from heights of one kilometre and plummet through the sky, they may reach speeds of 300 kilometres an hour or more.

▼ Saker falcons have bold markings while some Eleonora's falcons have rusty pink breast feathers.

Eleonora's falcon

Saker falcon

753 **There are about 35 species of falcon and most of them are speedy fliers.** They are medium-sized raptors with muscle-packed bodies, pointed wings and short tails. They usually nest in cliffs and lay several eggs at a time. Falcons prey upon birds and other small animals.

▶ Gyrfalcons are bulky birds with extra body fat that helps them to keep warm.

754 Gyrfalcons can cope with the cold and they live around the Earth's frozen north. Some gyrfalcons are brown or grey. The further north they live, the paler they become, so they are camouflaged against the snowy landscape. These are the biggest falcons, with a wingspan of up to 1.3 metres, so they can pursue large prey such as ptarmigans, gulls and geese.

▼ Lesser kestrels spend the winters in Africa, travelling into Europe for the summer. They mostly feed on insects, but in spring they hunt reptiles and small mammals.

755 Kestrels are types of falcon that hover before attacking their prey. These small birds of prey have rounded heads and large eyes. While male and female raptors often have the same colour plumage, male kestrels are usually more colourful than the females.

Hawks and harriers

▼ Goshawks live in forested areas of Europe. They mainly hunt birds that are weak or ill because sick animals make easier targets.

756 **Hawks, sparrowhawks and goshawks belong to a group of raptors called Accipiters.** They are medium-sized birds and live in forests and woodlands. Short, rounded wings and long tails help them to fly in short bursts between trees, darting through branches in pursuit of small mammals and birds.

757 **Most hawks hunt rodents, such as rats.** They are useful because they eat pests that damage crops. However goshawks hunt game birds and poultry. Game birds, such as pheasants, are bred by farmers to be hunted for sport. Poultry, such as chickens, are an important food for humans. Goshawks have been killed to stop them from hunting these birds.

I DON'T BELIEVE IT!

Sharp-shinned hawks of America take their prey to a special perch called a butcher's block. This is where the raptor plucks all the feathers or fur off its prey, so these bits don't mess up its nest!

760 **Harriers are raptors that look similar to hawks, with long legs and tails.** They often fly low over fields and meadows, scouring the ground for snakes, frogs, insects, small birds or mammals. Hen harriers live in Europe, Asia and North America, but the populations of birds on each side of the Atlantic are slightly different from one another. North American birds are usually called marsh harriers or northern harriers.

58 **Hawks may squeeze their prey to death.** Many raptors use their feet to hold prey and their bills to kill it. Cooper's hawks hold a captured animal with their sharp talons and fly with it until it dies. They have been known to hold prey underwater to drown it.

Common black hawks live near water in Central America

▶ Hawks have rounded heads with short bills. Their compact bodies help them to fly fast and change direction.

Red-tailed hawks of North America inhabit woods, deserts and mountains

759 **Eurasian sparrowhawks are one of the most common raptors in the world.** They live in forests, farms, woods and parks across Europe and Asia during the spring and summer, and travel south for the winter. Despite being common, sparrowhawks are so secretive that they are rarely seen. However when food is scarce they may investigate gardens, searching for song birds such as sparrows to eat.

Eurasian sparrowhawks hide their nests in woodlands

761 Most owls hunt at night. As well as having talons and sharp bills, owls have big eyes that face the front and can see depth and movement. Eyes have two types of cells – one detecting colours, the other just faint or dim light. Some owls only have light-detecting cells and can see in the darkness, but not colour.

762 Owls use feathers to help them hear and to stop animals from hearing them. Their ears are covered by feathers that direct sound into the ear canal. Downy feathers on the body and feet help to soften sound as the bird moves. Feathers on the wings are arranged in a way that deadens the sound of flapping, so the bird descends silently on its prey.

▲ Like some other owls, this great horned owl is nocturnal, which means that it is most active at night. It begins hunting at dusk and settles down to sleep when the Sun rises.

◀ Owls have three eyelids. The third eyelid is a special membrane that sweeps over the eye to clean it.

► Pellets can be opened and their contents studied to discover the diet of a bird of prey.

Pellet from a little owl

Pellet from a long-eared owl

Pellet from a barn owl

Pellet from a red kite

765 Owls eat a range of food, including insects, birds, bats and fish, and they often swallow an animal whole. Like other birds of prey, owls are not able to digest the hard parts of a body, such as bones, fur or feathers. They bring them up from their stomach and spit them out in the form of pellets. It takes about seven hours for one pellet to form.

763 Eurasian eagle owls have a wingspan of nearly 2 metres. The largest owls, they attack other birds to steal their territories. Tiny elf owls catch their prey in flight. They are the smallest owls, with a wingspan of just 15 centimetres.

764 Many birds of prey build their own nests, but owls do not. They either use old nests left by other birds, or they lay their eggs in a hole in a tree, a hollow in the ground or inside an abandoned building. Owls usually lay a clutch of up to seven eggs at a time and the chicks are called owlets.

► Tawny owls nest in tree hollows. They lay 2–6 eggs and the fluffy chicks do not leave the nest until they are about 35 days old.

Working birds

766 **Birds of prey can be trained to work with people.** This is called falconry or hawking, and is an old skill that has been around for about 2500 years. The first trained birds of prey were probably used to catch birds for people to eat. In some places it is against the law to catch wild birds for use in falconry, so birds are specially bred.

Traditional hoods are handmade from 1–3 pieces of leather that are moulded and stitched

The bird may be tied to a leash

Bells may be attached to anklets on the bird's legs or fitted to the tail

A falconer pulls the hood off using the top knot

▼ ▶ Falconers use a range of equipment to train and fly their birds, such as this peregrine falcon.

A swing lure is used to train a falcon and is made from the wing of another bird

Hood braces are gently pulled to tighten the hood on the bird's head

767 **Birds most commonly trained are Harris hawks, peregrine falcons, sparrowhawks and goshawks, because they are intelligent.** Training takes time and patience. The first step is to get the bird used to people. Next, it has to be trained to hop onto the falconer's gloved fist, then to fly away – and return. To start, the bird may be tied to a line, but as it learns to return, it is released. When the bird does what the falconer wants, it is rewarded with food.

SEE THEM FLY

Visit a place where birds of prey are kept, so you can watch them fly. This could be a nature reserve, wildlife park or a place where trained birds of prey display their skills.

768 Working raptors have been used to keep public places clear of pigeons. Pigeon poo can cause damage to buildings and spread diseases, so falconers and their birds visit city centres to stop the pigeons from nesting nearby. One sight of a swooping, soaring raptor scares the pigeons into flying elsewhere.

769 Birds of prey help farmers to control pests. Fields of berry-producing plants attract birds such as starlings. A flock can quickly strip the trees or bushes, leaving the farmer with no crop. Rather than covering the plants with expensive netting or spraying with chemicals, farmers ask falconers and their raptors to scare the smaller birds away.

770 Falcons can patrol airports to keep flocks of birds away from planes. If birds fly into a plane's engines, they can cause damage that is expensive to repair and can be dangerous. Airports sometimes play bird of prey calls to scare away flocks.

▶ Falcons have proved effective at keeping the skies clear of smaller birds at airports.

335

Bird tales

771 Throughout history, people have recognized the might and power of birds of prey and told stories about them. Native American legends tell of thunderbirds, which are large birds that create storms by flapping their wings. They also tell of an evil creature called Eagleman, which had the head of a man but the body and wings of an eagle.

▲ Native American wood carvings often showed thunderbirds with their huge bills and eyes.

▲ This ancient Greek coin is decorated with an owl.

772 Unlucky Prometheus was a character in Greek mythology. He stole fire from Zeus, the father of the gods, and gave it to mankind. This angered Zeus so much that he chained Prometheus to a rock and ordered that an eagle would eat his liver every day. By night, his liver grew back so Prometheus was destined to an eternity of pain and misery.

773 In ancient Egypt, Horus was a falcon god, worshipped as the god of the sky. According to legend, Horus's right eye was the sun and his left eye was the moon and, as he flew across the sky, the sun and moon moved with him. More than 2000 years ago, Horus' worshippers built the huge Temple of Edfu to honour him and it still stands in Egypt today, along the banks of the river Nile.

◀ Pictures of the falcon god Horus cover walls of ancient Egyptian temples and shrines.

In ancient times, a Greek poet died after an eagle dropped a tortoise on his head. The raptor was probably trying to break the tortoise's shell and mistook the man's bald head for a large stone.

774 **A story from Finland tells how an eagle created the Earth and the heavens.** A woman called Luonnotar was floating in a giant ocean when an eagle made a nest on her knee and laid its eggs. However the nest fell, breaking the eggs. The shells became the heavens and Earth, the yolks became the sun and the egg whites became the moon.

▶ Griffins represented godly power and were often used to guard treasure, or to protect from evil.

775 **Griffins have featured in mythology and legends from Asia to Europe.** These fabled creatures were usually shown as lions with the heads of birds of prey, especially eagles.

Watching and tracking

776 Birdwatchers are called birders, while people who study birds more scientifically are called ornithologists. They use hides to watch raptors without disturbing them. Hides are covered in natural materials, such as branches or grass, for camouflage.

▲ A bird is trapped using a hawk mist net. Data taken from the bird will help to follow its movements and how it has grown.

777 Observing birds of prey is a fascinating hobby, but it is also an important job for scientists. They collect information to learn about how the birds live, where they migrate to and how many breeding adults there are. This work can then be used to follow how populations of birds of prey in different places increase or decrease.

778 Some birds of prey are studied using leg rings and by tracking their movements. They may be captured using a mist net, which catches birds in flight without harming them. Information is collected about each bird, such as its age, sex and size before an identity ring is put around its leg, or a tag is attached to its wing.

▼ Birds like these red kites can be studied from a hide. Birders use binoculars and telescopes to zoom in and watch them closely, without disturbing them.

ORDER FALCONIFORMES

Family	Number of species or types	Examples
Accipitridae	236	Kites, hawks, goshawks, buzzards, harriers, eagles, Old World vultures, sparrowhawks
Falconidae	64	Falcons, falconets, merlins, caracaras, kestrels
Cathartidae	7	New World vultures
Pandionidae	1	Osprey
Sagittariidae	1	Secretary bird

ORDER STRIGIFORMES

Family	Number of species or types	Examples
Tytonidae	21	Barn owls, bay owls and grass owls
Strigidae	159	Burrowing owl, eagle owl, fish owl, horned owls, long-eared owl, snowy owl, hawk owl

▲ Owls are placed in the order Strigiformes. All other raptors are in a separate order, called Falconiformes.

779 Identifying birds of prey can be **difficult.** Birders look for clues to help them work out what type of raptor they are observing, such as wing, tail and head shape. Colours and banding on plumage can also be used to discover what sex a bird is and whether it is a young bird or an adult. The way a raptor flies can also provide clues to identifying it.

MAKE A NOTE
When you see any bird you do not recognize make a note of its size, the shape of its wings and tail, the way it is behaving and the type of habitat you've seen it in. Use this information to discover its identity from a birdwatching book or website.

Raptors in peril

780 Birds of prey face few natural dangers, except those posed by humans and their way of life. Around half of all the world's species of migrating raptors are threatened with extinction. Many of these may die out because they are hunted or because their habitats are destroyed or polluted.

781 Raptors are killed by people who believe they are pests. Poison can be added to their food and left out for them to eat, or they may be shot. Birds and eggs are sometimes stolen from the wild by collectors or people who want to train birds for hawking or falconry.

▼ At night, barn owls may be confused by lights on roads or near towns and fly into the path of oncoming vehicles. Raptors can also be pulled into the sides of fast-moving lorries or cars.

Normal egg   Poisoned egg

▲ When female birds eat poisoned food, the poisons travel through their bodies and may reach the eggs growing inside them.

782 Habitats are damaged by chemicals used in farming or waste products from factories. When these chemicals enter birds' bodies – often by eating prey that have already been affected by them – they may cause permanent damage. Some chemicals stop eggshells from growing properly, so birds cannot produce healthy chicks.

▶ Long-billed vultures, such as this juvenile, are endangered.

783 When birds of prey drop in number, the environment suffers. Three species of Asian vultures help to stop the spread of disease to humans and other animals by eating carrion, but millions of these birds have died in just over ten years. The vultures are dying because a drug that is used to treat farm animals is deadly to any raptors that feed on their bodies.

784 Bateleurs live in open country across Africa, but their numbers are falling fast. They are struggling to survive because their natural habitat is being turned into farmland. Some large farming organizations are also poisoning them on purpose.

▶ Bateleur nests are disturbed as people settle near their habitats. Many birds are also trapped to be sold abroad.

Rescuing raptors

785 The Philippine eagle is one of the rarest raptors, but people are working hard to save it. There are probably fewer than 250 breeding pairs in the wild, although scientists have managed to breed them in captivity. The largest of all eagles, these birds have lost their homes to farmland and mines. Now they are protected by law and their land, nests and eggs are guarded.

▲ Even if the numbers of Philippine eagles stop falling, it may be impossible for the species to recover in the wild.

▶ Californian condors died in huge numbers after eating animals that had been shot with lead bullets. Lead is a poison that is still found in the environment.

787 Californian condors are vultures with wingspans of nearly 3 metres. They do not breed until they are about nine years old and only have one chick every two years. These birds once lived all over the USA, but by the 1980s there were very few left. They were all taken into captivity, making a total of 22. Since then they have been bred in protected places and some have been returned to the wild.

786 People who are interested in birds work together to protect them. BirdLife International is an organization that operates in more than 100 countries. It helps local conservation agencies protect birds' habitats and teach people how to respect the environment.

788 In many countries, endangered birds of prey are protected. It is illegal to hunt, trap or poison them. When protected raptors breed, nest locations are kept secret and volunteers may keep watch to make sure thieves do not steal the eggs. In some places, birds' habitats are protected and forests or woodlands cannot be turned into farmland or homes for people.

789 There are 24 types of raptor on the island of Madagascar and half of those are found nowhere else. People have campaigned to protect areas of habitat, such as the Manambolomaty Lakes, which are where the Madagascan fish eagle lives. Similar projects, called Species Survival Programs, have been set up in Madagascar and other places.

▲ Hand-rearing birds of prey is extremely difficult. Feeding them is more successful when the chick thinks a parent bird is looking after them.

▼ Birds that have been raised in captivity or treated for injuries or ill-health are always returned to the wild whenever possible. This bald eagle's release is a time of celebration for local bird-lovers.

SNAKES

790 Snakes have lived on our planet for more than 120 million years. There are nearly 3000 different species (type) of snake alive today. These spectacular, slithering serpents are superbly adapted to life without legs – the word 'serpent' means 'to creep'. Snakes are shy, secretive animals that avoid people whenever they can and will not usually attack unless they need to defend themselves.

▶ The first snakes to evolve were constricting snakes, such as this huge anaconda, which squeezes its prey to death in its strong coils.

What is a snake?

791 Snakes belong to the animal family group known as reptiles. They are related to lizards, turtles, tortoises, crocodiles and alligators. Snakes may have evolved from swimming or burrowing lizards that lived millions of years ago, and are in fact very distant cousins of the dinosaurs!

792 Snakes have long, thin bodies, with no legs, eyelids or external (outside) ears. They can't blink, so they always seem to be staring. Some lizards also have no legs, but they do have eyelids and outer ears.

▼ More than three-quarters of snake species, such as this python, aren't poisonous.

REPTILE FAMILY

Over half of all reptiles are lizards – there are nearly 5000 species.

Amphisbaenians, or worm lizards, are burrowing reptiles that live underground.

Snakes are the second largest group of reptiles, after lizards. Hundreds of species of snakes are poisonous.

Tuataras are rare, ancient and unusual reptiles from New Zealand.

Crocodiles, alligators, gharials and caimans are predators with long, narrow snouts and sharp teeth.

Turtles and tortoises have a hard shell on their back, which protects them from predators.

793 Like all reptiles, snakes are covered in waterproof scales. A snake's scales grow in the top layers of its skin to protect its body as it slides over the ground. Scales allow skin to stretch when the snake moves or feeds.

TRUE
OR FALSE?

1. Snakes have no eyelids.
2. A snake's tongue is shaped
   like a spoon.
3. Snakes need to eat five or
   six meals a day.

Answers:
1. True 2. False, it is shaped like
a fork 3. False, snakes don't need to
eat often and may eat only five or
six meals in a year.

▲ Snakes are most closely related to lizards, such as the Komodo dragon. It is the largest lizard in the world and can grow up to 3 metres in length.

794 A snake has a forked tongue that it regularly flicks in and out of its mouth. The tongue is used to taste the air and pick up information about the snake's environment. Only a few animals have forked tongues – such as the Komodo dragon, and some other lizards.

795 All snakes are meat-eaters and swallow their prey whole. Since a snake's body works at a slow rate, it takes a long time to digest its food and so can survive for months without eating. A big snake in the wild may eat only five or six meals in a year.

▼ An African rock python opens its jaws extremely wide to swallow an impala, which is the size of a small deer.

Where do snakes live?

796 **Snakes live all over the world on almost every continent.** There are no snakes on Antarctica, because it is too cold for them to survive. Snakes rely on their surroundings for warmth so they are most common in hot places, such as deserts and rainforests.

▶ This python lives in the rainforests of northeast Australia. Its waterproof skin helps to stop its body from drying out in the heat.

797 **The greatest variety of snakes live in rainforest habitats.** These warm places contain lots of food for snakes to eat and provide plenty of places to rest and shelter. Rainforests are always warm, enabling snakes to keep their body temperature up, which allows them to stay active all year round.

798 **The most widespread snake in the world is the adder.** This poisonous snake lives across Europe and Asia in a variety of habitats, including cold places. The adder's dark colour helps it to warm up quickly when it basks in sunlight, and it sleeps, or hibernates, through the cold winter months.

◀ Adders usually live in undisturbed countryside, from woodland and heathland to sand dunes and mountains.

The sandy-coloured woma python is well camouflaged in its dry desert habitat (home).

799 In Australia there are more poisonous snakes than non-poisonous ones. Australia is home to the taipan snake, which has one of the strongest and most powerful poisons of any land snake. It is very secretive and lives in desert areas where there are very few people, so not many people get bitten.

Taipan

800 Sea snakes live in warm, tropical waters, such as the Indian and Pacific Oceans. Most sea snakes can take in oxygen from the water through their skin, but they have to come to the surface regularly to breathe air. When underwater, sea snakes close off their nostrils with special valves.

Sea snakes have glands under their tongues that collect salt from their blood. When the snake flicks out its tongue the salt goes back into the water.

SNAKE HABITAT POSTER

You will need:
pen   paper   pictures of snakes
glue   atlas

Using a pen and paper trace a world map from an atlas. Draw on the biggest mountains, forests and deserts and then draw or stick on pictures of snakes from wildlife magazines or the Internet.

Big and small

801 The six biggest snakes are all boas and pythons. They are the boa constrictor, the anaconda, the reticulated python, the Indian python, the African rock python and the scrub python. These snakes all take a long time to warm up and need to eat a lot to keep their massive bodies working.

802 The longest snake in the world is the reticulated python. An average adult can grow to around 6 metres in length, but it has been known to grow much longer. This snake has an effective camouflage pattern on its scaly skin to help hide its huge body, so it can lie in wait for its prey without being seen.

803 The heaviest snake is the anaconda. This enormous snake can be as thick as an adult human and weigh as much as five children! It lives in the rivers of the Amazon rainforest in South America, where the water helps to support its enormous bulk. An anaconda grows up to an impressive 7 or 8 metres long.

I DON'T BELIEVE IT!

The biggest snake ever to have lived was as long as a bus! Known as *Titanoboa*, it lived in the rainforests of South America around 60 million years ago.

▼ It has taken nine people to support the weight of this 5-metre-long anaconda, from South America.

Reticulated
python

304 Some of the smallest living snakes are blind snakes. They burrow underground to feed on insects and other soil-dwelling creatures. Most are about 0 centimetres long. Even the biggest blind snakes only reach lengths of around 0 centimetres.

A reticulated python's head is usually between 0 and 25 centimetres in length.

Adder

Eyelash viper

Western diamondback rattlesnake

Fer-de-lance pit viper

◀ The biggest snakes are up to 10 metres long, while the smallest are less than a metre in length.

Black mamba

African rock python

Reticulated python

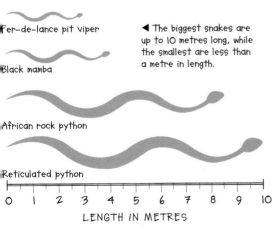

0	1	2	3	4	5	6	7	8	9	10

LENGTH IN METRES

▶ A Barbados thread snake looks more like a small worm than a snake.

Barbados thread snake

805 The world's smallest living snake is a type of thread snake, and is only 10 centimetres long. It usually lives under rocks on the island of Barbados in the Caribbean and probably feeds on termites. Females lay just one large egg and the young are about half as long as the adults.

Snake bodies

SHADOW SNAKES

You will need:
old socks   sticks   torch
white sheet
Make snake shapes by pulling l...
socks over your hands and arn...
Shine a torch onto the back of ...
white sheet and move your shad...
snakes behind the sheet to tell ...
scary snake story.

806 Snakes come in different shapes and sizes depending on their environment and lifestyle. They may be short, thick and slightly flattened, like a ground-dwelling rattlesnake, or long, thin and lightweight, like a tree snake. Burrowing snakes have tube-shaped bodies, which help them to slide through the soil.

Kidney

Kidne...

Intestines

Brain   Skull

Eye

Fangs

Venom gland

Tongue

Trachea (windpipe)

Triangular

Short, thick body

Loaf-shaped

Long, thin body

Tube-shaped body

807 Some snakes, such as rattlesnakes, have a distinct head and neck region. Others, such as blind snakes, look much the same at both ends. Pythons and vipers have short tails, while the tails of some tree snakes are longer than their bodies.

◄ The Texas blind snake's eyes are two dark spots under three small scales across the top of its head.

► A rattlesnake has an arrow-shaped head because of the venom (poison) sacs behind its eyes.

▲ These cross sections show five different snake body shapes, with the backbone and a pair of ribs inside.

808 There isn't much space inside a snake's body, so the organs are long and thin. Most snakes have only one working right lung, which does the work of two. A snake's skeleton consists mainly of a skull and a long, flexible backbone with up to 400 vertebrae (spine bones).

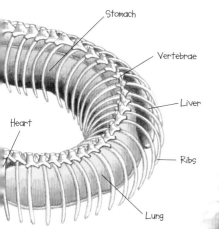

Tail

◄ The organs of this male water moccasin are elongated to fit into its long, thin body.

Rectum

Stomach

Vertebrae

Liver

Heart

Ribs

Lung

809 Like all reptiles, snakes are cold-blooded. They can't keep their bodies at a constant temperature, the way warm-blooded mammals and birds do. Their bodies stay the same temperature as their surroundings, so they bask in the Sun, or on warm surfaces to gain heat, and move into shade, underground burrows or cool water to cool down.

▼ In cooler parts of North America, thousands of garter snakes often emerge together from their hibernation dens in spring.

810 In colder places, snakes often sleep through the long winter months, waking up in spring when the weather is warmer. This winter sleep is called hibernation. Snakes often hibernate in caves, hollow trees, crevices under rocks or old burrows, where they are protected from the cold winter weather.

Scaly skin

811 A snake's skin is protected by a sheet of dry, horny scales that cover its body like a suit of armour. They are made from thick pieces of keratin – the substance that hair, feathers, nails and claws are made from. Snake scales are linked by hinges of thin keratin and usually fold back, overlapping each other.

▲ Some snakes have 'keeled' scales, with a raised ridge along the middle of each scale.

Head scales

Ventral scales on the underside of the snake's body

Scutes

Dorsal scales on the sides and back

▶ The number, shape, colour and arrangment of a snake's scales helps with identification.

Subcaudal scales under the tail

Scale

Outer layer (epidermis)

Lower layer (dermis)

▲ The areas of skin between a snake's scales allow the body to stretch, making it very flexible.

812 Most snakes have a row of broad scales called scutes underneath their bodies. These scutes go across the snake's belly from one side to the other and end where the tail starts They help the snake to grip the ground as it moves. Legless lizards don't have scutes, so this is one of the ways to tell them apart from snakes.

A few snakes polish their scales with a secretion from their nostrils. This may waterproof the scales or allow the snake to leave a scent trail as it slithers along.

814 As snakes move and grow their skin becomes scratched and damaged. Adult snakes slough (moult) their outer layer of skin up to six times a year, but young snakes shed their skin more often as they are growing quickly.

▲ Fluid builds up between the old and new spectacles (scales that cover the eye).

813 The texture of a snake's scales helps it to move and catch prey. The scales of coral snakes and burrowing snakes are smooth. This helps them slide easily through small spaces. Wart snakes are covered with rough scales, which help them to grip slippery fish.

815 A snake's eyes are protected by clear, bubble-like scales. These 'spectacles' or 'brilles' cloud over before a snake sheds its skin. Snakes become sluggish and bad-tempered just before their skin peels off, which may be because they cannot see well and their skin is itchy.

▲ The outer skin peels back from the head and comes off inside out, revealing the new layer of skin that has grown underneath.

◄ The shed skin of a snake is stretched, making it longer than the snake it covered.

355

Colours and patterns

816 **Some snakes are brightly coloured to warn predators that they are poisonous.** There are more than 90 species of coral snake, each with a different pattern of red, black and yellow or white bands. Birds have learnt to avoid snakes with these warning colours.

▼ The bright tail of the ring-necked snake distracts predators away from its fragile head.

817 **Some snakes shimmer with rainbow colours.** Snakes in the sunbeam snake family are named after the way their large, smooth, polished scales create a rainbow effect along their bodies. As they move, light strikes the thin, see-through outer layers of their scales, making their colours appear to change.

◄ The scales of the rainbow boa glimmer with different colours.

SNAKE BRACELET

You will need:
thin card   scissors
colouring pencils   hole punch
wool   beads
Cut a strip of card 20 centimetres long and 3 centimetres wide. Use colouring pencils to draw a snake pattern on it. Punch a hole in each end of the card then tie together with strips of wool. Once you have threaded beads onto the wool and tied a knot in each end it is ready to wear.

818 Some snakes use bright colours to startle or threaten predators. Ring-necked snakes are dull colours on top but have brightly coloured bellies. If threatened, this snake will curl its tail into a corkscrew, creating a sudden flash of colour and drawing attention away from its vulnerable head.

◀ The extraordinary nose shield of the leaf-nosed snake may help to camouflage it while it hunts.

819 Many snakes have colours and patterns that make them blend into their surroundings. Their camouflage helps them avoid predators and catch their prey. Patterns on their scales help to break up the outline of their bodies. The patterns on a gaboon viper make it look just like the dead leaves on the floor of an African rainforest.

▼ The gaboon viper is well camouflaged among the leaves as it lies in wait for its prey.

357

On the move

820 The way a snake moves depends on what species it is, its speed and the surface it is moving over. A snake may wriggle along in an S-shape (serpentine movement), pull half of its body along at a time (concertina movement) or pull its body forwards in a straight line (caterpillar movement).

◀ Tree snakes use an adapted form of concertina movement to move from branch to branch.

821 On smooth or sandy surfaces, snakes move by sidewinding. By anchoring its head and tail firmly on a surface, it can fling the middle part of its body sideways. A sidewinding snake moves diagonally, with only a small part of its body touching the ground at any time.

▼ Sidewinding snakes, such as this viper, leave tracks at a 45° angle to the direction of travel.

822 Tree snakes have strong, prehensile (gripping) tails, which coil around branches. Holding on tightly with its tail, a tree snake stretches forwards to the next branch, and then pulls up its tail. This is a sort of concertina movement

▲ Large, heavy snakes use their belly scutes to grip the ground and pull themselves forwards.

▲ Most snakes move in an S-shaped path, pushing forwards where their curves touch the ground.

▶ When using concertina movement, a snake bunches up its body (1) then stretches the front half forwards (2), and lastly, pulls up the back half of its body (3).

① ② ③

323 Sea snakes swim using S-shaped wriggles, rather like the serpentine movement used by many land snakes. To give them extra swimming power, sea snakes have broad, flat tails, which push against the water and propel them along.

▼ This high speed photo shows how a paradise tree snake flings its body into the air from a branch to glide for distances of up to 100 metres.

324 A few Asian tree snakes glide through the trees by spreading out their long ribs to create a sort of parachute. This slows down the snakes' fall, so that they float from tree to tree instead of plummeting straight down to the ground.

Super senses

825 Snakes rely on their senses of smell, taste and touch much more than sight or hearing. A snake's tongue is used to collect particles from the air and to touch and feel its surroundings. A snake has a special nerve pit called the Jacobson's organ in the roof of its mouth, which analyses tastes and smells collected by its tongue.

▲ A snake can flick its tongue in and out through a tiny opening even when its mouth is closed. An active snake will do this every few seconds, especially when it is hunting or feels threatened.

Jacobson's organ

Tongue

◄ A snake's tongue collects scent particles and chemicals from the air and places them in the two openings of the Jacobson's organ in the roof of its mouth.

826 Most snakes have well-developed eyes and some have good eyesight. Some tree snakes have a groove along the snout in front of each of their eyes, so they can see forwards to judge depth and distance. Coachwhip snakes are one of the few snakes to hunt mainly by sight, raising the front end parts of their bodies off the ground.

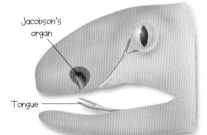

827 Day-hunting snakes usually have round pupils, whereas night-hunting snakes have vertical, slit-shaped pupils. Vertical pupils can be closed more tightly than round ones, helping protect the snake's eyes from bright light when it comes out to bask in the Sun during the day.

▶ The day-hunting oriental whip snake has a distinctive keyhole-shaped pupil.

▶ The round pupil of a Natal green snake is surrounded by a beautiful golden iris.

▼ By looking along grooves in its narrow, pointed snout, a vine snake can focus both eyes at once, giving it 3D vision.

▶ The eyelash viper has the typical slit-shaped pupil of a night-hunting snake.

828 Snakes have no outer ears or eardrums so they cannot hear sounds in the same way we do. They have an inner ear bone connected to the jaw, which helps them to sense ground vibrations. A snake can also pick up vibrations from the air through its skin.

829 Some snakes, such as pit vipers, boas and pythons, are able to sense the heat given off by their prey. They are the only animals that can do this and their unique sense allows them to track warm-blooded prey, such as rats, in the dark.

Heat pits

◀ Vipers have holes behind their nostrils that are lined with heat-sensitive cells. Boas and pythons have similar heat holes along their lips.

Hunting and eating

830 Most snakes eat a wide variety of prey depending on their size, the season and what is available. But a few snakes have very specific diets. Thirst snakes feed only on slugs and snails, queen snakes eat crayfish and children's pythons can move fast enough to catch bats.

▶ The common kingsnake can eat poisonous snakes. It can digest the venom so it is not harmed.

◀ The jaws of an egg-eating snake stretch to swallow an egg three times the diameter of its head.

◀ Once the egg has been swallowed, the snake arches its neck, forcing pointed bones in its throat to break through the shell.

◀ The snake then swallows the egg's nutritious contents, and regurgitates (coughs up) the crushed eggshell.

831 An egg-eating snake swallows eggs whole and uses the pointed ends of bones that jut into its throat to crack open the shell. Eggs are a useful source of food because they are rich in body-building protein as well as being easy to find.

I DON'T BELIEVE IT!

Large snakes can swallow prey up to a quarter of their own length. They have been known to eat leopards, gazelles and even small crocodiles!

832 Many snakes lie in wait to ambush their prey because they cannot move fast enough to chase after it. Snakes such as vipers, boas and pythons have wide bodies so they can eat big meals. They do not have breastbones, so they can move their ribs apart at the front to make their bodies even wider.

833 Some snakes, such as the king cobra, even eat other snakes! A snake's body is easier to swallow than other prey, such as mammals or birds, because it is a thin, smooth shape. Most snakes that eat poisonous snakes are immune to their poisons.

834 Some snakes set traps for their prey. The death adder has a brightly coloured tip to its tail, which looks similar to a worm. The adder wriggles this 'worm' to lure lizards, birds and worms within reach of its poisonous jaws.

▼ Young Mexican cantils have a bright green or yellow tip to their tail. They use this to lure prey, such as frogs, lizards or rodents.

363

Teeth and jaws

835 **Most snakes have short, sharp, curved teeth to grip and hold their prey.** The teeth are no good for chewing or tearing up food, which is why snakes swallow their prey whole. A snake's teeth often break as it feeds, but new teeth grow to replace broken ones.

836 **Many smaller snakes swallow prey alive, but larger snakes kill their food before they eat it.** Around 700 species of snakes use poison, called venom, to immobilize or kill their prey. The venom is injected into the prey through large, pointed teeth, called fangs, which are connected to glands (bags) of venom in the snake's head.

▶ Rear-fanged snakes need to chew their venom into their prey for 15 minutes or more before the poison takes effect.

837 **Snakes can have fangs at the front or back of their mouths.** Some fanged snakes, such as vipers and cobras, have fangs at the front, while a few snakes, such as the African boomslang, have fangs at the back. Back fangs may either just be large back teeth, or they may have grooves for venom.

▼ Fangs at the back of a snake's mouth help to kill prey as it is being swallowed.

Fangs are towards the rear of the mouth, below the eye

The large fangs of an eyelash viper swing forward to inject venom into its prey.

838 Snakes in the viper family, such as rattlesnakes and eyelash vipers, have moveable fangs. These can be folded back against the roof of the mouth when they are not in use. When the snake strikes, the fangs swing forwards and bite into the prey, injecting venom deep inside the victim's body.

Most poisonous snakes have hollow fangs at the front of their mouth.

The puff adder has long, folding fangs and strong venom. It is Africa's most dangerous snake.

839 Snakes can open their mouths wider than any other animal, thanks to hinged bones and a stretchy ligament joining the top and bottom jaws. The two sides of a snake's jaw can also move independently of each other, allowing the snake to 'walk' its jaws from side to side as it forces food down its throat, with first one side pulling and then the other.

The red arrow shows how the lower jaw is attached to the skull like a hinge, allowing the jaw to open widely. The blue arrows show how the two sides of the jaw can move backwards and forwards separately.

The lower jaw can stretch wide apart because it is in two halves, joined at the front by a stretchy ligament

Poisonous snakes

840 **Venom is a highly modified form of saliva (spit).** Saliva is a type of digestive juice, so venom contains enzymes (particles that break down food). These start to digest and soften the meal even before the snake has swallowed it. Snakes don't run out of venom, because their glands make more poison as they use it up.

▶ Eyelash vipers catch prey while hanging from tree branches. Small animals are overcome by venom in minutes.

VENOM KEY

① Venom gland sits in the side of the snake's head

② A tube leads from the gland down to the fangs

③ Fangs are hollow with a venom canal down the middle

④ Venom is injected deep into the prey's muscle tissue

841 **Snake venom is a complicated substance that works in two main ways.** Snakes such as cobras, coral snakes and sea snakes have venom that attacks the victim's nervous system, causing paralysis (stopping all movement) and preventing breathing. Snakes such as vipers have venom that destroys body tissues, attacking the circulatory system (blood vessels) and muscles.

842 Venom is useful because it allows snakes to overcome their prey quickly without being injured. Snakes with powerful venom, such as vipers, tend to bite their prey quickly and then retreat to a place of safety while their poison takes effect. If the victim crawls away to die, the snake follows its scent trail to keep track of its meal.

▲ The venom of the common krait is very powerful — these snakes are even more poisonous than common cobras.

▼ As the snake bites down, venom flows down its fangs and can be collected in the bottom of a jar.

844 If a person is bitten by a venomous snake the deadliness of the bite varies. The size and health of the victim, the size of the snake, the number of bites, the amount of venom injected and the speed and quality of medical treatment are important. Some of the most dangerous snakes in the world are the black mamba, Russell's viper and the beaked sea snake.

▶ The black mamba is the longest venomous snake in Africa and is named after the black colour inside its mouth, which it displays if threatened.

843 Venom is collected from poisonous snakes by making them bite down on the top of a jar. The venom is used to make a medicine called antivenin, which helps people recover from snake bites. Snake venom can also be used to make other medicines that treat high blood pressure, heart failure and kidney disease.

I DON'T BELIEVE IT!
The king cobra is the world's longest venomous snake, growing to lengths of over 5.4 metres. Its venom is powerful enough to kill an elephant!

845 **The two main groups of poisonous snakes are vipers and elapids.** The cobras of Africa and Asia belong to the elapid family, as do the colourful coral snakes of the Americas and the mambas of Africa. Elapids have short, fixed fangs at the front of their mouths, as do their relatives, the sea snakes.

846 **Cobras can spread out the skin around their neck into a wide 'hood' that makes them look larger and frightening to their attackers.** The hood is supported by long, movable ribs in the cobra's neck. Some cobras have huge eye-spots on the back of the hood, which probably startle predators.

847 **To defend themselves, spitting cobras spray venom through small slits in the tips of their fangs.** They aim for the eyes of an attacker and can spit venom for distances of up to 1.8 metres – the height of a tall man.

◄ Cobras follow the movement of a snake charmer's pipe. They cannot actually hear the music.

Spitting cobras spray their venom
pushing air out of their lungs while
rcing the venom through
les in the front of
eir fangs.

QUIZ

1. Do cobras have moveable fangs?
2. Why does a puff adder inflate its body like a balloon?
3. How far can spitting cobras spray their venom?

Answers:
1. No, cobras have fixed fangs 2. To defend itself 3. Up to 1.8 metres

348 The viper family of venomous snakes includes the dders, night adders, vipers, ush vipers, rattlesnakes, opperheads, asps and pit vipers. ll vipers have long, hollow fangs hat can be folded back inside their mouths. The largest viper is the ushmaster, which lives in the forests f Central and South America and grows up to 3.6 metres in length.

▼ The palm viper lives in trees and shrubs, often at the base of palm fronds. Its prehensile tail acts as an anchor.

849 The puff adder inflates its lungs when threatened, which makes its body puff up like a balloon, making it look bigger than it really is. The saw-scaled viper is also named after its threat display because it makes a rasping sound with its jagged-edged scales.

369

Crushing coils

850 Snakes that squeeze their prey to death by wrapping it tightly in their strong coils are called constrictors. All boas and pythons are constrictors, as are the sunbeam snakes and some of the snakes in the colubrid family, such as rat snakes and kingsnakes.

▼ 1. The snake holds its prey in its teeth and squeezes it to death in its strong coils.

▲ 2. When the animal is dead, the snake opens its mouth very wide and starts to swallow its meal.

851 Constricting snakes usually hold the head end of their prey with their sharp teeth. They then throw their coils around the animal's body and squeeze hard to stop it from breathing. Each time the victim breathes out, the snake squeezes a little harder, until it dies from suffocation or shock.

852 The time it takes for the snake's prey to die depends on the size of the prey and how strong it is. When the prey stops struggling, the snake relaxes its grip, unhinges its jaws and starts to force its meal down its throat.

853 Prey is usually swallowed head-first. The legs or wings of the animal fold back against the sides of the body and the fur or feathers lie flat – making it easier for the snake to swallow. Slimy saliva in the snake's mouth helps the prey to slide down its throat and into its stomach.

854 When it is swallowing a large meal, a snake finds it difficult to breathe. It may take a long time to swallow a big animal. The snake moves the opening of its windpipe to the front of its mouth so that it can keep breathing while it swallows.

▼ 3. A snake's meal forms a bulge in the middle of its body while it is being digested. It may take days, or even weeks, to be absorbed completely.

Boas and pythons

855 **Two powerful types of constricting snakes are boas and pythons.** Unlike many other types of snake, most of them have a working left lung, hip bones and the remains of back leg bones. Many boas and pythons have heat-sensitive jaw pits to detect their prey.

856 **Many boas and pythons have markings that give them excellent camouflage.** The patterns help them to lie in wait for their prey without being seen. The sand boa perfectly matches the rocks and sand of its desert habitat.

▲ The shape of the Kenyan sand boa's mouth and jaws helps it to dig through soft sand.

857 **The ball python, or royal python, from West Africa, coils into a tight ball when it is threatened.** Its head is well protected in the middle of its coils and it can even be rolled along the ground in this position.

▶ A ball python in a defensive ball shows off its camouflage colours. These snakes can live for up to 50 years.

358 The emerald tree boa and the green tree python look alike. These two snakes live in different parts of the world and are not closely related, but they look and behave in a similar way because they both live in rainforest environments.

Emerald tree boa

▲▼ Emerald tree boas and green tree pythons rest in the same way, coiled around branches. They grip tightly with their prehensile tails.

359 Boas and pythons live in different places around the world. Most boas live in Central and South America, while pythons live in Africa, southeast Asia and Australia. Another difference between the two snake groups is that all boas (except for one species) give birth to live young, while all pythons lay eggs.

I DON'T BELIEVE IT!

The smallest type of python in the world is the anthill python, which grows to a maximum length of 30 centimetres.

Green tree python

Survival skills

860 **Snakes have delicate bodies and are vulnerable to attack from a variety of predators.** Animals such as foxes, racoons, crocodiles, baboons and even other snakes will attack them. Predators that specialize in snakes include the secretary bird of the African grasslands, which stamps on snakes to kill them.

861 **Rattlesnakes warn predators to keep away by shaking the hollow scales on their tails, making a buzzing sound.** Each time a rattlesnake sheds its skin, an extra section of the tail remains, making its rattle one section longer.

◀ A rattlesnake's 'rattle' is a chain of hollow tail tips, which make a warning sound when shaken.

862 **Most predators prefer to eat live prey, so the hognose snake and the grass snake pretend to be dead if they are attacked.** They roll onto their backs, open their mouths and keep very still until the predator goes away.

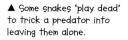

▲ Some snakes 'play dead' to trick a predator into leaving them alone.

863 The harmless milk snake copies the colour pattern of the venomous coral snake. The two snakes look so similar that predators can't tell the difference between them, and leave the milk snake alone.

Coral snake

Milk snake

◀ A mongoose is agile enough to kill snakes such as cobras. It is partly immune to the venom and is protected by its thick fur coat.

864 Spraying smelly liquid at a predator, or smearing itself with an unpleasant scent, is a good way for a snake to escape attack. Many snakes, such as the cottonmouth, the hognose snake and the Chinese stink snake, give off a nasty-smelling yellow or green fluid when they are picked up or attacked.

375

Courtship

865 At certain times of year, usually in the spring or the rainy season, mature male and female snakes search for a mate. They are ready to mate when they are between two and five years old. Male snakes find females by following their scent trails, which signal that they are ready to mate.

▶ Blue-banded sea snakes stay close to each other during courtship and females give birth to between three and five young in the water. The young can swim and feed as soon as they are born.

866 Male boas and pythons have small spurs on the ends of their tiny back leg bones. They use these spurs to tickle the females during courtship, and also to fight with other males. Females may also have spurs, but these are usually smaller than the spurs of the males.

867 Many snakes mate when they emerge from hibernation in spring. Male garter snakes emerge from hibernation first so they can warm up in the Sun and be ready to compete for the females when they emerge.

▲ During courtship, a male red-sided garter snake lies with its body pressed closely against the female and presses its chin against her head.

868 Rival male snakes of some species, such as adders, mambas, vipers and some rattlesnakes, compete for females in a test of strength that is rather like a wrestling match. They coil around each other, sometimes rearing up into the air, and try to push each other down to the ground. These tests of strength can last for hours.

► A fighting male rattlesnake sways to and fro, looking for a chance to coil his body around the rival and pin him to the ground.

869 Female flowerpot snakes are believed to be able to produce baby snakes without mating with males, using a form of reproduction known as 'parthenogenesis'. All the young produced in this way are females, but they can reproduce clones of themselves when the conditions are ideal, without having to wait for a male.

Laying eggs

870 About 80 percent of snakes reproduce by laying eggs. A snake's eggshell is tough, leathery, flexible and almost water-tight, protecting the developing baby inside from drying out. Female snakes usually lay about five to 20 eggs at a time.

871 Most female snakes don't look after their eggs once they have been laid. Only a few, such as the bushmaster snake, some cobras and most pythons, stay with their eggs to protect them from predators and bad weather.

▼ This cutaway artwork shows a female Burmese python laying eggs. She may lay up to 100 eggs in a single clutch (batch).

872 The female king cobra is the only snake known to make a nest for her eggs. She builds a mound of rotten leaves, twigs and plant material, lays her eggs in the middle and then perches on top to prevent predators, such as wild boars, from eating them.

873 Female grass snakes and rat snakes lay their eggs in compost heaps or manure heaps. The warmth given off by the rotting plants helps to speed up the development of their eggs.

▲ The grass snake is the only snake in Britain that lays eggs. Females lay 10–40 eggs at a time.

① When fully developed, a baby snake uses the egg tooth on the tip of its snout to tear a hole in the egg.

② The snake tastes the air with its forked tongue. It may stay in the shell for a few days.

③ Eventually, the snake decides to uncoil its slim body and begins to wriggle free of the egg.

874 Baby snakes develop inside eggs for six to 12 weeks, feeding on the yolk stored inside. When it is ready to hatch, a baby snake makes a slit in the eggshell with a sharp egg tooth on its snout. A few hours after hatching, the egg tooth drops off.

④ The baby snake slides along in S-shaped curves to begin its life in the wild.

Giving birth

875 About 20 percent of all snakes give birth to live babies. Boas, rattlesnakes, garter snakes and adders don't lay eggs. Instead, the babies develop inside the mother, and are contained inside clear, tough sacs called membranes instead of shells.

▶ Baby eyelash vipers are about 15–18 centimetres long when they are born. They stay with their mother for about two weeks until they moult their skin for the first time.

The babies have white tips to their tails to lure prey close enough for them to capture

876 Snakes that give birth to live young often live in cold climates. The warmth inside the mother's body helps the baby snakes to develop. The mother can also look for warm places to soak up the Sun's heat, which speeds up the development of her young.

877 Baby snakes that develop inside their mother are better protected than eggs that are laid on the ground. A pregnant snake is heavy, so she often hides away to avoid predators. The extra weight of her developing babies also makes it harder for her to chase prey.

878 Most sea snakes usually give birth to live young, which means they do not have to come onto land to lay eggs. The baby sea snakes are born underwater and have to swim up to the surface to take their first breath. Yellow-bellied sea snakes breed in warm oceans and females give birth to between one and 10 young after five to six months.

879 Most snakes that give birth to live young do not look after their babies when they are born. Venomous snakes are born with their venom glands full of poison, so they can give a dangerous bite to predators soon after birth.

Save our snakes!

880 The biggest threat to snakes comes from humans who are destroying their natural habitats. Many snakes are killed by cars and trucks on the road. They are also killed to make tourist souvenirs or for use in traditional medicines.

▲ Some snakes are used to make traditional medicines by soaking them in rice wine, or another type of alcohol.

881 One reason snakes are important is because they control insect and rat populations. To find out the best ways of protecting and conserving snakes, scientists fit them with radio transmitters or tags to mark individuals and collect data about their secretive lives.

882 During the Hindu festival of Nagpanchami, thousands of snakes have traditionally been trapped and killed. Volunteers now rescue the snakes, which are protected by Indian law, and return them to the wild if possible.

▼ Radio-tracking snakes helps conservationists work out why a species is becoming rare and to plan the management of wildlife parks.

SNAKE CONSERVATION

Visit the International Reptile Conservation Foundation's website at www.IRCF.org to learn how conservation groups help save endangered snakes and other reptiles.

▲ In 1995, only about 60 Antiguan racer snakes survived in the wild. Now conservation efforts have increased numbers to around 300.

883 The world's rarest snake is probably the Antiguan racer. The species nearly died out when people introduced rats and mongooses to its habitat. It was also killed by people who wrongly thought it was dangerous. Removing the predators, educating the public and breeding these snakes in captivity may help them survive.

884 There are many rare snakes all over the world. They include the San Francisco garter snake, which is the most endangered reptile in North America and the eastern indigo, the largest snake in the USA. The king cobra of Asia is rare, as is Dumeril's boa, which is only found on Madagascar. The broad-headed snake is Australia's most endangered snake and the rarest snake in the UK is the smooth snake.

▶ Visting a zoo with snakes is a good way to learn about these fascinating creatures.

383

CATS AND KITTENS

885 Cats make great pets. Perhaps your family has a cat? These creatures can be warm, friendly and funny. They are quite independent and don't need as much attention as dogs do. However, cats still need our care – fresh food and water every day, a safe place to sleep and someone to look after their health.

◀ A mother cat, or queen, relaxes with her kittens. The female cat is one of the animal world's best mothers. She watches over her kittens day and night, feeds them with her milk, and licks, cleans and grooms them.

Feline family

886 All the cats in the world form one big family — what animal experts call the family Felidae. This includes about 38 different kinds or species of cat, from massive tigers and lions to our own pet cats. The cat family belongs to the larger group of mammals called carnivores, along with dogs, foxes, wolves, stoats and weasels.

▼ The sabre-tooth cat *Smilodon* was bigger than a tiger and lived in North America. It died out about 10,000 years ago.

887 Big cats include lions, tigers, leopards, snow leopards, clouded leopards, jaguars and cheetahs. The biggest are tigers, especially the Siberian tiger that lives in cold, snowy northeast Asia. It can grow to 3 metres long including its tail, and weigh up to 350 kilograms. That's 100 times heavier than a pet cat!

◀ The tiger's dark stripes help it to hide in long grass and tangled undergrowth.

888 The cheetah is the world's fastest runner, at 100 kilometres an hour. In ancient times rich people raised cheetahs in North Africa and the Middle East. They were put on leads, like dogs. However, they were never truly tamed, and often escaped.

889 The large cat with the most names is the cougar – also called the mountain lion, puma or American panther. People tried to tame young cougars and keep them as pets. But as they grew, their wild instincts, or feelings, become stronger. A fully grown cougar can be very dangerous.

▲ Cougars live from the north of North America, all the way down to the south of South America.

890 There are about 20 kinds of medium-sized cats. Lynx live all around the north of the world and hunt hares and deer in cold forests and on icy mountains. In Africa the spotted serval preys on rats and birds. In Southeast Asia the fishing cat swims after frogs, crabs and fish.

▲ The serval has a slim body and long legs. It runs very fast, like its bigger cousin, the cheetah.

▲ The cheetah has a very bendy back that arches up and down as it runs, giving extra speed.

MAKE A SABRE-TOOTHED CAT MASK

You will need:
cardboard paints elastic scissors
1. Ask an adult to cut out a cat's face shape from card.
2. Cut out holes for the eyes and paint on whiskers and fur.
3. Attach some elastic to go around the back of your head.
4. Put on your mask and growl!

Small cats in the wild

891 All kinds, or breeds, of pet cats belong to the same single type, or species, which scientists call *Felis cattus*. Some kinds of cats that live in the wild are even smaller than our pet cats. Most live in forests and jungles. Their fur is spotted and striped so that they blend in with the trees, branches and leaves, and their shadows. This means they can creep up on prey without being noticed.

892 The jungle cat of southern Asia is slightly larger than a pet cat. It is also called the reed or swamp cat since it hunts along the banks of rivers, swamps, pools and ditches. Its main food is rats, birds, lizards, snakes and fish. It also eats frogs and even toads. Unlike many cats, the jungle cat does not mind prowling about looking for food during the day. It often lives near villages and towns and does not seem to mind people nearby. However, it usually stays hidden among bushes and undergrowth.

▼ An adult jungle cat. Jungle cat kittens have close-set stripes and look like tiny tigers. However, the stripes fade as they grow up.

893 Nearly all cats are good climbers, but the margay of South America is one of the best climbers of all. It can run straight up a tree trunk – and run head-first straight down again! The margay is about the same size as a pet cat. Like all cats, it is a hunter. It catches squirrels, tree rats, possums and small birds.

▲ The Andean cat wraps its furry tail around itself when it sleeps, to keep warm in the bitter cold of the mountains.

▼ The black-footed cat has dark spots on its body that lengthen into rings on its legs and tail. It lives in hot, dry, rocky grasslands.

895 The Andean cat is small, only the size of a pet cat – but very tough. It lives high in the Andes Mountains of South America, like a tiny 'mountain lion'. Its thick fur protects it from the icy winds as it hunts small creatures.

894 The black-footed cat of southern Africa can weigh less than 2 kilograms. That's smaller than most pet cats, which usually weigh 3 to 4 kilograms. Because it is so little, the black-footed cat catches little prey too, such as small lizards, baby birds, spiders, and even worms and termites.

I DON'T BELIEVE IT!

Many cats were once hunted for their fur coats, which were used to make hats, boots, gloves and similar items. Today most cats in the wild are protected by law.

The first pets

896 **All pet or domestic cats probably came from the cat species known as the wildcat (*Felis silvestris*).** It looks like a slightly larger, heavier version of the pet cat known as the tabby. The wildcat still lives naturally in many places today, including Scotland, Europe, Africa and Asia. Sometimes wildcats breed with pet cats.

▶ A wildcat pauses to crouch on a branch, looking and listening for prey — or danger.

897 **The first pet or domestic cats were tamed from the type of wildcat that lives in and around Egypt in north Africa.** This is called the African or Abyssinian type of wildcat. It still survives today in the wild. If its kittens are taken in by people and reared from a very young age, they become friendly pets. In fact, this is how the first domestic cats gradually evolved. The European or forest type of wildcats, as found in Scotland, are much more 'wild' than their African cousin — they are fierce and almost impossible to tame, even if people raise them from tiny kittens.

◀ In ancient Egypt people worshipped a goddess called Bastet, who was kind and gentle. She looked after women and cats. Bastet sometimes appeared with the head of a lioness, when she was supposed to be protecting the king in battle.

898 We think the first domestic or pet cats date back to ancient Egypt, more than 5000 years ago. Perhaps this happened when African wildcats waited around houses or food and grain stores, attracted by pests such as mice and rats. The cats gradually got used to people, and the people became friendly with the helpful, pest-killing cats. When the Great Pyramids and temples of Egypt were built, important rulers or pharaohs were preserved as mummies – so were many cats.

899 There are pictures, statues and carvings of cats from ancient Greece and Rome, more than 2000 years ago. The Roman city of Pompeii was mostly destroyed when the volcano Mount Vesuvius erupted in the year AD 79. A mosaic picture that was undamaged shows a tabby-like cat attacking a bird.

▲ The bodies of some Egyptian cats were preserved as mummies and buried in special tombs.

◀ The Abyssinian breed of pet cat is clever and friendly. It also likes freedom, so does not like being kept in a small place such as a town house.

900 Today the pet cat that is most like the very first domestic cats is probably the Abyssinian breed. It usually has large pointed ears, orange eyes, and brown or tawny fur with faint patches of darker brown or black.

Pet pampering

901 A cat can make a great pet — but only for certain people. A pet cat that receives care, comfort and companionship will be a loving friend for many years. However, some people simply don't like cats. They become nervous or worried when a cat is near. The cat senses this and becomes nervous too.

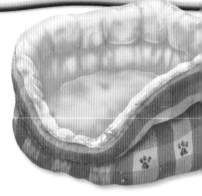

▲ A comfy cat basket is a safe place for warm naps.

◀ ▼ Small moving toys are fun to chase. A flea collar, comb and brush keep the cat's fur clean.

902 When people plan to get a pet cat, they should ask — 'Do we have time?' Like any pet, a cat needs regular food, water and comfort. Some people say that female cats are friendlier and less trouble, while males or toms are more independent and roam further. But every cat, like every human, has its own personality.

I DON'T BELIEVE IT!

Every year, thousands of cats are abandoned or made homeless by thoughtless owners. They are left to live as stray cats. This is why there are cat rescue centres.

903 It is a good idea to buy a basic 'cat kit' before your new pet arrives. This includes strong plastic bowls or dishes for food and drink, cat food, a brush, and usually a litter tray or box (toilet tray) for droppings. Some owners buy their cat lots of toys and a warm padded basket for sleeping. But part of the fun with cats is that they don't always do what we want, and they may ignore these luxuries!

904 There are many places to obtain a new pet cat, such as pet shops, friends, rescue centres, cat breeders and cat dealers. Generally, it's best to get a cat from someone who knows a lot about them and who can give proper advice. A new cat should be checked by a knowledgeable person such as a vet or local cat breeder.

906 Sometimes a cat does not want to be picked up, in which case it's best not to try — otherwise, you might get a scratch. If a cat does not mind, then it can be picked up carefully with both hands under the body, and held against our own body with the rear legs supported by our hand or arm. A cat must feel well supported and confident, or it will be frightened.

◀ Food and water can be put in two separate bowls or one double bowl, using the cat's own fork (rather than your own) for the food.

▶ A cat's lower body must be supported by one hand, so the cat feels safe and does not 'dangle'.

905 Cats are naturally clean animals. However, we should always wash our hands after handling them, their food and their litter trays. Otherwise we could catch something from them — or they might catch something from us!

◀ A litter (toilet) tray must be checked every day, especially for cats that live mainly indoors.

Mealtime

907 Cats are carnivores – their basic food is meat. This includes fish, and poultry such as chicken, as well as animal meat. Most pet foods made for cats contain much of the goodness they need. Dry cat biscuits are useful because they do not go rotten or bad as quickly as fresh meat if uneaten. Cats like to eat and drink without interference, so it's best not to stroke a cat when it is eating – just leave it alone.

908 It's best to give a cat different foods, so that it gets a wide range of nourishment. It's also best to feed a cat in the same place each time, preferably somewhere quiet and calm like a corner of a room, using its own clean feeding bowl and mat. Usually two meals each day are best – morning and evening. Kittens and young growing cats need to have smaller meals more often as they are using a lot of energy as they run around and grow.

▼ Two cats must get to know and trust each other before they will eat and drink close together. In the wild, they could be very hungry and try to steal each other's food.

909 Some owners give their cat treats such as specially cooked rich meats, cream and other titbits. This is fine now and again, but not every day. Cats may seem to be 'fussy eaters', always wanting the most expensive foods. But if they are hungry, they will soon eat cheaper foods.

910 Overweight cats can be unhealthy just like overweight people. Cats are naturally sleek hunters, and if they get too fat, they are at risk from various problems such as stiff joints and heart disease. It's unwise to give a cat too much food. Leftover meat soon goes smelly and rotten, and attracts pests such as flies. Adjust the amount you give so the cat's food bowl is virtually empty by the time of its next meal.

QUIZ

1. What are overweight cats particularly at risk of?

2. How often should you feed an adult cat?

3. Why is it a bad idea to leave leftover cat food lying around?

Answers:
1. Stiff joints and heart disease. 2. Twice a day, once in the morning and once in the evening 3. It attracts pests such as flies

Supreme hunter

911 Everything about a cat is designed for silent, stealthy hunting — especially when it's dark. A pet cat is smaller than most other cat species, but is just the same in its body build and structure, or anatomy. It has strong muscles, padded paws for silent walking, excellent senses of sight and hearing, and sharp claws and teeth.

912 Inside its body, a cat has the same main parts as a dog, rabbit, horse, monkey and you — in fact, any mammal. It has a skeleton made of bones, a heart to pump blood, lungs to breathe air, and a stomach and intestines (guts) to digest food.

▲ A cat creeps towards its prey very slowly, bit by bit. It tries not to make any noise and crouches low to stay mostly hidden. If it feels the prey has noticed it, the cat may 'freeze' completely still, even for several minutes.

913 A cat has five clawed toes on each front paw, and four on each back paw. The innermost toe on the front paw is higher up on the side of the foot, more like a thumb. Usually, muscles pull the claws up and into the toe, hiding them in small pockets or sheaths. This prevents the claws becoming worn and blunt. When a cat wants to extend or unsheath its claws, foot and toe muscles pull the claws out and down, ready for action. Claws are used for grabbing prey, gripping when climbing, scratching in defence and grooming.

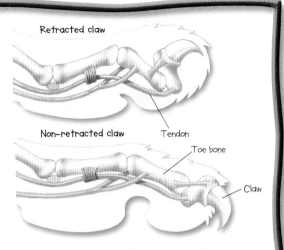

Retracted claw

Non-retracted claw   Tendon

Toe bone

Claw

▲ Normally the claws are pulled up or retracted. To extend them, muscles in the legs pull ropelike tendons to move the toe bones and tilt the claw down.

914 Cats often leap, run and climb up trees or along ledges, walls, fences and branches – yet their amazing balance means they hardly ever fall. The tail is very important at these times. The cat can swish or bend its tail to help its balance when walking along a narrow ledge or branch.

▼ A cat's skeleton has most of the bones that we have. The main extra ones are in the tail.

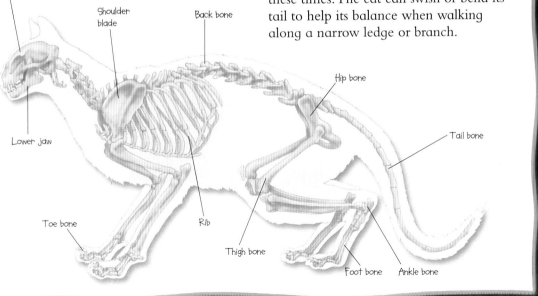

Skull

Shoulder blade

Back bone

Hip bone

Lower jaw

Tail bone

Toe bone

Rib

Thigh bone

Foot bone   Ankle bone

Feeling sensitive

Pupil closed

▲ In bright daylight the cat's pupil narrows to a slit, allowing less light in.

Pupil open

▲ In darkness the pupil widens to let in as much light as possible, and may become a circle.

Nictitating membrane

◀ A cat has a 'third eyelid' called the haw or nictitating membrane, on the inner side of its eye. This can move partly across to protect the eyeball.

915 Cats have better hearing than us — especially for high-pitched noises such as mouse squeaks. Also, a cat can twitch and move its ears to find out which direction a sound is coming from. It does not have to turn its whole head, as we have to.

916 A cat has large eyes to see well in the dark. At the front of the eye is a black area called the pupil. If it is nighttime, the pupil opens wide to let in as much light as possible. In daytime the pupil narrows to a slit, to stop too much light damaging the eye. Also, there is a mirror-like layer at the back of the eye called the tapetum. This bounces or reflects light within the eye, which helps the cat to see better in darkness.

THE CAT'S WHISKERS

You will need:
drinking straws   sticky-tape
1. Fasten some drinking straws to the edges of your sabre-toothed cat mask (page 387) with sticky-tape.
2. Put the mask on and walk around. Can you feel when your whiskers touch something, even with your eyes closed?

917 A cat's sense of smell is better than ours, but not as good as a dog's. Cats sniff food and drink to check they are safe. They also smell the scents of their owners, other people, other cats, and any animals nearby. Familiar scents mean a cat is happy and relaxed. Strange scents make it nervous.

918 Cats often rub their faces against their owners, as well as furniture and other objects around their home. The cat is spreading its own scent substances from parts called glands around its face and cheeks. This marks out the cat's home area or territory and warns strange cats to stay away.

919 A cat's tongue not only tastes food and drink, it's also used for cleaning and grooming. The tongue has a very rough upper surface, like a file or rasp. The cat uses this to scrape meat off bones, drink, and clean its own fur and skin. When a cat drinks, its tongue becomes spoon-shaped to scoop up the liquid. This is called lapping. The tongue can also be pushed out a long way so that the cat can lick around its mouth, whiskers and nose.

920 The extra-long hairs on the sides of a cat's nose are its whiskers. The skin at their bases detect any movements of the whiskers. This helps the cat to 'feel its way' in the dark.

▶ A cat rubs scent from its cheeks onto familiar objects – from a chair to its owner. This is the cat's way of saying: 'I live here and own these things – so other cats should keep clear!'

Do cats have nine lives?

921 There is an old saying that 'a cat has nine lives' – but of course this is not really true. It actually means that cats often seem to survive dangers and hazards that other animals can't. This is because of a cat's keen senses, quick reactions, strong muscles and great balance.

▲ Cats may seem to get stuck up trees, especially when young and not experienced in climbing. However, if left alone, and not frightened by noisy people crowding around below it, the cat can often work out how to climb down safely.

922 Another old saying is 'curiosity killed the cat'. This has some truth. Cats are naturally curious. They want to find out what is around corners and above or below things. This probably comes from their wild behaviour long ago, when looking for food. Cats sometimes squeeze into narrow spaces, but after a time they usually get themselves out of these tight spots.

923 A cat's excellent balance and fast reactions mean that it can fall from high places yet usually lands unhurt. The cat twists its body around as it falls. Then it straightens its legs to point downwards, and immediately gets ready to bend its legs as it touches down on all four feet, to cushion the shock of landing.

924 A cat is quick to defend itself against enemies. Its hair stands on end, so the cat looks twice as big. It also snarls and hisses and bares its teeth, showing off these sharp weapons. This serves as a warning to the enemy to keep away or risk being harmed. It is best not to get too close to a cat that is behaving like this, as it may strike out in fear and self-defence.

I DON'T BELIEVE IT!

Occasionally, cats have been accidentally locked in their houses by owners going on holiday. Some cats have lived without food for more than two weeks, surviving only on water in drops of condensation on glass windows.

▼ A frightened cat crouches with ears flattened and teeth bared, ready to defend itself.

▼ Stray cats can make litter problems worse by tearing open waste bags and dragging old meat from bins.

925 There are various names for pet cats who have no human owners or safe homes, and so 'live wild'. These names include feral, stray and alley cats. They sometimes attack and harm pet cats and can also cause a nuisance and health hazard by spreading pests such as fleas and raiding dustbins and rubbish heaps for leftover food.

Cat habits

926 Cats are usually very clean animals and spend a couple of hours each day grooming or 'washing' themselves. The cat bends and twists to lick almost every part of its body with its rough tongue. This gets rid of dirt, old skin, loose fur and tiny pests. The cat may also lick its paw, rub this on a body part to clean it, then lick its paw again. And it may run its claws through its fur to get rid of dirt.

927 Most cats like being brushed by their owners. This is especially important for long-haired cats, which cannot keep their thick fur clean by themselves. Getting a cat used to being brushed takes time and patience. Start with a few gentle strokes of the brush, stay calm, make no sudden moves, and stroke and fuss the cat afterwards. Over many days the cat will get used to being brushed and begin to enjoy it.

▲ When washing itself, a cat pays special attention to its paws. Bits of dirt, twigs or small stones may get stuck between its toes. The cat must carefully remove these and also lick clean any small nicks or cuts.

◄ Long-haired cat breeds, like this American Curl, should have regular grooming sessions from their owners. Otherwise tangles, dirt and pests start to collect in its long, thick fur.

I DON'T BELIEVE IT!

Cats sometimes eat grass! This is natural. Grass gives cats extra nutrients. Plants also help a cat to cough up stuck food or furballs.

928 **Cats often seem to be sick – but they are really coughing up, or regurgitating, furballs or hairballs.** These are lumps of fur that the cat swallows while grooming, and that mat together as a slimy mass in its stomach. Coughing up furballs is healthy. Otherwise the furball might block the cat's intestines and cause real sickness.

929 **Cats like to scratch – in fact, they need to.** The cat usually stretches out its front legs and pulls with its claws at something rough and hard, like wood. This is not so much to keep its claws sharp, but to stretch and exercise its muscles and joints. For cats kept indoors, a purpose-made scratching post helps to save the curtains!

▲ A scratching post can be purpose-made, or simply be an old piece of wood.

Cat comforts

930 **Most cats like being stroked.** But, like picking up a cat, you should start by doing this carefully and calmly, so the cat comes to trust you. Sudden moves or noises, or forcing a cat to be stroked, only make it more wary and nervous. Along the back, the cheek and behind the ears are good places. This is where cats 'stroke' us by rubbing themselves against our legs. Always stroke a cat in the same direction that its fur lies in.

▼ Let a cat come to you, rather than rushing after it. Stroke it gently and calmly. This way the cat will gain confidence and soon come to enjoy it.

931 **A cat's miaow can mean many different things.** A loud, high-pitched miaow may mean, 'I'm hungry!' A quieter, short miaow like a squeaky door, may be a welcoming sign, like saying 'Hello friend!' The sounds a cat makes come from its voice-box or larynx which, like our own voice-box, is in the neck. Some cat breeds miaow more than others. Siamese cats are well-known for being noisy.

▲ A happy purring cat may narrow its eyes and stretch its front paws forwards one after the other as if 'paddling'.

932 Cats usually purr when they are happy, relaxed and content. The purr comes, not from the cat's voice-box, but from its breathing muscles deep in its chest. The rattling or vibrating sound can also be felt if you touch a loudly purring cat!

CAN YOU PURR?

Try various ways to copy a cat's purring sound. For example, let your loose tongue rattle against the roof of your mouth as you breathe out.

933 Cats are famous for their cat-naps – short periods of snoozing and dozing. The cat is usually quite alert when napping, and will leap up at the slightest worry. In general, cats prefer warm, quiet places for napping and sleeping. This is why they often sleep behind chairs or in corners. They also like places that smell right – often of their owners. This is why cats may curl up on their owner's clothes, chairs or beds. Cats like to fall asleep in the sunshine too, seeking out sunny spots to keep warm.

▶ This Abyssinian cat has found a sunny spot on a draining board. Cats don't find the most practical places to fall asleep, but that's all part of their character.

Friend or foe?

934 Cats have moods, like us, and it helps if we recognize these. A tiny movement, faint sound or smell that we cannot detect, can worry a cat. It may suddenly become alert and ready for action. A scared cat crouches low, flattens its ears, opens its mouth, hisses, bristles its fur and swishes its tail low. Then it's best to leave the cat alone, so it can run off or hide if it wishes.

◄ Cats wail, screech and cry to tell other cats of their presence, saying 'This area is not free – I live here'.

935 Cats may seem to bring home 'presents' of small creatures such as half-dead mice and wounded birds. Often the cat does not kill its victim, but chases, pounces and 'plays' with it. This may seem cruel to us, but the cat is simply following its natural behaviour and instincts. It is practising its hunting skills in familiar surroundings.

◄ Kittens play with almost anything that moves, such as falling leaves, to rehearse their hunting actions.

936 Cats often 'caterwaul', making loud wails and screeches – especially at night. Usually they are warning other cats away from their territory. A cat's territory is its home area, where it likes to roam, rest and hunt without fear of interference by other cats. Territories vary greatly in size. They may be just a room in the owner's house, or the whole house, the garden too, or even part of a street, park or wood.

▶ A young cat and dog who grow up in the same place often become excellent friends — perhaps even more so than two young cats.

937 A cat and dog can be best friends, especially if brought up together as kitten and puppy. But if a cat and dog are strangers, they are often less friendly. The cat may bare its claws, fluff its fur, and get ready to hiss in self-defence. But like any animal, it usually prefers to avoid danger and escape.

938 Some cats, especially toms (males), spray urine around their territory — and this may include the house! The urine has scents that other cats detect, and which warn these cats to stay away. A vet's advice may be needed for a troublesome tom who sprays urine in the house.

I DON'T BELIEVE IT!
Cat flaps can have computers! One design of cat flap only opens when a computer chip comes near — and the chip is on a safe elastic collar around the cat's neck.

Keeping healthy

939 Cats sometimes fall ill, but we can prevent some serious illnesses by giving them injections called vaccinations. The two main injections protect against feline influenza or 'cat flu', and feline infectious enteritis, an infection by virus germs. The vet advises when to give these, usually in kittens from the age of eight weeks.

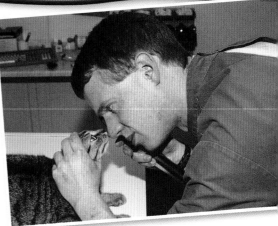

▲ Vets are experts at handling animals, and soon put a worried cat at ease so it can be checked and examined.

940 Cats can show various signs of illness. These may include coughs, sneezes, fluids such as pus or discharge from the eyes, nose or ears, being sick or vomiting, diarrhoea, trembling and fur loss.

941 Cat owners should stay alert for signs of illness in their pets. Sometimes these are obvious, such as a runny nose. Other signs are difficult to pinpoint, such as loss of appetite or being 'off food', and a dull coat rather than shiny fur.

942 Apart from an occasional cough or sneeze, if a cat seems ill then it's best to contact a vet by phone and describe the signs. The vet can advise on home treatment or whether to take the cat to the veterinary centre for a proper examination.

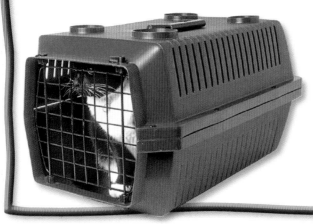

◀ A cat-carrier (cat-cage or cat-conveyor) keeps the cat safe on journeys such as to the vet. Trying to hold a nervous, ill cat in your arms is far too risky.

943 A cat that scratches lots, often quite suddenly, may have tiny pests such as fleas, lice, mites and ticks. They can sometimes be seen crawling in the fur or their droppings may look like dark dust. Also, they can spread and bite us! Most kinds of pests can be killed with special powders, shampoos or sprays. Fleas can be kept away with a cat flea collar.

944 A cat that seems to eat lots but stay thin and 'off colour' may have worms. These include long, ribbon-like tapeworms and smaller, squirmy roundworms. Sometimes the worms or their eggs are seen in the cat's droppings. Pills or injections can kill these worms.

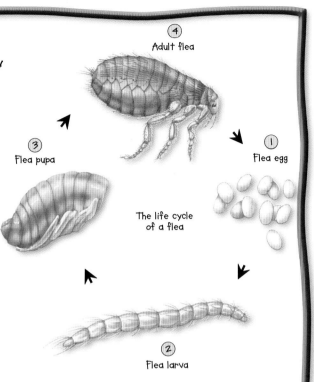

④ Adult flea

③ Flea pupa

① Flea egg

The life cycle of a flea

② Flea larva

▲ Cat fleas are dark brown and not much larger than a pin-head. The adult flea lays tiny eggs which hatch into worm-like larvae or grubs. These grow hard casings and become pupae, then the adult flea breaks out of the case.

QUIZ
Which of these signs would need a vet's attention?
A. Coughing and fast, shallow breathing that goes on for hours
B. Short single cough
C. Drinking lots of water or other liquid whenever possible
D. Small single sneeze
E. Lots of sneezing plus a runny nose and eyes

Answers:
B and D are not too worrying provided they are one-offs. The other signs could mean a serious illness. Contact the vet without delay.

945 A tiny worm called toxocara can spread from cats, usually from their droppings, to people and occasionally cause blindness. This is why it's important to wash your hands after handling cats and their equipment, especially litter trays.

Starting a family

946 Pet cats breed like most other animals. A male (tom), and a female (queen) mate. The female becomes pregnant with developing babies – kittens. This can happen only at certain times of the year. The female is ready to mate around March to April, then through midsummer in June, and around September. Usually the female does not mate until she is 7 to 12 months old, and a male before 10 to 13 months of age.

I DON'T BELIEVE IT!
Most mother cats have about four to six kittens in a litter. But sometimes there can be as many as 12.

947 After mating, a mother cat is pregnant (which is known as her gestation period) for an average of 65 days. But this varies from 60 to 70 days, depending on the breed of cat, the mother's age and other features.

948 An expectant mother cat gains one to two kilograms in weight and her tummy grows in size. Near the birth she searches for a nest or den where she can have her kittens in peace and quiet. This can be almost anywhere she feels comfortable and safe – from the corner of a shed, a clump of grass at the end of the garden, or behind the sofa. Most owners try to provide a kittening box or basket and hope the mother will give birth there.

949 Usually a mother cat gives birth to all her kittens within a day. At first she pants and purrs. Then the kittens arrive one by one, along with the bag-like membranes they grew within, inside the womb. The mother bites through the umbilical cord, which joins the kitten's tummy. This carried nourishment to the kitten when it was in the womb. Then she licks and cleans each kitten in turn, and finally feeds them before resting.

◀ Giving birth to a litter of hungry, squeaking new kittens is hard work, and may take all day and night. When they have all been born, the mother allows her kittens to suckle her milk while she rests.

New kittens

950 **New baby kittens are almost helpless.** Their ears are folded back and their eyes are closed, so they cannot hear or see. They cannot walk or even crawl. These bundles of fluff depend fully on their mother, who stays with them and keeps them safe in their nest or den. The mother licks and cleans them often, and their eyes start to open after about a week.

◀ Newborn kittens are tiny, weak and unable to see or hear properly.

951 **One of the few things a new kitten can do is suckle – feed on milk from its mother.** Each kitten in the litter has its own teat (nipple) on the mother's underside, which it sucks to obtain the milk. If a kitten is hungry, it makes small squeaking noises to let its mother know.

▲ Once kittens are one week old their eyes are just opening and their legs can stretch and scrabble.

▼ At three weeks kittens look around, listen, and are able to crawl or shuffle.

952 **Every few days, the mother cat may move her kittens to a new nest or den.** She picks up each one in her mouth by the loose skin on the back of its neck (the scruff) and carries it quietly to the new nest. This often happens if the mother is disturbed or feels the existing nest is unsafe.

954 A mother cat's milk gives her kittens all the nourishment they need for the first three or four weeks after birth. Then the kittens start to eat other foods as well, called solids. By about eight weeks old, the kittens usually stop suckling. This changeover from milk to normal foods is called weaning.

◀ When they are four weeks old kittens are able to walk and start to run and play.

QUIZ
How old are kittens when the following stages of kitten growth usually happen?
1. Eyes start to open
2. Begins to crawl or shuffle
3. Starts to walk
4. Starts to eat solid foods
5. Stops taking mother's milk

Answers:
1. 1 week 2. Three weeks 3. Four weeks 4. Four weeks 5. Eight weeks

953 The mother cat and kittens soon come to know each other in many ways. As they lie near each other, their body scents spread between them, so they can all recognize each other by smell. The mother also knows her kittens by sight and sound as they mew for milk.

◀ Once a kitten is eight weeks old it is active, playful, entertaining and just about ready to continue life without its mother.

413

Growing up

955 **From about four weeks of age, kittens can run and jump — and then they start to play!** They race about, spring up and leap down, climb almost anything, and sometimes bump into things or fall over.

▼ A mother cat 'rescues' lost kittens and carries them back to safety. She gently holds the youngster by the loose skin at the back of the neck, known as the 'scruff'.

956 **By six or seven weeks old, the kittens start to 'play-hunt'.** They chase each other's twitching tails, and pounce on small objects such as fluffy balls or toy mice. They use their teeth and claws to scratch and grab.

957 **After about a month, the kittens are strong enough to 'go walkabout' with their mother.** They follow her as they wander about, sniffing and pawing at things. They watch her tail as a guide to where she is.

958 **If a kitten gets lost or separated, it usually makes a squeaky mewing noise.** The mother cat miaows back, or comes to find the lost kitten and carry it back to the nest. As the kitten gains in confidence and begins to explore, the mother cat will need to 'rescue' it less.

959 Most kittens are ready to leave their mother and be taken to a new owner by eight weeks of age. If they stay with the mother, they may leave by themselves after about six months.

960 Some people do not want their young cat to have kittens. So they take it to the vet for a small operation, which removes the body parts that are used for breeding. This is called spaying for female cats and can be done after 15 weeks of age. It is known as neutering for male cats and can take place after 35 weeks.

961 Kittens can get so excited as they play that they use their tiny sharp teeth and claws on almost anything — including us. If a kitten feels in danger it will hiss, spit and scratch. So an adult should always be around when young children play with a kitten, and warn the children not to put the kitten near their faces.

▼ Kittens who are litter-mates (sisters and brothers) usually stay good friends. They play together well, even though their 'games' may become rough as they get older.

Different breeds

962 **All pet or domestic cats belong to one kind, or species.** Within this species there are many different types (breeds) of pet cats. They vary in size, body build, coat colour and pattern, fur length, eye colour and other features. Some breeds weigh an average of less than 2.5 kilograms, while others are twice as heavy.

▲ The Manx breed with no tail at all is called a 'rumpy' Manx. If it has just a tiny short stump for a tail it is known as a 'stumpy' Manx.

963 **The many breeds of cats have been decided by people.** Cats with certain features, such as a new fur colour or pattern are selected to mate and have kittens. Then people choose which of the kittens should breed, and so on. This is called selective breeding. Over many years it has produced more than 100 cat breeds.

▲ The tabby is the 'original' colour for a pet cat. If all pet cats were allowed to breed with each other for several years, and not be selected by breeders, then most would end up as tabbies.

964 **One of the most common cat coat colours is a mix of black, brown and tawny swirls, stripes and spots.** This is called the tabby or 'moggie'. The first domestic cats, thousands of years ago, were probably a similar colour to this.

965 One of the most famous cat breeds is the Siamese. It is long and slim, with small paws and intense blue eyes. About 500 years ago these cats were kept by the kings of Siam, the region now known as Thailand. Siamese cats tend to be very affectionate to their owners. They can also be quite noisy, with a loud miaow.

◀ A Siamese cat has slim, elegant body proportions.

COLOUR YOUR OWN CAT

You will need:
large sheets of card coloured pens
crayons or paints.
You can make a new breed of cat in a few minutes – but only on paper. Draw a cat outline. Colour the fur with your favourite shades and patterns. Choose an eye colour too, like blue, green or yellow. What will you name your new breed of cat?

966 The British Blue is the best-known of the breeds called British Shorthairs. In fact its 'short hair' is quite long and thick, with a grey-blue sheen. It also has striking orange or copper-coloured eyes, small ears and short legs. This breed was one of the first to be displayed when cat shows started over a hundred years ago.

▶ The British Blue's fur is dense, meaning the hairs grow very close together.

967 The Persian breeds of cat are also known as Longhairs. Their fur is long and thick, and they need help from their owners with their grooming. There are many colours of Persians, from pure white to jet black, and also tabby and tortoiseshell breeds. Their name comes from the region once known as Persia (now Iran) in west Asia. The earliest Persian breeds of cats arrived in Europe during the late 1500s.

Strange breeds

968 The Scottish Folds breed began in 1961 with 'Susie', a white kitten who lived on a farm near Coupar Angus in Tayside, Scotland. Her unusual ears were bent forwards and down. A shepherd named William Ross noticed Susie. He bred her with a local male cat. Two of Susie's kittens had folded ears too, and so this new breed began.

▶ It takes a while for a new breed like the Scottish Folds to become established, and to be accepted by the organizations who run cat shows and the official lists of breeds or pedigrees.

▼ The tail of the Japanese Bobtail has hairs growing out all around, giving a fluffy effect like a rabbit's tail.

969 The Japanese Bobtail breed is named after its very short or 'bobbed' tail. Most of these cats have a tortoiseshell-and-white colour pattern known in Japan as Mi-Ke. Other colours include black-and-white and red (brown)-and-white. Often when this cat sits upright, it raises one of its front feet as though about to 'shake paws' – a gesture which Japanese people say means good luck. The Japanese Bobtail has a sturdy body, long back legs, large ears and big eyes. Its tail measures around 10 centimetres and is usually curled in, close to the body.

970 **The Maine Coon was one of the first cat breeds from North America.** It is large and strong, with a thick shaggy coat that is usually brown and black, and a white chest and paws. It is named after the northeast US state of Maine, where it probably began, and it has similar colouring and hunting methods as the raccoon. Maine Coons probably started as farm cats. They still search out strange places to sleep, like on rooftops or under floorboards.

◄ The Maine Coon can make a strange, quiet miaowing sound, similar to a bird chirping.

971 **The Sphynx breed is perhaps the most unusual pet cat – it has no fur.** It started in Canada in 1966 when one kitten in a litter was born without fur. The Sphynx is friendly and quiet, but it is not keen on being held or cuddled too much. It has large ears and small paws. The only hairs are short, dark, fine 'down' on its face, ears, feet and tail tip. It is an ideal cat for people that are allergic to animal fur.

I DON'T BELIEVE IT!
Longhaired cats that become homeless have particular trouble surviving in the wild, because their fur gets dirty, tangled, wet and full of pests.

▲ Most pet cats, if they lost their fur, would have a similar shape to the Sphynx breed.

Showtime!

972 There are many official clubs and organizations for breeding cats and showing them in competitions, displays and exhibitions. They include the British Governing Council of the Cat Fancy (GCCF), the Cat Fanciers' Association (CFA) of America, and others in almost every country. People who run these groups include cat breeders, cat exhibitors and cat fanciers (cat fans).

▲ The Supreme Cat Show is licensed by the GCCF. It is held each year in Birmingham. There is also a section for non-pedigree cats.

▼ London's Crystal Palace was the site of the first major cat show. Today, shows held in huge exhibition halls and conference centres attract thousands of cats and owners.

973 The first proper cat show was organized by Harrison Weir in London in 1871. It was held at the Crystal Palace and included 25 different competitions or classes for Persians, British Shorthairs and other breeds. Soon after, cat shows were held in the New England region of northeast North America, mainly for the Maine Coon breed.

974 Today there are countless cat shows around the world. They vary from huge international gatherings, where cats and owners fly in from many countries, to local shows in a town or village, where children can show off their family pets.

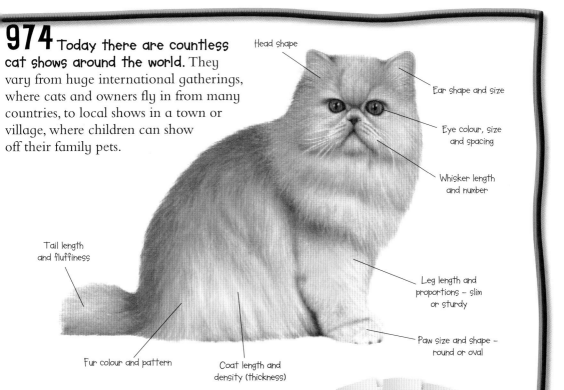

Head shape

Ear shape and size

Eye colour, size and spacing

Whisker length and number

Tail length and fluffiness

Leg length and proportions – slim or sturdy

Fur colour and pattern

Coat length and density (thickness)

Paw size and shape – round or oval

▲ Cats, such as this Persian, are judged on every feature of their head, body, legs, tail and coat, as well as their behaviour and temperament — from relaxed and friendly, to nervous, shy or scared.

975 The main show in Britain is the GCCF Supreme Cat Show. This began in 1976 and only cats that have won at other championship shows can enter. It takes place every November at the National Exhibition Centre, Birmingham. The International Cat Association, TICA, organizes shows in North America, Europe and many other regions, from Brazil and Argentina to Korea and Japan.

MAKE YOUR CAT A CHAMPION!

You will need:
large sheets of card   safe scissors
coloured pens or crayons.
Pretend your cat has won top prize at an important show. Real champions receive a rosette, an official certificate, and perhaps a cup. You can make these from cut-out paper or card, and colour them, perhaps on a computer.

DOGS AND PUPPIES

976 Dogs are special animals that have earned a place in our hearts and our homes. They have been close companions for people since the earliest times and they still work and play with us today. That's why they are often called 'man's best friend'. Dogs are clever creatures with strong, athletic bodies. They are alert and playful and they can move with great speed and agility.

◄ From fearsome wolf to favourite pet, all members of the dog family are fascinating creatures. They have lots of energy, like these puppies, and are highly intelligent.

In the family

977 There are wild dogs and domestic dogs, but they all belong to a family of animals called canids. There are 36 different types (species) of canids, which includes wolves, foxes, coyotes and jackals, as well as the domestic dog. Canids are intelligent animals with long, lean bodies, slender legs and bushy tails.

▲ By mating two different types of domestic dog, it is possible to create an entirely new breed.

978 Domestic dogs are tame and live with people. They are all one species of animal, which means that they can breed (mate) with one another. Different types of domestic dog are called breeds and there are around 200 recognized breeds, but new breeds are always being created.

◀ Jackals live in Africa, Asia and southern Europe. They will sometimes move into cities in the search of food and scraps.

979 Wild dogs are found almost all over the world. Many species of wild dog are in danger of dying out because they are being hunted, or due to the places they live being taken over by people. Domestic dogs live almost everywhere that humans live.

Grey wolf

Fennec fox

◀ The tiny fennec fox and huge grey wolf may differ in size, but they are both members of the dog family and share many characteristics.

980 The smallest wild dog is the fennec fox. It is as small as a pet cat and lives in the desert lands of North Africa where it hunts lizards and bugs. The fennec fox has very large ears in relation to its body size, which allow it to pick up very quiet sounds, even over long distances.

981 The largest wild dog is the grey wolf. This magnificent creature can measure up to 1.5 metres in length, from its nose to its rump, and can weigh up to 60 kilograms. Some domestic dogs are almost as huge. Great Danes are one of the tallest breeds and they can easily measure more than 2 metres in length.

Call of the wild

982 African wild dogs live in huge packs that have more than 30 members. They used to roam across the African plains hunting zebra, antelope and wildebeest. Sadly, there are not many packs of African wild dogs left now, as many have been caught in traps, shot by humans, or died from diseases spread by domestic dogs.

▲ African wild dogs have lost their homelands (habitat) to people or other animals and they are now in danger of extinction.

983 The red fox is a very common member of the dog family. It is found all over Europe, Asia, North America and Australia. Like other foxes, these animals dig underground burrows where they can raise their cubs and stay warm. A fox's burrow is called an earth or a den.

984 The Arctic fox is pure white in winter to blend in with the snow. Its fluffy winter coat is warm, and thick tufts of fur cover the fox's paws. During the summer the fox grows a thinner coat that is grey or brown in colour.

▲ Red foxes are very adaptable and can live almost anywhere, and eat almost anything.

985 **Most foxes will eat almost anything!** Foxes that live in the countryside usually eat rabbits or young hares. They lie in wait in tall grass or bushes, and creep close to their prey – before suddenly leaping into action. They will also eat beetles, fruit, mice, berries, worms, frogs or food left around by humans.

▲ Coyotes live alone, in pairs, or in packs. Males may fight one another to protect their territories or hunting areas.

986 **Coyotes are very fast runners and can reach speeds of 65 kilometres an hour when chasing their prey.** These wolflike wild dogs live in North and Central America, and at night their howling can be heard across mountains and plains. Coyotes often live near to humans and have been known to attack family pets and even children.

987 **Wild dogs in Australia are called dingoes.** It is thought that dingoes might have been domesticated at some point long ago, and have returned to living wild. They are now regarded as pests by many farmers, who build large dingo-proof fences to protect their sheep.

Wolves

988 Grey wolves are the largest wild members of the dog family. However, there are not many grey wolves left in the wild because their habitats have been destroyed by humans. Wolves have also been hunted for centuries, partly because people are scared of them – even though it is very rare for a wolf to attack a human.

▼ Grey wolves mate towards the end of the winter and litters of 2 to 10 pups are born 9 weeks later. Other females in the pack help to look after the pups.

989 Grey wolves live in family groups. Each group is called a pack and usually contains between 8 and 12 wolves, although some packs may have up to 20 members. Each pack has a leader, called the alpha wolf. The alpha wolf is usually a female and she rules the group. The alpha female and her mate are the only wolves that have cubs.

990 Grey wolves work as a group to catch their prey. By hunting together, the wolves can chase, attack and kill animals that are much larger than themselves, such as moose and caribou. They also eat small animals including beavers, hares and rabbits. Wolves find their prey using their powerful senses of smell and hearing.

991 There may be as few as 100 red wolves alive in the wild today. Red wolves are smaller than their grey cousins and they only live in North Carolina, USA. They mostly eat mice, rats and rabbits, but they will also eat berries and insects.

TELLING TALES

You can probably think of some stories or fairy tales where the spotlight is on a bad wolf. Can you make up a story where the wolf is the hero instead? Use words that describe the wolf's appearance and character. Draw a picture to go with your story.

Taming the dog

992 **Dogs were probably first tamed by humans around 12,000 years ago during the last ice age.** These first 'pet' dogs were probably bred from wild wolves and dogs. They may have been used to hunt, or to scare off more dangerous wild animals, such as bears. Dogs were also used as protection on long journeys.

▲ The Spanish explorer Vasco de Nuñez Balboa took his dog Leoncico on all his expeditions and even paid him a wage.

993 **Ancient Egyptians had their dogs mummified so they could accompany them into the next life.** Dogs were prized as pets by Egyptians, but they also worked as guard dogs or hunters. Their proud owners gave them leather collars and names such as 'Blacky' or 'Brave One'.

◀ The ancient Egyptians mummified many animals, including dogs, cats, snakes and lions.

994 **Dogs have been treated like gods and used in worship.** Statues of lionlike dogs are often placed outside temples in the Far East, where they are believed to stand guard and protect the building from evil spirits.

▶ Called a Chinese Foo Dog, this statue rests his paw on a ball that represents the Earth.

995 About 300 years ago the Japanese ruler Tokugawa Tsunayoshi changed the law to protect dogs. He was so fond of his canine friends he decreed that any person who mistreated, or even ignored, a dog could be put to death. In one month alone, more than 300 people were executed as a result.

996 The Romans bred huge, vicious dogs, called Molossians, to fight in battles. These 'dogs of war' were similar to modern Rottweilers and, according to legend, Alexander the Great (a hero of the ancient world) owned one beast that fought and killed an elephant and a lion. Romans also set up fights between dogs and slaves.

I DON'T BELIEVE IT!

Nine hundred years ago the king of Norway handed his throne to a dog! The royal pet ruled for three years and signed important papers with a paw print!

997 Dogs helped to protect travellers. Highwaymen used to hold up horse-drawn carriages and rob the people travelling in them. Dogs were trained to run alongside the carriages, and attack or frighten the highwaymen.

◀ Dalmatians were often used to protect the travellers in coaches because they are excellent guard dogs.

A dog's body

998 **The first doglike animal lived about 30 million years ago.** Around 300,000 years ago the first wolves appeared, and all of today's dogs descend from them. The way that animals change over time is known as evolution.

▼ Like all mammals, a dog's skeleton is made of bone – a tough but lightweight material. Muscles are attached to the skeleton by rubbery ligaments and tendons.

Backbone

Hipbone

Ankle

Rear foot bones

▼ The brain, skeleton and muscles work together to create movement. A long tail helps a dog to keep its balance as it runs at speed.

999 **All members of the dog family are similar in important ways.** Most canids have deep, muscle-packed chests, long bodies and strong, slender legs. Dogs are endurance runners. This means that they can keep running at a steady pace for a long time without tiring.

1000 A dog's back paws have just four claws each, but its front paws have five claws. Domestic dogs, however, sometimes have extra claws on their back paws, called 'dew claws'. They are shorter, and are not used for walking.

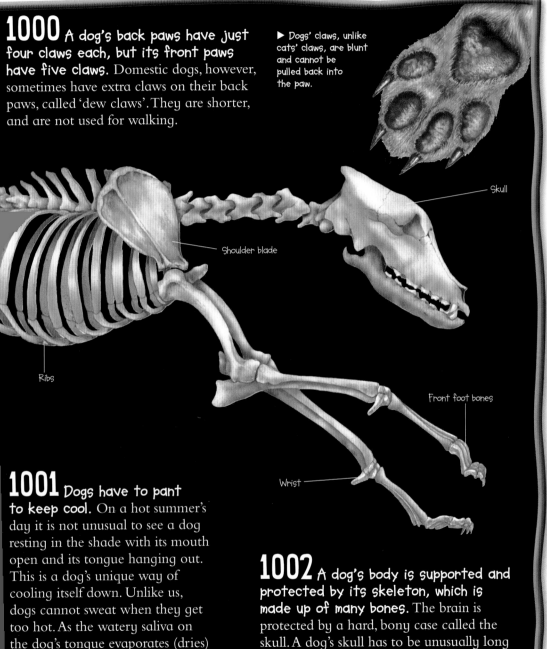

▶ Dogs' claws, unlike cats' claws, are blunt and cannot be pulled back into the paw.

Skull

Shoulder blade

Ribs

Front foot bones

Wrist

1001 Dogs have to pant to keep cool. On a hot summer's day it is not unusual to see a dog resting in the shade with its mouth open and its tongue hanging out. This is a dog's unique way of cooling itself down. Unlike us, dogs cannot sweat when they get too hot. As the watery saliva on the dog's tongue evaporates (dries) the tongue cools. This lowers the dog's body temperature.

1002 A dog's body is supported and protected by its skeleton, which is made up of many bones. The brain is protected by a hard, bony case called the skull. A dog's skull has to be unusually long to make room for its muzzle, which contains the nose and mouth.

433

Scratch and sniff!

1003 Dogs have a much better sense of smell than humans. They are particularly good at sniffing out certain scents such as sweat. In fact, it has been estimated that domestic dogs are one million times better at smelling sweat than us and they can even match a person to the smell of their sweat!

▼ Dogs such as this Basset hound have around 220 million smell-sensing cells in their noses. Humans have only 20 million.

▼ Pointer dogs are popular hunting dogs. When they smell a game bird they stand still and 'point' with their bodies.

1004 Dogs can follow a trail using only their sense of smell. Dogs such as bloodhounds have been used for centuries by police to find missing people and criminal suspects by tracking their scent. Bloodhounds have followed four-day old trails over distances of more than 120 kilometres.

1005
A strong sense of smell helps wild members of the dog family to survive. Wolves sniff the air to find out if other wolves are invading their territory. Wolf packs mark their territories with urine, and the smell contains a message telling other wolves to stay away. They also use their sense of smell to find a mate or their prey.

▼ The outer part of an ear is called the pinna. Many canids can move the pinna so it 'catches' a sound and directs it towards the eardrum, which sends the message to the brain.

Pinna

1006
Members of the dog family have eyes that help them follow the movement of other animals. This helps them chase down their prey. Some dogs, such as greyhounds, have very good eyesight but most types of dog can see less well than humans. Like cats, dogs are able to see some colours and have good vision in the evening and early morning when there is little natural light.

Grey wolf

Great Dane

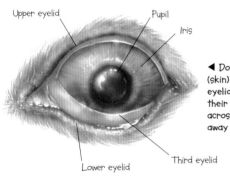

Upper eyelid   Pupil
Iris

◀ Dogs have a membrane (skin) called the 'third eyelid' that protects their eyeballs. It sweeps across the eye to clear away dust and dirt.

Lower eyelid   Third eyelid

Irish terrier

1007
Wolves' ears are large, upright and pointed, but modern domestic dogs have ears in a huge variety of shapes and sizes. Wild dogs can move their ears in the direction of a sound, to help the animal hear it better. Some dog breeds have long, drooping ears that cannot be so easily moved.

Pug

Body language

1008 **Dogs are social animals.** This means that they like to live with other animals, or humans. In the wild, a group of dogs usually has a leader – the 'top dog'. The 'top dog' decides what the group will do, and the 'underdogs' follow his, or her, lead. Pet dogs treat their owners as if they are the 'top dogs' of the pack, and that's why they can be trained to be obedient.

1009 **Dogs show how they are feeling using their mouths, ears and tails.** Frightened dogs will put their tails between their legs. They flatten their ears against their heads and may even roll over onto their backs. This is a dog's way of showing that it does not want to fight.

Tail down between legs

Ears flattened

Head lowered

◄ A dog's body language can show how it is feeling. This dog is scared and, by making its body seem small, it is asking other dogs – or humans – to leave it alone.

1010
Growling, barking and howling are a dog's way of sending messages to other animals. Wolves howl and dogs growl to warn other animals to stay away. Barking is a dog's way of telling other members of its pack that something strange is happening, and to be alert and on guard.

▶ Wolves howl rather than bark and some pet dogs communicate this way too. Howling can be heard over great distances.

1011
Young puppies do not wag their tails. Dogs usually start tail-wagging when they are four to six weeks old, normally when they are feeding on their mother's milk. Older dogs often wag their tails when they are excited about seeing another friendly dog or a person that they know.

Tail arched

Hair raised

eth bared

1012
An angry, aggressive dog will bare its teeth in a menacing way, while growling. If it can prick its ears they will be erect and pointing forward and its tail will be held out straight or arched up behind. This shows the enemy animal or person that the dog is alert and ready for action.

◀ Angry dogs look bigger and more threatening. Their fur stands on end and they show their 'weapons' by baring their teeth to scare other animals away.

A dog's dinner

1013 All canids are hunters. Dogs, both wild and domestic, have a natural instinct to look for creatures to chase, kill and eat. Animals that hunt other animals are called 'predators' and the animals they hunt are called 'prey'. Both dogs and cats are predators, but dogs (unlike cats) rarely live on a diet of meat alone and may eat fruit and insects too.

1014 Pet dogs do not need to hunt for their food. Dog owners give their pets regular meals – usually cooked meat and biscuits with added vitamins and minerals. Dogs are often given small treats to reward them for good behaviour, but these should only be given as part of their training, as they are not part of a healthy diet.

▶ Pet dogs eat a range of food, not just meat. Biscuits and rawhide chews provide extra vitamins and help keep a dog's teeth clean. Dogs need plenty of fresh water every day.

1015 Many dogs enjoy chewing beef bones and this helps to keep their teeth clean and their gums healthy. Bones can break and splinter, however, so pet dogs should only be allowed to chew bones for a short while. It is better if they chew on special toys that are designed to massage their gums. These can be made of meat, biscuit, rubber, nylon or braid.

1016 Chocolate is dangerous to dogs. Although many dogs like the taste of chocolate they shouldn't be allowed to eat it, because even a tiny amount is enough to poison a small dog. Dog treats will normally contain very little chocolate, or none at all.

DINER OR DINNER?

These animals are either predators, or prey.

Find the predators and the prey:

a. wolf b. rabbit
c. polar bear d. cheetah
e. rhinoceros f. zebra

Answers:
Predators: a c d
Prey: b e f

1017 Dogs can suffer from gum disease and bad breath — just like people! Dog owners can brush their pets' teeth to help keep them clean and avoid decay. You shouldn't use human toothpaste on a dog's teeth as it contains fluoride, which can poison a dog, but you can buy special toothpaste for dogs, which you can get from vets. You should check a dog's mouth regularly, looking for bad and broken teeth or swollen gums and lips.

Starting a family

1018 **Female dogs are usually pregnant for between 60 and 70 days.** During this time the pups grow slowly inside her. A pregnant female needs to be treated with care. She will tire more easily and needs short exercise periods. Pregnant dogs need more food towards the end of their pregnancy.

▲ This Labrador puppy is a newborn, and cannot survive without its mother's care. She feeds it with milk and keeps it warm, clean and safe.

1019 **In the wild, most dogs have their puppies (cubs) in a safe place called a den, or an earth.** The den may be a hole in the ground, or a cave. It needs to be dry, dark and hidden so that the youngsters are protected from other animals. Domestic dogs will also make 'nests' where they feel safe enough to give birth. The ideal place is in a quiet corner where they will not be disturbed.

▶ When a puppy is 2 weeks old its eyes and ears should be working, so it will begin to take more interest in its surroundings, although it cannot yet stand properly or walk.

▶ At 3 weeks old a puppy can move clumsily and snuggles up to its littermates to sleep. Like human babies, puppies need plenty of rest.

1020 **When female dogs are ready to give birth they often stop eating.** Most will also become very restless for a few hours before birthing begins. They need to be kept away from other animals and allowed to settle quietly into their nest. When they begin to give birth they are said to be 'whelping'.

1021 A mother dog usually gives birth to a group, or litter, of between three and eight pups, and looking after them is hard work. All dogs are mammals – this means that their babies grow inside them, and feed on their mother's milk when they are young. As soon as the puppies are born their mother licks them clean. At this age, puppies cannot eat solid food – they can only suck milk from their mother.

1022 Puppies are born deaf and blind and they rely on their mother to look after them. During its first weeks of life a puppy spends most of its time asleep while its body grows and develops. After 10 to 14 days a puppy's eyes begin to open and after 14 days most puppies can sit up. They can't stand for another week, and a few days after that a puppy begins to walk.

▲ When a puppy reaches 5 weeks of age its mother begins to push it away when it tries to feed from her. At 6 weeks of age it will begin to eat solid food.

▼ Playful, curious and noisy – an 8-week-old puppy has its own personality. Soon it will leave its mother to meet a new family.

441

Puppy love

1023 Puppies should stay with their mothers until they are about 10 weeks old. From this time they can be given to a new family. Looking after a puppy is a lot of work. They need four meals a day and lots of affection.

1024 Puppies love to play. Young puppies play with their brothers and sisters, but as they grow older they play with people, too. When they play, puppies are practising skills they might need later in life – such as hunting, chasing and fetching.

▶ Young puppies play-fight with their brothers and sisters. Play-fighting may look aggressive, but it is just a dog's way of asserting its dominance and personality.

1025 Puppies and adult dogs can get bored and restless if they do not get enough exercise. All dogs – especially youngsters – need to spend plenty of time outdoors where they can explore using all their senses. Dogs love to follow the trail of a new smell and enjoy sniffing the ground and plants. Some dogs are natural 'diggers' and enjoy scratching at the ground, particularly on flowerbeds and lawns!

▲ Puppies must learn that they should play only with their own toys.

▶ Puppies love chewing toys, especially ones that squeak! Never give a dog a toy with small parts, as they could choke on them.

1026 Toys are a great way to keep a puppy happy. Most dogs love to play with toys that they can chase and catch, such as balls and Frisbees. You can teach a dog to bring its toy back to you by rewarding it with a small treat or by praising it every time it fetches. When they are at home, puppies can turn almost anything into a toy and they love chewing on shoes and furniture.

Dogs are for life

1027 **Deciding to buy a dog is an important decision.** Caring for an animal is a big responsibility – it takes work and can be expensive. Before getting a dog you should find out how much care it will need by talking to other dog owners and vets, and by reading books and looking at websites.

1028 It can be best to buy a puppy rather than an adult dog, as you can make sure it has the best training and care from a young age. It's a good idea to buy a puppy from a breeder, or a person recommended to you by a vet, because it is essential that the puppy has been well looked after in its first weeks of life.

1029 Dogs are sometimes abandoned by owners who don't want them anymore. Occasionally, people realize, after getting a dog, that they are unable to look after their pet. Responsible owners will find a better home for their animal, but it is not unusual for dogs to be turned out into the street. Dogs that are abandoned are known as strays.

1030 Dogs usually live for between 10 and 15 years, depending on their breed. They need to visit the vet for vaccinations, which will help protect them from disease, and to be treated for any injuries or illnesses they get during their active and busy lives. Good owners will check their dog regularly for any scratches, cuts or other signs of illness.

▶ Vets give dogs and puppies vaccinations to help protect them from a range of diseases such as distemper and kennel cough.

▼ Which of these Staffordshire bull terrier puppies would you choose? It is important to check a puppy for signs of good health, alertness and a pleasing personality. Try to visit a litter of puppies several times before making a choice.

1031 Dogs need time, patience and attention. They need to be stroked, fed, walked and played with – every single day. Young dogs should not be left alone all day as they can become lonely and difficult to train.

COUNT THE PUPPIES!

1. Three bitches have puppies. One of them has six puppies, while the other two have four puppies each. How many puppies are born altogether?

2. Daisy is a Dalmatian dog. She has five puppies every year for three years. How many puppies has she had altogether?

Answers:
1. 14   2. 15

Caring for a dog

1032 A new puppy settles quickly into a home where preparations have been made for its arrival. At first, it should be kept in one room, with a bed provided. This can be a cardboard box to begin with, lined with old towels or pullovers to keep it warm.

▲ Cardboard boxes make good dens for a new puppy, but baskets are more suitable for older dogs.

1033 Exercising a puppy on a lead helps it learn how to obey you. It is important that puppies and dogs learn to behave well and obey your commands, especially when they are outdoors with other animals and people. There are four basic commands – Sit, Stay, Come and Lie Down. Once your dog has mastered these, you may want to try him or her out on a few more complicated instructions.

▶ When a dog follows a command correctly it is important to praise him or her. This Dalmatian is waiting patiently for his reward.

1034 Dogs and puppies need to be kept safe when they are playing. They should not be allowed on the streets without a collar or a lead, in case they run into the road or scare people. If a dog lives in the countryside it must be kept away from farmers' animals. Responsible owners always clear up their pets' droppings.

1035 A puppy has to be house-trained. This means that it needs to learn to go to the toilet outside the house. A very young puppy cannot control when it passes its waste. Whenever a young puppy wants to relieve itself it should be placed on newspaper and rewarded when it finishes. Most puppies are house-trained by the time they are six months old.

PLAY THE GAME!

This is a game for a group, played just like musical bumps. When the music stops, the leader must shout a command ('Sit', 'Stay', 'Come' or 'Lie down'). Everyone must follow the command correctly – the last person to do the correct action is out. The last person still playing is the winner.

▶▼ Puppies should wear collars from an early age to get used to them. They can begin training to walk on a lead from the age of 12 to 15 weeks.

1037 Dogs need to be groomed every day, especially long-haired breeds. Brushing a dog's fur helps remove dead hairs and dirt, and keeps its coat glossy. Dogs also need baths sometimes to give them a deep-clean and keep them smelling sweet.

▶ Dog food contains vitamins and minerals that are an important part of a dog's daily diet. This complete food can be moist or dry.

▶ Regular grooming using a brush or a comb helps to keep a dog's coat clean and healthy.

1036 All dog equipment, such as feed bowls and toys, should be kept clean and germ-free. Puppies need to have regular meals and it is possible to buy specially prepared dog food for them. Breeders usually give new dog owners a diet sheet that tells them which types of food are best for their pet.

Dog breeds

1038 **There are many types (breeds) of domestic dog.** Dog breeds are divided into groups, according to their type. There are six groups – working dogs, toy, terriers, herders, hounds and sporting dogs. Some dogs are suited to family life and make good pets, but others thrive on a farm or enjoy a working life.

▼ Afghans are hounds. This word is used to describe dogs that have been used to hunt wild animals in the past.

1039 **Afghans are famous for their long, shaggy coats.** These tall and leggy dogs are an ancient breed that originally came from Afghanistan. Harsh winters meant that dogs from this area needed to have thick, warm coats. Afghans were once trained to hunt wolves, leopards and jackals, but now they make popular family pets.

1040 **The Rottweiler is an intelligent breed of working dog.** Originally from Germany, they are strong and powerful. The temperament of the Rottweiler can be unpredictable and they have been known to attack people, but with good training and control they can make excellent guard dogs.

◄ Like German shepherds, Mastiffs, Boxers, Dobermans and Dalmatians, the Rottweiler is a strong working dog.

1041 The Chihuahua is the smallest breed of dog.
In fact, they are not just small, they are tiny, reaching to between just 16 and 20 centimetres in height! These dainty toy dogs need little exercise and they must be kept out of the cold.

▼ Chihuahuas are known as toy, or companion dogs. They are famous for their lively intelligence.

1042 Herding dogs have been bred for their great intelligence and energy.
They often work on farms, where they help the shepherds control the sheep, but many herding dogs are also used to do police work or are kept as family pets.

1044 Sporting dogs are also known as gundogs.
These animals were first bred to work with humans and flush out birds, hares and other animals to be shot. The dog then collected, or 'retrieved', the dead animal and brought it back to the hunter.

◄ Golden retrievers rarely work as gundogs today. They are popular family pets as they love being with children and are easy to train.

1043 Terriers were bred to run underground and chase other animals out of their holes.
Jack Russell terriers were named after the parson who first bred them. They were trained to run with the hounds during foxhunts, and chase the foxes out of their hiding places so the hounds could catch them.

▲ Terriers can be quite snappy in nature and some bark a lot. Although some breeds love children, not all types suit a young family.

449

Pedigrees and mongrels

1045 A dog whose ancestors — parents, grandparents and great grandparents — were all the same breed is called a pedigree, or **purebred.** Pedigree dogs are usually very expensive to buy, but one advantage is that their owners know how large they will grow, and what their personalities will be like.

1046 Bulldogs might look fierce, but they are actually sweet-natured and make good pets for **children.** Unfortunately they tire very easily and cannot walk long distances before needing a rest. They also get uncomfortable in hot weather and tend to breathe quite noisily. Bulldogs were originally bred to tackle bulls by grabbing their noses with their front teeth!

▲ Bulldogs have huge skulls and folds of loose skin, especially around their heads, necks and shoulders. They walk with a peculiar 'rolling' motion on their short, sturdy legs.

1047 Greyhounds lived over 4000 years ago in ancient Egypt, and pictures of them were drawn on the walls of the pyramids. These slender and athletic pedigrees are famous for their love of running and they are often bred and trained to take part in races. They have gentle natures and enjoy being with children.

◀ Thousands of greyhounds are retired from racing every year and have to find new homes. Many become family pets.

1048
Dogs that are not pedigree or purebred are called mongrels. Usually the breed of their parents is not known and they may be a mixture of lots of different breeds. Mongrels are often healthier than pedigree dogs. If a dog of one breed mates with a dog of another breed, the puppies are called cross-breeds.

◀ Mongrels can make great pets, but without knowing about their background it is difficult to know how their personalities will develop.

1049
Bloodhounds are famous for their droopy ears. It is thought that they were first brought to Britain in 1066 by William the Conqueror. Bloodhounds have a fantastic sense of smell, and are often used as tracker dogs.

WHAT'S MY BREED?
Rearrange the letters to find the names of dog breeds:

1. Gup 2. Gorci 3. Rexbo
4. Doolpe 5. Tearg aned

Answers:
1. Pug 2. Corgi 3. Boxer
4. Poodle 5. Great Dane

▲ Bloodhounds are large dogs, weighing up to 50 kilograms, and they need a lot of food to fuel their powerful bodies.

Snow dogs

1050 For hundreds of years St Bernard rescue dogs searched through the Alps for people who needed their help. Stranded by bad weather and avalanches, many climbers and walkers owed their lives to these noble dogs who braved the mountains to save them.

▼ There are several dog breeds that suit a cold climate. Pyrenean mountain dogs are a giant breed and can weigh up to 65 kilograms! Once working dogs, Samoyeds are now popular as pets.

Pyrenean mountain dog

Samoyed

1051 Some breeds of dog have lived in the cold lands of the north for hundreds of years. In these regions the winters are severe and thick snow makes it difficult for people to travel. By using a sledge, pulled by a team of dogs, it is easier to cover long distances and transport goods and food.

▶ All St Bernard rescue dogs are now retired from work. Rescues in difficult conditions are now carried out by helicopter patrols with heat-seeking equipment.

1052 Huskies are one of the world's best known breeds of snow dogs. They can cope with cold weather because they have thick fur and can survive on much less food than other dogs of their size. Huskies have changed very little through breeding and are still very similar to their ancestor, the wolf – they howl, rather than bark, and they live in packs. Although Huskies will pull sledges, they are difficult to train in any other way.

▼ A team of Huskies can pull a sledge up to 130 kilometres in one day. Some Huskies are specially bred to take part in speed sledge racing while others are bred to travel long distances.

1053 Alaskan malamutes, Eskimo dogs and Samoyeds are all breeds of snow dog. Alaskan malamutes are similar to Huskies but they are more affectionate. Eskimo dogs are now one of the rarest breeds, but they have worked alongside the Inuit people of the Arctic for thousands of years. Samoyeds are pale-coloured, good-natured dogs that are now most often kept as family pets.

Unusual breeds

▼ The fluffy Chow Chow belongs to one of the world's oldest dog breeds. They were first bred as herding dogs in Mongolia. Chow Chows have black tongues.

1054 There are many strange breeds of dog. Some of these unusual breeds came about because they suit the places where they live, but others have been especially bred to exaggerate their most peculiar characteristics.

▼ Chinese Crested dogs are about 30 centimetres tall. They make popular pets as they are intelligent and do not need much exercise.

1055 The Chinese Crested dog is one of the most unusual-looking pets you will ever see. This breed is small and almost completely hairless, except for sprouts of hair on its head, feet and tail. Chinese Crested dogs make great pets but they must be covered in sunscreen on hot days and have to wear a coat on cold days.

I DON'T BELIEVE IT!

The hair of Hungarian Puli dogs grows to form thick cords that reach to the ground. Their fur needs constant combing to prevent it from forming a frizzy, knotted clump!

1056 **The wrinkliest dog is the Shar Pei.** It has folds of skin around its head and face, a frowning expression and a bristly coat. Shar Peis were bred in China to herd sheep and hunt boar but they are now kept as pets. Shar Peis almost became extinct in their native China and were once considered the rarest dog breed in the world. The line was continued by breeders in Hong Kong and they have become more popular in recent years.

▲ Shar Peis are born with wrinkles all over their skin. As they get older, many of these wrinkles disappear, except for those around the face, neck and withers (shoulder area).

1057 **The dog with the strangest name is the Xoloitzcuintle.** Known as Xolos for short, these dogs are completely hairless. By the 1950s it was thought that this breed was so rare that it was going to die out, but since then it has become much more popular as a family pet.

◀ Poodles need to have their thick, curly hair shampooed and clipped regularly.

1058 **Poodles come in all shapes, sizes and haircuts!** It is thought that Poodles could be one of the oldest dog breeds in the world, and their pictures appear on ancient Greek and Roman coins. There are three main types of Poodle: Standard, Miniature and Toy. Poodles do not moult (shed their hair), making them a good choice of dog for people with asthma.

Clever clogs

▶ Dogs that attend obedience trials perform tricks such as jumping over obstacles, coming when called and finding items touched by their owner.

1059 **Dogs are smart enough to learn new tricks.** They can learn how to roll over, beg and even shake hands. Dog owners can enter their dogs into competitions, where they are judged for their appearance or for their obedience skills. More than 20,000 dogs compete every year at the world's most famous dog show – Crufts.

1060 **Dogs can predict earthquakes and thunderstorms.** When they know that a big natural event is going to happen, dogs may become alarmed, start panting and rush madly about the house or garden. They may get very distressed and begin to whimper and shake. It is possible that dogs are sensitive to tiny changes in air pressure before thunderstorms, or can hear an earthquake's first rumbles before humans can.

▲ Border collies crouch down and fix their gaze on the sheep. They herd the sheep without needing to bark or nip.

1061 **The world's cleverest dogs are Border collies, Poodles and German shepherds.** These breeds of dog are often chosen to work with humans because they can learn new commands very quickly and are usually very obedient. Border collies are often used as sheepdogs and they are able to follow instructions to help herd an entire flock of sheep into a pen.

1062 Grey foxes can climb trees. You might usually expect to see cats in trees, but the grey tree fox, which lives in southern USA and Mexico, often makes its den in a hollow tree. It will climb trees to find its food – insects, birds and fruit – or to escape from danger. Grey foxes live in pairs rather than in a pack.

▶ Grey fox cubs start to climb trees when they are only four weeks old.

Doing good work

1063 **Some dogs have important jobs to do.** Dogs are easily trained, so they make excellent companions for people and many work in hospitals. It is thought that patients who have contact with animals recover faster than patients who do not.

◀ Guide dogs allow people who have little or no eyesight to be more independent.

▲ A building has been reduced to rubble, but this specially trained dog can use its great senses of smell and hearing to find any survivors.

I DON'T BELIEVE IT!

Service dogs can be trained to open doors, turn on switches and even help their owners take off their shoes and socks.

1064 **Service dogs are trained to help people.** During the First World War dogs were trained to help blind soldiers who'd been wounded in battle. Since then, hundreds of thousands of dogs around the world have learned how to help people who can't see. Their work means that blind people have more freedom to get out and enjoy life.

1065 Dogs can be used to find dangerous chemicals, including bombs. Labrador retrievers and German shepherds are often used for this sort of work because of their extraordinary sense of smell. In the USA dogs are trained to sniff out more than 19,000 different combinations of exploding chemicals that can be used to make bombs. They can also detect drugs that are being smuggled in planes, cars, lorries and boats.

▶ Dogs that work with the police are trained to frighten and capture criminals as well as controlling crowds, or finding lost people. German shepherd dogs are popular because they are strong, intelligent and have an excellent sense of smell.

1066 Dogs were used to carry messages during World War I. Many human messengers were killed so dogs were trained to do this task instead. Stray dogs were trained and sent to the front. Messages or food were put in tin cylinders and the dogs carried them between soldiers. The dogs probably saved many lives, but 7500 of them were killed in action.

▲ 'Trench dogs' were popular with soldiers because they provided companionship and killed rats.

HORSES AND PONIES

1067 Strong, elegant and patient — horses have been loyal companions to humans for thousands of years. People have used horses to help them pull loads, plough fields and fight wars — without the help of horses, the story of human history would be very different. Today many people still rely on horses, ponies, donkeys and mules for transport. When they are free to gallop in a field, or live in the wild, we can truly appreciate the beauty and energy of these magnificent animals.

▶ All horses, wild or tame, enjoy the thrill of galloping at speed. They are sociable animals and prefer to live in groups, or herds.

1068 Horses, ponies, zebras and asses all belong to the same animal family – the equids. All members of this family have a single toe on each foot, and are called 'odd-toed' animals (unlike cows and deer, which have two toes on each foot). Like other animals with fur, horses are mammals and they give birth to live young, which they feed with milk.

▲ Zebras are easily recognized by their stripy coats. These wild equids live in Africa.

1069 Ponies are smaller than horses. Although horses and ponies are the same type of animal, they are different sizes. Horses are measured in 'hands', not centimetres, and a pony is a horse that is less than 14.2 hands (or 148 centimetres) tall. Ponies also have wider bodies and shorter legs than horses.

▶ A horse's height is measured from its feet to the top of its shoulders, which are known as 'withers' (see page 465).

1070 Equids live all over the world. Wild equids, such as zebras, live on grasslands where they can graze all day on plants. Horses that live and work with humans can be found almost everywhere across the world, and these are known as domestic horses.

1071 Equids have manes of long hair on their heads and necks, and thick, tufted tails. Their long legs, deep chests and powerful muscles allow them to run a long way at great speed without getting tired.

MEASURE IN HANDS

Normally we use centimetres and metres as units of measurement, but you can use anything you like – even your hands.

Measure the height of a table using your hands. Then ask an adult to measure it as well. Did you get the same measurement? If not, why not?

1072 Wild horses live in large groups called herds. All horses, wild or domestic (tame), are very loyal to one another and can form close bonds with other animals, including humans. Since it is natural for horses to have company, domestic horses should always be kept together, or with other animals such as sheep and cows.

1073 Horses are intelligent animals. They can communicate with each other by whinnying or braying, but, like many other animals, horses also sniff and smell one another to communicate. They also enjoy nuzzling and grooming each other's fur.

▼ In a herd, horses who get on well with each other will groom and nuzzle one another.

Inside out

▼ The features of a horse's skeleton, including extended leg bones and a rigid spine, allow it to run at speed for great distances.

Skull

Spine

Femur

Ribs

Knee

Fetlock

1074 **Horses have a bony framework called a skeleton.** The skeleton supports their bodies and protects their organs. The skull protects the brain, and the ribs protect the lungs and heart. Bones are made from a hard material called calcium, but are full of tiny holes, which make them lightweight.

Croup

Dock

1075 Domestic horses all belong to the same species, which means that they can mate with one another. Within the horse species there are lots of different types of horse, and these are called breeds. Breeds of horse differ in their appearance and in their personalities. A carthorse, for example, might have strong bones and a muscular body that is suited to pulling heavy loads, whereas a racehorse needs long legs and slender bones to run very fast.

Tail

Stifle

Thigh

Hock

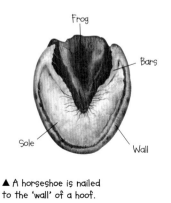

Frog

Bars

Sole

Wall

▲ A horseshoe is nailed to the 'wall' of a hoof.

1076 All equids have hooves, which are made from keratin. Keratin is the same material that is found in fingernails, hair, fur and claws. Hoof edges can be trimmed without causing any pain to the horse. Domestic horses can be prone to having sore and damaged feet, because they often walk and run on hard, paved surfaces. It is important that their hooves are well looked after.

Fetlock

1077 The parts of a horse's body that you can see are called 'the points of a horse'. Each point is given a special name and people who work with horses and ponies, or ride them, have to learn these names.

▼ Recognized terms or 'points' are used to pinpoint particular areas of a horse's body.

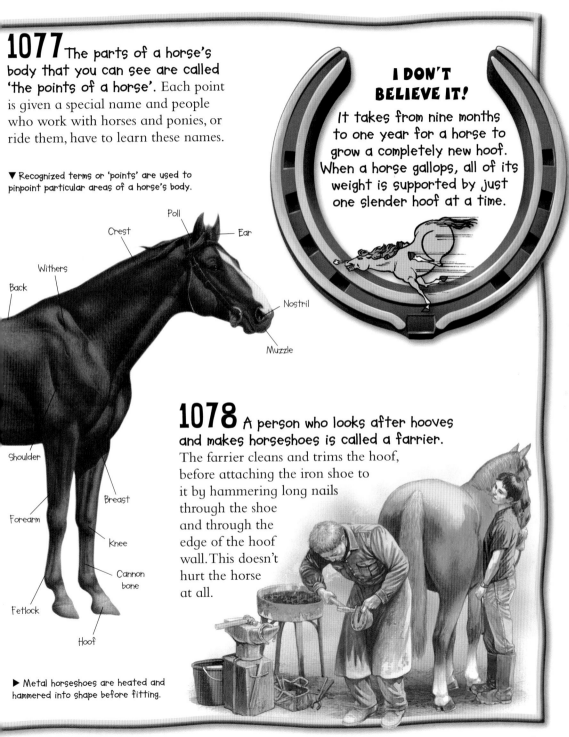

Poll

Crest

Ear

Withers

Back

Nostril

Muzzle

Shoulder

Breast

Forearm

Knee

Cannon bone

Fetlock

Hoof

I DON'T BELIEVE IT!

It takes from nine months to one year for a horse to grow a completely new hoof. When a horse gallops, all of its weight is supported by just one slender hoof at a time.

1078 A person who looks after hooves and makes horseshoes is called a farrier. The farrier cleans and trims the hoof, before attaching the iron shoe to it by hammering long nails through the shoe and through the edge of the hoof wall. This doesn't hurt the horse at all.

▶ Metal horseshoes are heated and hammered into shape before fitting.

Colours and markings

Star

Stripe

White face

Blaze

Snip

1079 **The fur of horses and ponies comes in a wide range of colours.** The most common are bay (red-brown), chestnut (red-gold), grey (which can be almost white to dark grey), brown (dark bay) and black. There are also many other colour variations, such as dun (sandy brown), bright bay (light bay) and liver chestnut (dark chestnut).

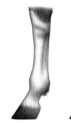

Over knee (stocking) Mid-cannon Fetlock

1080 **Horses often have markings on their lower legs.** These are called socks. White socks that extend above the knee are called stockings. Horses may have white marks elsewhere on their bodies – a white mark on the belly is called a 'flesh mark'.

Half-pastern (sock) Crown Coronet

▲ White leg markings are described using the points of anatomy that the white hair covers.

1081 White patches of fur on a horse's face are often used to help identify a horse. A 'stripe' is a narrow band of white that runs down the face, a 'blaze' is a broad band, a 'star' is a white mark on the forehead and a 'snip' is a patch of white between the horse's nostrils.

◀ A full description of a horse would include natural marks.

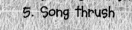

ODD ONE OUT!

Find the animal that has neither stripes nor spots:

1. Cheetah 2. Hover fly
3. Walrus 4. Coral snake
5. Song thrush

Answer: 3. Walrus

1082
Some wild equids have stripes or dark marks along their spines. Zebras are the most famous of all striped animals, but other wild equids sometimes have stripy legs, or a stripe of black fur running from the mane to the tail. This darker stripe is called an 'eel stripe'.

1083
Horses' hooves can also be different colours. A horse with dark legs is likely to also have dark hooves. Pale horses, or those with white socks, often have hooves that are a pale colour – usually cream. Dark hooves are called 'blue' and pale hooves are called 'white'.

Wall

Heel

Toe

▲ A horse's hooves may be dark, light, plain or striped.

1084
Some breeds of horse have large patches of different colours on their coats. These horses are called 'part-coloured'. Horses with patches of white and black fur are called 'piebald'. Horses with large patches of white and any other colour, apart from black, on their coats are called 'skewbald'.

▶ Horses that are referred to as 'piebald' usually have large, irregular patches of white and black hairs on their coat. Pinto horses are popular piebalds in the United States.

467

Hold your horses!

▼ Wild horses often run, or gallop, when they are scared. A stallion usually leads the way.

1085 A horse's body is packed with muscles. These help it to run fast, jump and leap, and pull heavy loads. The world's fastest wild equid is the onager – an ass that can reach an incredible top speed of 78 kilometres an hour!

1086 The way in which a horse moves is called the 'gait' or 'pace'. In the wild, horses move at their own pace and only have two gaits, walking slowly as they graze and galloping when they are frightened. Domestic horses are trained to perform at least four different gaits.

Walk

Trot

1087 The 'walk' is the slowest gait. It has a four-beat rhythm. The horse places its left foreleg forwards, then its right hind (back) leg, followed by its right foreleg and then its left hind leg. The 'trot' is the next fastest gait and it has a two-beat rhythm. As the horse moves, two legs (for example, the left foreleg and the right hind leg) touch the ground at the same time, while the other two legs (the right foreleg and the left hind leg) are in the air.

I DON'T BELIEVE IT!

At full gallop, Thoroughbred racehorses can reach speeds of over 60 kilometres an hour, even with riders on their backs.

1088 The canter and gallop are the fastest two gaits. When a horse canters it has a three-beat rhythm, and there is a moment when all four of the horse's feet are off the ground. Galloping is the most exciting of the gaits. It is similar to the canter, but faster and with longer strides. Each foot strikes the ground separately. The moment when all four feet are in the air at the same time is called the suspension.

▼ A rider can control their horse's gait. To change from one gait to another a rider presses their legs into the horse's body and pulls gently on the reins.

Canter

Gallop

Colts and fillies

1089 Only a few hours after they are born, baby horses (foals) are able to stand up and walk around. Like the young of other hoofed animals, foals born in the wild are at risk of being hunted and caught by predators. For this reason, foals spend a long time – about 11 months – developing inside their mothers so they are ready to move and feed soon after they are born.

1090 Mares – female horses – usually give birth to just one foal at a time. When a foal is born it rests for a few minutes, but soon attempts to stand and feed from its mother. The mare licks her newborn clean. She sniffs her foal to get used to its smell and the mother and foal whinny to one another, learning the sounds of each other's voices.

▶ In the first weeks of its life a foal stays next to its mother at all times. Mares can even sleep standing up, and are easily wakened if their youngster needs protection or reassurance.

1091 Foals stay close to their mothers for the first two months of their lives.

After this time the foals become braver and more adventurous, and will move away to investigate other members of the herd. Soon after this they begin to groom and play with other horses. When a young horse is between 12 and 24 months old, it is called a yearling. A female yearling is known as a filly, and a male yearling is known as a colt.

1092 An expert can tell how old a horse is by looking at its teeth.

The front, cutting, teeth are incisors and they are used to slice grass and other tender plants. As a horse ages, its incisors change from an oval shape to round, then become triangular and flattened. By examining the length and shape of a horse's teeth, it is possible to estimate its age.

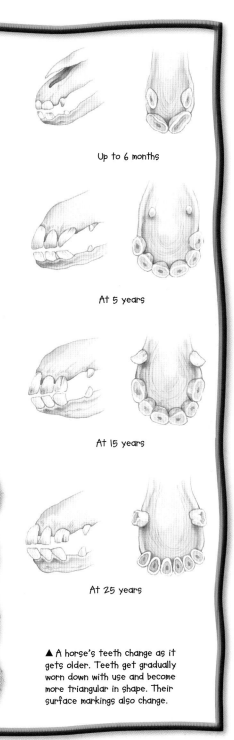

Up to 6 months

At 5 years

At 15 years

At 25 years

▲ A horse's teeth change as it gets older. Teeth get gradually worn down with use and become more triangular in shape. Their surface markings also change.

WHAT TYPE OF ANIMAL AM I?

The young of animals are often given special names, like foal or calf. Use a dictionary to find out what type of animals these other youngsters are:

1. Eaglet 2. Gosling
3. Leveret 4. Maggot

Answers: 1. Eagle 2. Goose 3. Hare 4. Fly

Sensitive and smart

1093 Horses have better senses of sight, hearing and smell than humans. Long ago the grasslands of the world were home to thousands of herds of equids, such as horses, zebra and asses. These grazing animals made good meals for predators. In order to keep themselves safe, horses needed to have highly developed senses of hearing, sight and smell so that they could detect any lurking predators.

▲ Grooming, stroking and talking all help to build a special friendship between horse and rider.

1094 Domestic horses and ponies like and need company. They can often become very close to the people who care for them, or ride them. Talking to horses may feel silly, but it isn't. They are such intelligent animals that they quickly begin to recognize voices, and can learn to understand simple words, such as 'no', 'stop' and 'go'.

1095 A horse's eye is twice as large as a human's eye, and is even bigger than an elephant's eye. Horses' eyes are positioned on the side of their heads, which means they can see in almost every direction. That's helpful when you always need to be on the look-out for a hungry predator.

I DON'T BELIEVE IT!

Horses have such good hearing that they have been known to sense earthquakes before humans are aware of them.

1096 Horses are able to recognize friends, both human and animal, by smell alone. Animals that live in groups have to be able to communicate with each other, and horses are no exception. Horses use the position of their ears to communicate their feelings – when their ears point backwards, horses are showing that they are scared or anxious.

1097 A herd of wild horses includes only one adult male, called a stallion. There are normally only about seven horses in a herd – one stallion with his mares and foals. The stallion protects his family and fights any other males that come too close to the herd.

▲ Stallions start to fight when they are four to five years old. They will rear up and kick their rivals, and aim bites at the throat, neck, ears or tail.

473

Hungry as a horse!

1098 **Wild horses can spend between 16 and 20 hours a day feeding.** The main bulk of their food is grass, which is difficult to digest. This means that horses need to eat a lot to get the energy that they need. Horses even eat during the night because they can see well in the dark and they only need a small amount of sleep. They will often nap for just a few minutes at a time, while still on their feet.

▶ Different types of teeth are used in eating. A horse's incisors cut and pull up plants. Its molars and premolars grind and mash the food. The surface of the teeth is worn down by about 3 millimetres every year.

1100 **Horses are fussy eaters.** They will spend time looking for a good patch of plants before they settle down to graze. Although they like grass, horses enjoy other plants such as cocksfoot, wild white clover, dandelions and chicory. They use their flexible top lips to grab the plant, then bite off a clump with their incisor teeth.

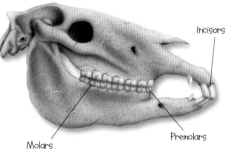

Incisors

Premolars

Molars

1099 **Horses can't bring up food, so if they eat something poisonous it can kill them.** Horses can poison themselves with the natural vegetation found in their fields, or in the trees and hedges surrounding their paddocks. Horses learn to avoid plants that taste bad, or cause them stomach pain, but not all dangerous plants have these obvious effects. Domestic horses and ponies should be kept in fields from which poisonous plants such as foxglove, yew, bracken, buttercups, laurel and laburnum have been removed.

◀ ▶ Ragwort, oak leaves and acorns are dangerous to horses. These plants should be removed from a horse's field.

Oak

Ragwort

1101 Some domestic horses are given their food, so they do not have to graze all day. Their normal diet of grass and fresh plants is replaced with hay and other food. Horses have small stomachs, so they need to be given lots of small meals, rather than a few large ones. Hay is dry grass, so although horses enjoy it, they have to be given plenty of fresh water to help them digest it easily.

▼ Food such as oats, barley, sugar beet and bran are known as 'hard feed'. They may be mixed with chopped hay and straw and given to a horse or pony.

1102 Removing a horse's or pony's droppings is called 'mucking out'. Horses produce lots of manure (waste) every day and clearing this away is an important job for anyone who owns a horse or pony. Manure is useful stuff – it can be left to rot, and then used in gardens or farms to put goodness back into the soil.

CHOOSE THE CORRECT WORD

1. Are animals that are active at night nocturnal or nautical?
2. Are rotting plants or manure called compost or comical?
3. Is tomahawk or toxin another name for poison?

Answers: 1. Nocturnal 2. Compost 3. Toxin

Habitats and homes

1103 The first equids are thought to have lived in the area we now call America, when it was joined to other continents. A continent is a big region of land, such as Africa or North America, and long ago the continents were connected. From America, horses were able to spread to Europe, Asia and Africa.

1104 After the last ice age, which ended about 10,000 years ago, millions of wild horses roamed the grasslands of Europe and Asia. They probably lived in herds, travelling great distances in search of food and water. The numbers of horses gradually decreased as the climate changed. Horses were also hunted by people, who used them for food and fur.

▼ Zebras now live in Africa but, like other equids, they originally came from North America.

1105 Domestic horses are found all over the world. There are very few equids living in the wild now, but there are millions of domesticated horses that live or work with people who depend on them for transport or pulling loads.

▶ Most types of horses are domestic, but some wild horses still roam free.

1106 The place where an animal lives is called its habitat. Wild horses are usually well-suited to their habitat. Those that live in cold areas may have very thick fur. The tarpan was an ancient type of horse with a coat that turned white during the snowy winter weather of its north European home.

1107 Wild asses are found in western Asia and the Middle East. Asses are the ancestors of modern donkeys, which first lived in North Africa. Since then, donkeys have spread to other parts of the world, and are common in Europe.

▼ The ancestors of the shire horse had to develop bulky bodies to help them survive the cold winters of northern Europe.

I DON'T BELIEVE IT!

About 10,000 years ago horses became extinct (died out) in the Americas. They were reintroduced by Spanish travellers about 500 years ago.

The first horses

Hyracotherium
50 million years ago

Mesohippus
36 million years ago

Parahippus
24 million years ago

Merychippus
17 million years ago

1108 The very first horse-like animal is thought to have lived about 50 million years ago. It is called *Hyracotherium*. By looking at its remains and teeth, scientists have decided that *Hyracotherium* probably lived on a diet of leaves. It had four toes on its front feet and three toes on its hind feet.

▼ The horse has adapted to changing conditions over millions of years. By the time of *Equus*, horses had grown larger, their necks were longer and their extra toes had disappeared.

Pliohippus
5 million years ago

Equus
1.5 million years ago

1109 It is believed that *Hyracotherium* is the ancestor of modern horses. Over millions of years animals can change so that they are better suited to the environment in which they live. This process is called evolution.

◀ Palaeontologists are scientists who study ancient animal remains.

MAKE A FAMILY TREE

You probably have some ancient relatives too! Look through old photograph albums and talk to your parents and grandparents to find out about members of your family. See how many years back you can trace. Do you look similar to any of your relatives?

1110 There are only ten species of equids, but hundreds of different breeds of domestic horse. A species of animal includes any members of a group that can mate with one another to produce healthy young that are the same, or very similar. Breeds are different types, or varieties, of animals in one species.

1111 Gradually, *Hyracotherium* evolved so that it could survive in a changing world. By 36 million years ago this ancient creature had disappeared, but a different horse-like animal lived – *Mesohippus*. It was the size of a sheep and had three toes on each foot, a long neck and a slender face.

▼ Unlike modern horses, who prefer to live on open grasslands and plains, *Hyracotherium* was a forest dweller.

Asses, donkeys and mules

1112 An ass is a wild horse that is sure-footed and able to survive in very harsh conditions. Asses are shorter than most members of the horse family, and they are famous for their ability to live in places where there is little food or water. Wild asses are found mainly in Africa and Asia, where rain rarely falls and the ground is stony. Asses can survive on a diet of dry grass and thorny shrubs and bushes.

1113 Long before farmers had tractors, they used animals to work in their fields. Onagers, which are a type of ass, were probably the first animal that were used to pull ploughs and carts. They are extremely fast runners, strong and reliable. Today, these gentle creatures are in danger of extinction.

1114 Przewalski's wild horse looks similar to an ass, with its short stocky body. The last free Przewalski's horse was seen in the 1970s, in Mongolia. Today, these unusual beasts are mostly kept in zoos or parks, but a small herd has now been put back into the wild.

◄ Przewalski's horse is heavily built. It has a large head, thick neck and short legs.

▶ Donkeys and mules have often been used to carry heavy loads. This mule train, under attack, is carrying treasure.

1115 Donkeys are asses that have been domesticated. They are used to carry people or goods, and for farming. They are very strong and can live in harsh habitats, often walking for many miles in the heat with little food or water.

▼ Donkeys are popular with tourists at the seaside, where they carry children down the beach.

MATING GAME

When two different species of animals are mated, their youngster (like a mule) is called a 'hybrid'. Can you guess the parents of these hybrids?

1. Geep 2. Tigon
3. Wholphin

Answers: 1. Goat and sheep
2. Tiger and lion. 3. Whale and dolphin

1116 If a female horse mates with a male donkey, the foal is called a mule. Mules combine the horse's strength with the donkey's ability to keep working in difficult conditions. If a male horse mates with a female donkey, the foal is called a hinny. Mules and hinnies are sterile, which means that they cannot have any foals themselves.

On the African plains

1117 **Zebras are wild horses that have startling patterns of black-and-white striped fur.** They are found in Africa, where they live on the huge grasslands known as the savannah, along with other grazing or browsing creatures such as giraffes, wildebeests and antelopes.

1118 There are three types, or species, of zebra — Grevy's, mountain and Burchell's. A Grevy's zebra lives further north than the other two species. It is the tallest of the three types and has very thin stripes, particularly on its face. The mountain zebra has a dark muzzle and thick black stripes on its rump. It is in danger of becoming extinct. The most common of the three types is Burchell's zebra.

Grevy's zebra

Burchell's zebra

Mountain zebra

▲ Zebra types can be identified by the pattern of stripes on their fur.

▼ The common, or Burchell's, zebra has broad horizontal stripes that extend under the belly.

1119 No one knows for sure why zebras have stripes. It was thought that the patterns might confuse predators. Or it may be for purposes of identification – each zebra has a unique pattern of stripes, and a zebra can recognize another member of its herd just by its pattern of stripes.

1120 There was a fourth type of zebra – the quagga – but it is now extinct. Quaggas lived in southern Africa, in herds of up to a hundred individuals. Like other zebras, they lived on grasslands and spent most of their day grazing. They were ruthlessly hunted by European settlers and the last one died in 1883.

Horses and ponies in the past

1121 No one knows for sure when horses and ponies were first used by people for riding, pulling or carrying things. However, there are pictures of men on horseback that are more than 4000 years old! Since ancient times, horses, ponies, asses and donkeys have helped humans explore their world.

▼ This horse–drawn machine, called a 'seed drill', dropped seeds in to a ploughed field and helped make farming more efficient.

1122 For thousands of years, horses went to war. In ancient Persia (now Iran) and Rome, horses pulled chariots, which took soldiers wielding swords and spears into battle, or to entertain crowds in large arenas.

◀ In the Middle Ages, kings and knights led their armies to war on horses chosen for their strength and obedience.

1123 Horses have been used in farming and for carrying or pulling heavy weights. The strongest members of the horse family have been chosen by farmers to help them move carts weighed down with crops, or to plough fields and carry water. In most modern countries, machinery has replaced horses, but across the world many people still rely on their horses to help them grow their crops.

1124 **The United States of America was explored by settlers with horses.** The USA covers a vast area. Without horses and mules it would have been very difficult for European travellers to make their way across the huge continent. Hundreds of horse-drawn wagons formed a winding trail as they travelled west to set up new towns and farming communities.

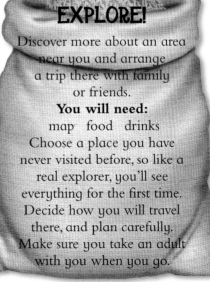

▶ Annie Oakley was an American rodeo star and sharp shooter.

EXPLORE!

Discover more about an area near you and arrange a trip there with family or friends.
You will need:
map food drinks
Choose a place you have never visited before, so like a real explorer, you'll see everything for the first time. Decide how you will travel there, and plan carefully. Make sure you take an adult with you when you go.

1125 **A thousand years ago, medieval soldiers took part in tournaments on horseback.** They sat astride their large and powerful horses, which had to carry their riders and heavy metal armour too, as they jousted with one another to prove their courage and strength.

Wild ponies

1126 Ponies are usually smaller than horses, with wider bodies and shorter legs. They often come from areas of the world where they have had to struggle to survive, so they show great stamina. Ponies are usually sure-footed, which means that they can easily get about on steep hillsides and rocky plains. Wild ponies have often lost their habitats to humans, but some breeds still live on the moors and grasslands of the world.

▲ The Highland is the largest of the Scottish breeds and can survive where food is scarce.

1127 Connemara ponies originally came from Ireland, but they are now bred throughout Europe. Connemaras have been bred with Arab and Thoroughbred horses, and they have inherited speed and good jumping ability from these famous horse breeds. Connemaras are strong, sturdy and intelligent. They make good competition horses and are popular with both adults and children.

▶ Wild Connemara ponies have lived on the moors of western Ireland since the 16th century.

1128 Tiny Shetland ponies first arrived in Scotland about 10,000 years ago, from Scandinavia. They live in harsh conditions, which has led to the breed developing great strength. Shetland ponies are measured in inches, not hands, and they stand up to 40 inches (102 centimetres) tall. For their size, Shetlands are probably the strongest of all horse and pony breeds.

▼ Shetland ponies have thick fur and manes to protect them from the cold. They have large noses and nostrils so they can warm the air before it reaches their lungs.

1129 New Forest ponies have been living wild for about a thousand years. They live in protected woodlands and heaths of Hampshire in southern England. The ponies can graze and mate freely. This type of pony can also be tamed and used in riding stables, where it is particularly popular with children.

1130 Two of the most famous breeds of wild pony are the Dartmoor and Exmoor. These sturdy ponies can survive the difficult conditions found on the moors – they have to be tough enough to cope with rain, snow, biting winds and the poor grazing. The Exmoor is one of the oldest breeds in the world, and dates back as far as the last ice age – 10,000 years ago! Tame Dartmoor ponies are often used for riding lessons, as they are strong and they jump well.

Ponies as pets

1131 In the past, ponies were used to haul carts and work on farms, but today they are most often kept as pets. Children who want to learn how to ride usually have their first lessons on a pony. Ponies are good-natured animals. They are reliable and patient, so boys and girls can often form very close friendships with them.

1132 Fell ponies are famous for their ability to work very hard. They were once used in mines and on farms, and could travel hundreds of kilometres in one week, pulling carts. Fell ponies are only 14 hands (142 centimetres) high, but they are strong enough to carry adults and they are popular ponies for children.

◀ Fell ponies are usually black or dark brown, occasionally with small white markings. Their bodies are deep, their legs are short and strong and they have long, thick tails.

▲ Falabella horses are so small they can even be dwarfed by a dog! Falabellas have large heads, slender legs and thick manes and tails.

1133 The little Falabella is the smallest of all the horse breeds. It is a very new type of horse, which has been created by the Falabella family of Argentina, who mated Shetland ponies with Thoroughbred horses. A Falabella only stands about 7 hands (71 centimetres) tall, but it is often called a miniature horse rather than a pony because of its horse-like character and body shape. Falabellas are too small to be ridden, but they are popular as pets. Falabella foals are usually only 4 hands (41 centimetres) tall.

▶ Welsh cobs make good driving ponies – this means they can be used for pulling a cart or trap.

1134 Welsh mountain ponies make excellent riding ponies. They are divided into four different types – Section A, B, C and D. Welsh Section A ponies come from the Welsh mountains. Section B, C and D ponies have been developed by breeding Section A ponies with other types of horse or pony. They are often used for jumping or driving.

Hotblood horses

1135 Horse breeds are divided into three main groups, called hotbloods, warmbloods and coldbloods. Hotbloods are ancient and very pure breeds that originally came from North Africa and the Middle East. They are very elegant and fast runners. Coldbloods come from northern Europe and they are large, heavy, strong horses. Warmbloods were developed by mating hotbloods with coldbloods.

1137 Although horses come in all sorts of shapes and sizes, they are divided into breeds. Within each breed, the horses are similar in personality and appearance. By mating a horse from one breed with a horse of another breed, people (called breeders) have been able to create new and different types of horse, such as warmbloods.

1136 The most famous of all hotbloods is the Arab. These lively and speedy horses first lived in the desert regions of the Middle East. They are said to be the oldest domestic horse breed in the world, as well as the most beautiful. Arabs are small, but they are famous for their stamina. Like Thoroughbreds and Akhal-Tekés, Arabs are a high-spirited breed and are not usually considered suitable horses for young or inexperienced riders.

▼ Although Arabs are not as fast as Thoroughbreds, they gallop with a wonderful, flowing movement and they can run for a long time before getting tired.

1138 Thoroughbreds are the world's fastest domestic horses. These hotbloods were first bred in England about 400 years ago, to create fast horses for competitions. They are still used as racehorses, or to breed with other types of horse and pony. Thoroughbreds are both strong and quick, and for these reasons they are thought of as one of the best horses to ride, but they can have difficult personalities and are hard to handle.

1139 The Akhal-Teké is a hotblood horse that has been bred in the Middle East for thousands of years. These brave and tough horses are unusual looking, with long and slender bodies that are coated in a thin layer of golden fur. Akhal-Tekés are the world's greatest long-distance runners, and can even cope with the extreme heat and dryness of the desert.

I DON'T BELIEVE IT!

Akhal-Teké hotbloods have been known to travel over 4000 kilometres in just 84 days, surviving on only a tiny amount of food and water.

Warmblood horses

1140 **Most horse breeds of the world are warmbloods.** Despite their name, the blood of warmbloods is exactly the same temperature as that of hotbloods and coldbloods! The name refers to where different types of horses come from. Hotbloods first came from desert areas, while coldbloods came from cold countries of the north – and warmbloods are a mixture of both!

▼ A Lipizzaner stallion performs a movement called the 'levade'.

▼ Quarter horses have become famous for being those ridden by cowboys when they tend their cattle. They were bred for riding and farm work.

1141 The Quarter horse is said to be the most popular horse in the world. It works hard, but it also has a calm and patient personality. Quarter horses were first bred in the USA, about 350 years ago. They combine great strength with agility – they can stop, start and change direction very quickly.

1142 The Spanish Riding School of Vienna is known throughout the world for the athletic tricks performed by its Lipizzaner horses. These grey warmbloods have Spanish ancestors (which is how the Riding School got its name) and they are trained to perform special movements, such as jumps and kicks. The movements are said to be based on medieval tricks of war that were used to evade enemy soldiers. It takes many years to train just one horse.

1143 Camargue horses have been called the 'wild white horses of the sea'. These beautiful white warmbloods come from the bleak and windswept Rhône region of southern France. As a result, they are extremely tough. It is thought that they are related to the primitive horses that appear in French cave drawings, which are about 17,000 years old. There are herds of wild Camargue horses, but domesticated ones are used by local cowboys to round up wild black bulls.

MAKE TASTY HORSESHOES

You will need:
packet of bread mix

1. Follow the instructions carefully to mix the dough and knead it.
2. Make small balls that you can then mould into strips and shape into horseshoes.
3. Leave the dough to rise, then sprinkle with sesame seeds and bake in the oven. Eat the horseshoes with butter and jam while they are still warm.

1144 One of the most unusual-looking warmbloods is the Appaloosa. It is known for its strikingly patterned coat, which can be a variety of different colours. This American breed got its name from the Palouse River in the USA. It was bred during the 18th century by a Native American tribe, who wanted to create strong and agile working horses.

▶ There are five Appaloosa coat patterns: marble, blanket, leopard, snowflake and frost. Shown here are blanket (white quarters and loins, sometimes with dark spots) and frost (dark background with white speckles).

Coldblood horses

1145 Coldblood horses come from the cooler regions of the world, and they are the largest and strongest of all horse types. Coldbloods have been bred for their immense power, and they have been used to pull heavy loads for hundreds of years, particularly on farms. They have wide backs, muscle-packed bodies and thick, short legs. They usually have very calm, docile natures.

▼ Heavy horses carried medieval knights into war. They are the ancestors of breeds such as the Shire horse (in Britain) and the Percheron (in France).

1146 Coldbloods are also known as 'heavy' or 'draught' horses. Before trains and motor vehicles were invented, these horses worked hard as they ploughed fields, pulled boats along canals or hauled carts. In medieval times, these heavyweights were needed to help carry knights to fields of war.

1147 Heavy horses are often dressed up and shown in competitions. The owners of these magnificent creatures often travel to country shows and fairs where they give demonstrations to show their horses' strength and power. The horses' manes are braided and plaited, and they are decorated with brasses and gleaming harnesses.

1148 The Shire is often called the greatest of all draught horses. It is tall, strong and very gentle. It gets its name from the English counties of Derbyshire, Lincolnshire, Staffordshire and Leicestershire, where it was first bred. Shire horses carried English Medieval knights into battle, and also worked on farms and in cities.

I DON'T BELIEVE IT!

Horses rarely live to be older than 30 years, but an English draught horse, called Old Billy, is said to have made it to the grand age of 62!

▲ Shire horses can stand more than 18 hands (180 centimetres) tall and are probably the largest heavy horses. They are usually black, bay, brown or grey in colour, and their legs often have long white stockings. Most heavy horses have wispy fur, called feathers, around their hooves.

1149 Suffolk Punches are coldbloods that are all related to a single male horse, which was born in 1768. Suffolks were bred to work on farms but their distinctive chestnut colour makes them a popular breed at shows and competitions.

Horses for courses

1150 Horses and ponies have to learn how to be ridden, or how to pull a cart, wagon or trap. Horses begin this training while they are still young foals. Teaching a horse how to carry a rider, and follow the rider's instructions, is called 'breaking it in'. When a horse is being broken in, it gets used to a saddle and reins, and all of the other equipment it will wear.

I DON'T BELIEVE IT!

The first known horse races with riders took place 2000 years ago at the Olympic Games in Greece. The men rode bareback – without saddles.

▼ A show-jumper aims to clear a round of fences without knocking any of them over, and without the horse refusing to jump.

1151 Many riders love to teach their horses and ponies how to jump, and show-jumping is a very popular sport. At a show-jumping event, or competition, riders are expected to take their horses around a course, jumping over fences on the way, in the fastest possible time. Both horse and rider enjoy the challenge of jumping, and to do it successfully takes real partnership and trust.

1152 Horse racing is said to be the sport of kings. All around the world, horses compete in speed competitions, and their owners are rewarded with prize money if they win. Training and keeping a racehorse is very expensive, and riding a racehorse at top speed can be dangerous – but the thrills make it worthwhile for the people who love this sport.

▲ Thoroughbreds are considered the perfect racehorses – fast, light and comfortable to ride.

▶ During a flag race the rider has to lean over and reach a flag whilst still moving at high speed.

1154 Horses can enter competitions where they are tested on the way they can follow the rider's signals and instructions. This is called dressage, and it is a sport that requires plenty of practice and a beautifully turned-out horse and rider. Marks are awarded for presentation, and the horse's or pony's paces and behaviour.

1153 Horse and pony riders often meet to take part in games, races and displays, called gymkhanas. Gymkhanas are great places for young riders to meet other horse-lovers, while testing themselves and their riding skills in a variety of competitions.

1155 In cross-country competitions a rider and his or her horse or pony must jump over obstacles. These are usually things that you might find in the countryside, such as hedges, ditches and pools of water. Riders are allowed to walk around the course before the competition, so they can look at each jump and decide how they will approach it.

Saddle up!

1156 **Keeping a horse or pony is a big responsibility.** Horses and ponies are herd animals, so they need attention and company. They also need to be kept warm, sheltered and well fed. A farrier needs to tend to their hooves and feet, and a vet needs to give a horse or pony regular worming treatments and vaccinations.

1157 **Ponies can live outdoors in a field, but only if they have a place to shelter.** Many people keep their ponies at a livery stable or yard – a place where many ponies are looked after for a fee. A pony's stable needs to be kept clean and warm, and that means mucking out every day. New bedding needs to be laid and fresh water provided.

▲ Ponies love tasty treats such as juicy apples and carrots.

1158 **Ponies love to have their fur brushed.** Brushing keeps a pony's coat clean and glossy. Cleaning a pony's fur, mane and hooves is called grooming, and this is an important job. Grooming helps remove dried mud and grease from a pony's coat, and also helps the animal keep free from infection.

◄ Grooming a horse requires special equipment, including brushes, combs, hoof picks, sponges and hoof grease or oil.

1159 Few people can ride without saddles, reins or bridles. These are all special pieces of equipment – called 'tack' – that make riding easier and more comfortable, for both the rider and the animal! A Russian tribe, called the Sarmatians, are thought to have invented leather saddles in around AD 365.

Cantle

Seat

Girth

Pommel

Skirt

D–ring

Lining

Numnah

Stirrup iron

Stirrup leather

▶ A general-purpose saddle suits most riders, but other types are available for specialist sports, such as racing or jumping.

1160 Learning how to ride well can take years of practice. Riders are taught how to control the horse or pony by using their voices, hands, seat, legs and feet. In this way, a rider can tell the horse to change its pace or direction and to start or stop.

TACKING UP

Only three of these words are real names for part of the tack. Find the fakes!

1. Noseband 2. Nozzlestrap
3. Snaffle bit 4. Smooch lip
5. Throatlash

Answers: 2 and 4 are fakes.

1161 If you don't have your own horse or pony, then riding schools are a great place to learn more and get some hands-on experience. Riding schools and city farms often welcome interested people who want to learn more about these noble creatures. They also welcome volunteers who are willing to help with jobs such as cleaning the tack, feeding, filling haynets and water buckets, mucking out and grooming the horses and ponies.

Index

Entries in **bold** refer to main subject entries. Entries in *italics* refer to illustrations.

Index

Index

Index

Index

Acknowledgements

All artworks are from the Miles Kelly Artwork Bank

The publishers would like to thank the following sources for the use of their photographs:

(t = top, b = bottom, l = left, r = right, c = centre)

Alamy 92 Photos 12; 145(br) John Glover; 146 Mary Evans Picture Library; 169(c) Picture Press; 172(t) Photos 12; 255 Deco; 316–317 A & J Visage; 327 blickwinkel; 339(t) Peter Arnold, Inc.

Ardea.com 343(t) M. Watson; 353 Francois Gohier/Ardea London Ltd; 355(cr) John Cancalosi; 364 Chris Harvey

Burpee Museum of Natural History 127 Jane: Courtesy of Burpee Museum of Natural History

Corbis 102(b); 118 Bettman; 119 Bettman; 121 Layne Kennedy; 122 DK Limited; 126 Louie Psihoyos; 128 Louie Psihoyos; 141(t) Jonathan Blair; 143(br) Alex Hofford, (b) Patricia Fogden; 169(b) Martin Harvey; 182(b) Martin Harvey/ Gallo Images; 190 Frans Lanting; 192 Fernando Bengaechea/Beateworks; 194(t) Karen Kasmauski; 195(br) George Steinmetz; 196(t) momatiuk-Eastcott; 199 Owen Franken; 201(b) Keren Su; 203(t) Jeffrey L Rotman; 210(b) Theo Allots; 211 Martin Harvey; 216 Natalie Fobes; 217 Theo Allots; 223 Kevin Schafer; 320(bl) Arthur Morris; 330–331 W. Perry Conway; 335 Sandor H.Szabo/epa; 340 Ralph Clevenger; 366 David A. Northcott; 453 Wolfgang Kaehler; 456 Kevin R. Morris; 458 Stephanie Sinclair

Dreamstime.com 137(tr) South China tiger Trix1428; 160(c) Photoinjection; 167(b) Naluphoto; 355(tr) Picstudio; 361(top inset) Sharkegg

FLPA 144 Gerard Lacz; 172(b) Simon Littlejohn/Minden Pictures; 176 Frans Lanting; 184 Winfried Wisniewski; 193 Panda Photo; 204(b) Tui De Roy/Minden Pictures; 205(t) Linda Lewis; 206 David Hosking; 209 Flip Nicklin/Minden Pictures; 210(t) David Hosking; 212 Katherine Feng/Globio/Minden Pictures; 213(b) John F. Binns, www.IRCF.org; 214 Philip Perry; 215 Yva Momatiuk & John Eastcott/Minden Pictures; 218 Frans Lanting/Frans Lanting PL; 220 Tui de Roy/ Minden Pictures; 221(t) S D K Maslowski, (c) Terry Whittaker; 224(b) Frans Lanting; 228 Tui de Roy/Minden Pictures; 234(t) Roger Wilmshurst; 236 Fred Bavendam/Minden Pictures; 244 Jurgen & Christine Sohns; 247 Mitsuaki Iwago/ Minden Pictures; 253(b) Michael Quinton/Minden Pictures; 257(t) Malcolm Schuyl, (b) Frans Lanting; 259 Derek Middleton; 287 Mark Moffett/Minden Pictures; 292(t) Panda Photo 325 Imagebroker, Bernd Zoller, Image; 329 Ramon Navarro/Minden Pictures; 333 Roger Tidman; 341(t) Frans Lanting; 343(b) Mark Newman; 348(tr) Norbert Wu/Minden Pictures; 349(tr) Michael & Patricia Fogden/Minden Pictures; 354(l) Michael & Patricia Fogden/Minden Pictures; 376 Colin Marshall; 448 Mark Raycroft/Minden Pictures

Fotolia.com 137(cr) Sumatran tiger Vladimir Wrangel, (br) Malayan tiger Kitch Bain, (br) Indochinese tiger Judy Whitton; 140(bl) clearviewstock; 145(c); 164(t) sisu; 167(c) Jefery; 227(t) EcoView; 231 Audrey Eun; 234 Cosi; 265 Carlton Mceachern; 275 Eric Gevaert; 283 Ami Beyer; 288 Reiner Weidemann; 318 javarman; 346(panel, clockwise from top right) Becky Stares, Vatikaki, Eric Gevaert, reb; 348(b) Paul Murphy

Getty 131(t) Handout; 156(b) National Geographic; 173(t) AFP; 183 Art Wolfe; 202(b) Karen Kasmauski; 213(t) National Geographic; 227(b) Joel Sartore/National Geographic; 368–369 Digital Vision; 377(b) Marc Crumpler

iStockphoto.com 351(t) Ameng Wu; 354(tr) Mark Kostich; 356(bl) Seth Ames; 358(tl) lara seregni; 361(b) Mark Kostich; 367(cr) Mark Kostich; 372(br) Eric Isselée; 374(bl) Dave Rodriguez; 377(t) Claude Robidoux; 382(t) Roman Lipovskiy

Mark Henry 420(t)

Naturepl.com 158–159 Eric Baccega; 168 Andrew Harrington; 200 Luiz Claudio Marigo; 205(b) Andrew Murray; 254 Martin Dohrn; 273 Bruce Davidson; 302–303 Wild Wonders of Europe/Nill; 306(t) Igor Shpilenok; 307(t) Tony Heald, (br) John Cancalosi; 311 Markus Varesvuo; 312 Juan Carlos Munoz; 320-321 Markus Varesvuo; 323 Luis Quinta; 342 John Cancalosi; 350(b) Daniel Gomez; 359(b) Tim MacMillan/John Downer Pr; 383(t) John Cancalosi

NHPA 159(b) Bruce Beehler; 167(t) Photoshot; 182(t) Jonathan & Angela Scott; 195(t) Mark Carwardine; 198(t) Jonathan & Angela Scott; 203(b) Martin Harvey; 204(t) Martin Wendler; 225(b) Martin Harvey; 252 Simon Booth; 256 Martin Harvey; 285 Daniel Heuclin; 299 Martin Harvey; 372(tl) Daniel Heuclin; 382(b) Tony Crocetta

Photolibrary.com 102(t) Robert Clark; 112 Salvatore Vasapolli; 125 Steve Vider**;** 202(t) Nick Gordon; 140(c) Paul Nevin; 141(b) Stouffer Productions; 157 Howard Rice; 170–171 Purestock; 235 Don Brown/Animals Animals/Earth Scenes; 238 Marian Bacon/Animals Animals/Earth Scenes; 250(c) Animals Animals/Earth Scenes; 251 Tim Shepherd; 300; 344–345 Berndt Fischer; 347(b) Werner Bollmann; 349(b) David B Fleetham; 355(b) Zigmund Leszczynski; 356-357 Jack Goldfarb; 362-363 John Cancalosi; 363 Carol Farneti Foster; 379(tr) Morales Morales; 383(b) Imagesource; 468

Photoshot 306(br) Andy Rouse; 319 Jordi Bas Casas; 326 Jordi Bas Casas

Pictorial Press 420(b)

Reuters 124 Ho Old

Rex Features 130 © 20thC.Fox/Everett; 132 Nils Jorgensen; 147 Icon/Everett

Science Photo Library 123 Volker Steger; 134–135 Richard Bizley; 172(b) Philippe Psaila

Shutterstock.com 222 Ryan M. Bolton; 239 Glenn Young

Still Pictures 245(t) BIOS - Auters Watts Dave

Topfoto 131(t) Topham Picture Point; 156(t) Artmedia/HIP; 160(b) The Granger Collection; 161(t) The Granger Collection, (b) Topham Picturepoint; 459; 489

Warren Photographic Pages 422, 442, 443, 444 Jane Burton

All other photographs are from:

Corel, digitalSTOCK, digitalvision, John Foxx, PhotoAlto, PhotoDisc, PhotoEssentials, PhotoPro, Stockbyte

Every effort has been made to acknowledge the source and copyright holder of each picture. Miles Kelly Publishing apologises for any unintentional errors or omissions.